D1029017

Quest
for Past
and Future

Essays in Jewish Theology

Quest
for Past
and Future

Essays in Jewish Theology

E M I L L. F A C K E N H E I M

Indiana University Press
Bloomington & London

Published in Canada by
Fitzhenry & Whiteside Limited, Scarborough, Ontario

LIBRARY OF CONGRESS CATALOG CARD NUMBER: 68-27346
MANUFACTURED IN THE UNITED STATES OF AMERICA

TO

Herman E. Schaalman
*after more
than three decades*

Contents

vii

Preface

The essays collected in this volume are republished, except for minor, mostly technical changes, in their original form, and with the kind permission of the original publishers listed on the first page of each essay. The first essay, written especially for this volume, is an account of how my thinking has changed over a period of no less than twenty years, and of why it has changed so little. To facilitate the reader's own judgment in this matter the arrangement is chronological, despite the inevitable disadvantage that the more mature thought is thus found toward the end of the volume.

It is fitting that *Quest for Past and Future* should appear in the same year, and with the same publishers, as my *The Religious Dimension in Hegel's Thought*. The two works (which have occupied me during the same years) are related in their very difference. In the philosophical work all religious commitment is suspended by reflection; in the theological work all philosophical thinking is geared to a commitment. The first could be and had to be one book, for philosophical reflection can and must wait until it is complete. The second could be and had to be a book of essays, for theology cannot wait but must speak whenever the time is ripe, even at the price of fragmentariness. In tranquil times perhaps even theologians can wait. But to the present generation of Jewish theologians apply Hillel's words—"if not now, when?"

Toronto, October 4, 1967
Erev Rosh ha-Shanah 5728   E.L.F.

ix

Quest
for Past
and Future

Essays in Jewish Theology

1

These Twenty Years:
A Reappraisal

The mid-twentieth century is pregnant with momentous changes. The rise of the nonwhite, non-Christian world, marking the end of the two millennia of European-Christian hegemony, and the emergence of the threat of nuclear extinction, a new aspect of the human condition ever after—these are but the two most dramatic of the processes making contemporary men aware of the historicity of all—or most—things human. This is a generation to which even a God dying in history is more significant than one who dwells, unmoving, in eternity.

At a time such as this, a religious thinker who republishes essays spanning twenty years would have cause for a reappraisal even if his subject were timeless verities. Moreover, if he is a Jewish religious thinker, this is not his subject. In the nineteenth century Jewish theologians may have abstracted a "universalistic" Judaism from the "particularistic" existence of Jews. In the twentieth century dichotomies such as these are destroyed. It is now again revealed what always was true—that a Jew can be a faithful witness to his universal God only in his particular, singled-out Jewish condition, not through some manner of flight from it. At Auschwitz in the 1940s, and at Jerusalem in 1967, Jews were singled out and alone. Those Jews bodily present were singled out physically, in the one case with no choice but death, in the other with none but to fight for life. All Jews not bodily present were singled out spiritually, left with no authentic choice but solidarity with their brethren. Today, no Jew, however deeply involved in universally human concerns, can go on pretending to himself that he is a man-in-general. The universal and the particular are inextricably intertwined; he cannot be present at Selma and Hiroshima unless he is present at Auschwitz and Jerusalem. How then could a Jewish theologian go on perpetuating the unreal categories of "universalism" and "particularism"? How could he avoid the question of what it means, after Auschwitz and Jerusalem, to be a Jewish witness to the world?

To avoid Auschwitz, or to act as if it had not occurred, would be blasphemous. But how face it and be faithful to its victims? No precedent exists either within Jewish history or without it. For a Jewish religious thinker merely to begin to face Auschwitz is to see the possibility of a desperate choice between the faith of a millennial Jewish past and faithfulness to the victims of the present. At the edge of this abyss there must be a great pause, a lengthy silence, and an endurance.

II

I begin with an expression of debt to Martin Buber and Franz Rosenzweig. Much has changed in my Jewish thinking over the past twenty years. Thanks to the influence of these two thinkers I need not repudiate any part of my past writing as simply wrongheaded or wholly false.

I link Buber and Rosenzweig advisedly. Some of Rosenzweig's doctrines are overrun by events less than fifty years after his death.[1] Much of Buber's teaching is not Judaism, but only an option within it. In the basic concerns shared by these two men, however, the whole future of Jewish theology is at stake.

Before the twentieth century, Jewish theologians, if responding to the challenge of modernity, resorted to compromises. These occurred in many points, but the central point was the divine-human relation, crucially specified in a divine covenant with Israel. Modern thought seemed to leave no room for such a relation. It allowed no room for a God dwelling beyond the world, yet entering into it to seek out man: He was an irrational incursion into a rational universe. At the same time, in its more congenial moods modern thought gave substitute offerings—a Deistic First Cause or Cosmic Process outside man and unrelated to him, or an idealistic God-idea within him. Faced with this basic challenge and these substitute offerings, orthodox and liberal Jewish theology both compromised. Orthodoxy held fast to the Jewish God, but confined His essential activity to a conveniently remote Biblical and Talmudic past, acting as though the sacred documents of that past could be exempted from modern criticism. Liberalism for its part, wishing a present God, compromised the Jewish God Himself, now using the terms of Deism, then those of idealism, and in its still surviving forms the terms of a cosmic evolutionism.

Buber and Rosenzweig gave a radical Jewish response to the challenge of the modern world. Their response was radical negatively, for they faced up to such forms of modern thought as know neither benevolent First Causes or Cosmic Processes outside man, nor idealistic God-ideas within him. It was also radical positively, for they sought nothing less than a modern presence of the ancient God. What was needed was no less than a counter-challenge of modernity by the Jewish faith, transcending in its significance all divisions between liberalism and orthodoxy. What was and is at stake is the survival of Judaism in the modern world.

Perhaps it is not accidental that this response occurred in central Europe in the first half of the twentieth century. Perhaps religious thought may come to rest with compromises so long as it is challenged only mildly, superficially, or, ultimately, irrelevantly. Thus homiletical idealism (a mild challenge) encourages the view that there is, after all, no serious difference between divine revelation and human inspiration, or between divine commandments and human ideals. Historical evolutionism (a superficial challenge) provokes the protest that not all religions are superseded merely because they are past, coupled with efforts to bring one's own religion up-to-date where it is superseded. As for social-science relativism (ultimately an irrelevancy), it calls forth irrelevant proofs that religion can be wholesome. But in the central Europe of Buber and Rosenzweig the God of Judaism and Christianity was the target of graver attacks. Marxism, Nietzscheanism, and atheistic existentialism all confronted the God of Abraham, not that of philosophers or scientists, and they all rejected Him. They did so, moreover, not by means of marginal attacks on scriptural authorities, three-storey universes, or proofs of His existence, but rather by means of a frontal assault on the central Jewish and Christian commitment—a God on high, directly related to man below. Such a relation was viewed as acceptable only to pre-modern, authority-bound man, and intolerable to modern, emancipated man. Modern man was autonomous and self-active, and he could not be both self-active and subject to God. For modern man to be free, the ancient God had to be nonexistent, absent, or dead.

A Jewish religious thinker cannot face this challenge without facing the whole modern challenge. And when he does face it, there arises a stark alternative. Either the whole, long history of Jewish faith—one of no mere theoretical affirmations but of untold devotion, sacrifice, and martyrdom—rests, in the end, on a fundamental and tragic mistake or else there is need for a radical turning—a turning to the ancient God in the very midst of modernity.

Is such a turning a real possibility? Is it compatible with modern thought, and capable of bearing fruit in modern life? The strength of the Buber-Rosenzweig turning is that no problems of modern thought or life are denied, avoided, or supplied with a once-and-for-all solution. Biblical criticism and comparative religion, scientific rationalism and technological secularism, indeed, the crucial modern claim to autonomy itself—all these remain problems, only they are taken into a thought and an existence which are open to the presence of God. The problems of both life and thought are not behind but still ahead. What then is gained? Nothing but a ground on which one may stand. The Jewish believer may stand on it as he tries to enter into a relation with his ancient God in a modern world. And the Jewish theologian may stand on it as he tries to understand that relation, in terms intelligible and acceptable to modern thought.[2]

III

My first Jewish writing was occasioned by the experience of a clash between European Jewish realities and American Jewish theology. The Germany from which I had fled was an inferno of hate that persecuted Jews and forced believers among them to go back behind nineteenth century liberalistic platitudes to the roots of their faith. In the America to which I had come, Jewish theology was still arrested in nineteenth century euphoria. Man was still infinitely perfectible, God still an inspiring idea, and Judaism still no more than an admirable force for progress, democracy, and mental health. Nothing had changed.

More precisely, nothing had changed in religious thought. In the sphere of life the change was considerable, for American Jews, shaken by the European Jewish fate, were even then beginning to make a historic commitment to Jewish group survival, the religious significance of which I did not then understand.[3] Even so, American Jewish theology was so remote from a radical reappraisal that a symposium of liberal rabbis, held in 1953, could still arrive at the patronizing overall conclusion that Buber and

Rosenzweig did not, after all, veer too far from the tenets of liberalism.[4]

The need for polemic occasioned my first Jewish writing. It also led me to some conclusions which I must now repudiate. That Judaism is a history of encounters between God and Israel of which the evolution of ideas is a mere human reflection; that revelation differs qualitatively from human inspiration; that, because revelation is an event of divine incursion shot through with human interpretation, all liberal-orthodox conflicts within Judaism are secondary—to these and other fundamental theological affirmations I am now as before committed. Indeed, what I now repudiate in my first group of essays[5] is only secondarily specific errors, and primarily a standpoint apt to generate such errors. I then stood, as it were, *between* an apologetic, compromising liberalism which I saw as dissipating into humanism, and the covenantal reaffirmation of revelation, largely understood in the terms of Buber and Rosenzweig; my thought, therefore, was essentially polemical. Had I then stood *within* the covenantal affirmation I would have been freer to take modern life and its problems into it; also, my argument with conflicting positions would have been only accidentally polemical, if indeed polemical at all.

My former standpoint, I now think, is the prisoner of its self-imposed limitations. Confined to polemics, it cannot make necessary discriminations in either the attacked or the defended position. More seriously, it is vulnerable to the danger of special pleading.

The first of these faults is evident in my earlier essays in three main points. First, attacking what is wrong with the old-fashioned liberalism they pay no attention to what is right with it—the refusal to despair in an age rife with despair. Second, bent on affirming classical Judaism against external criticism they virtually disregard internal criticism—how classical Judaism, once reaffirmed, is to come to terms with the modern world. Finally, I then set up extremes of "humanism" and "supernaturalism," and staked all on a radical leap from the one to the other. But I now think that modern religious life is more complex and subtle than the extremes set up by such a theological polemic.

More serious than lack of discrimination is outright error. Most of the errors in my earlier essays are implicit in a definition of faith which I would still value were it not for these errors. I then defined faith as "the positive answer, given by way of personal commitment, to existential questions of ultimate significance, which reason can still raise, but no longer answer."[6]

Does the human condition give rise to ultimate existential questions answerable only by faith? This is for the impartial philosopher, not for the theologian to say, and as a philosopher I would no longer be so sweeping.[7] In any case, the theologian impairs the philosopher's freedom if he speaks on his behalf, as well as his own freedom when he makes faith and theology dependent on specific philosophies. A Tillich-style correlation of philosophical questions and religious or theological answers never quite escapes the suspicion of attributing to unbelief questions which are asked —as well as answered—only by belief.

My earlier definition, then, is faulty philosophically. It is faulty theologically as well. I would now categorically reject all theological attempts to set up alternatives of faith and despair: there is both despair within faith and serene confidence without it. My point is not that of Harvey Cox's *The Secular City*, which cuts off ultimate questions such as death and guilt, making the voice of American pragmatism the voice of God.[8] My point is that agnostics and atheists must be allowed to cope with these questions in their own terms, and be protected from theologians who ascribe to them either a faith or a despair of which they are not aware. Such theological devices now seem to me contrary to the spirit of Judaism which will let God, but not the theologian, lead man into contrition and say, "return, ye children of man." Even God's recourse to such a stratagem at times calls for Jewish protests.

A still graver theological fault in my earlier definition of faith is the elimination of radical surprise. The miracle at the Red Sea and the revelation at Sinai were not answers to already known questions. May a theology of revelation confine all radical surprise to the past? Not in Judaism, if only because of the Messianic future, for this must mingle the unexpectable with the expected. Indeed, even from the pre-Messianic future radical surprise cannot be eliminated, unless it is prejudged to be a barren sameness of working and waiting. This point may have been academic for most Jewish generations, but not for the generation which has witnessed Auschwitz and the first Jewish state in two thousand years.

Such, then, are the effects of self-imprisonment in theological polemic. A liberation occurs when the Jewish theologian takes his stand *within* the Jewish faith, and understands it as committed openness to the voice of God.

IV

The liberation occurs in two related ways. First, philosophy, no longer subject to theological exigencies, is free to go its own way, and encounters between philosophy and Judaism—if and when they occur—are more likely to be genuine ones; they are no longer suspect of being theologically staged. Second, theology, freed of its polemical posture, is freer to inspect its own domain, and philosophical thinking, or something akin to it, can take place within that domain. The general standpoint I first adopted in an essay published in 1957[9] I have seen no reason to change till this day.

In the medieval world, encounters between philosophy and Judaism (or Christianity or Islam) were most significant when what was called for was harmonization or synthesis. This is because most philosophers and theologians could then agree that there were, or might be, two sources of truth, reason and revelation, the problem being merely how to reconcile their respective content. In the modern world, however, encounters are most significant when the conflict is most radical, for modern philosophy questions revealed authorities, supposed actual revelations, and the very possibility of revelation. Indeed, so radically critical is modern philosophy of religion—or, at any rate, of revealed religion—that it may well seem that this latter is foredoomed to destruction the moment it risks self-exposure. Such a view, however, rests on the secularist dogma that self-exposure should be unilateral, when in fact, to be fully critical, it must be mutual. When there is mutual self-exposure in an encounter between Judaism and modern philosophy, only one thing is known in advance— that light will be shed on both.

One brief illustration must here suffice.[10] Judaism and modern empiricism are in radical conflict, for the one, being a religion of revelation, affirms a God whose presence can be experienced, and the other surveys all experience but finds no God in it. To bring about a truly mutual self-exposure, one must note, first, that there are here two sets of categories, not one set only. It is true that the empiricist philosopher observes the believer's feeling of a divine presence, and maintains that his belief in an actual such presence is an inference or interpretation on the believer's part. But it must not be overlooked that in the believer's own mind there is no inference and no interpretation: Divinity is immediately present. This being the case, second, empiricism and Judaism may each indulge in unilateral criticism of the other. The empiricist may detect an unconscious inference or interpretation in the mind of the believer which only he, the empiricist philosopher, brings to the light of criticism. The Jewish believer on his part may assert that the presence of Divinity is a publicly observable datum which the empiricist, had he been present at Mount Sinai (or were he more sensitive now) would observe as well.

But, third, a truly mutual self-exposure results in two disclosures. One is that the empiricist already stands outside the circle of a believing openness when his "datum" is not the presence of God but merely a feeling of such a presence. The other is that the believer already stands within that circle when he hears the voice of God or even only accepts that it has somewhere been heard.

These two disclosures do not necessarily end the conflict. They do, however, alter the argument. The philosopher is forced to abandon all empiricist criticism of religious "data," undertaken from a standpoint of detachment, in order, instead, to inquire into the rational meaning and legitimacy of a religious commitment. The theologian on his part must recognize that there must already be a believing openness if the voice of God is to be heard, and that the nonbeliever cannot come to hear it through an experience which is of public "data," but only through a converting experience.

Still more important than encounters between Judaism and philosophy is what I have ambiguously referred to as "philosophical thinking, or something akin to it," within Judaism itself. The ambiguity is deliberate. I have in mind an inquiry into religious meaning, structure, essence, which is in principle abstractable from a commitment to religious truth, and which thus ought to qualify as uncommitted, impartial, and therefore philosophical. But the matter is not quite so simple. There surely is a difference between a phenomenological inquiry into Jewish, Christian, and Muhammadan prayer conducted by a philosopher who is himself neutral or even hostile to any religious commitment, and a reflection on the meaning and structure of Jewish prayer emerging from the immediacy of Jewish prayer itself, and undertaken with a view to what Kierkegaard calls "immediacy after reflection." Perhaps the future of Jewish philosophy is bound up with this difference.[11]

To call for an investigation of meaning in principle abstractable from a commitment to truth is, in a way, to call for a revival of the nineteenth century essence-approach to religion, despite twentieth century existentialist protests. I have in fact come to believe that the protests of men such as Buber and Rosenzweig are meant to be absolute only against caricatures of an essense of Judaism, and that their own existential affirmations are by no means devoid of structure. An existential commitment open to any content would raise the spectre of anarchism. And since this spectre is also raised by an historical positivism prepared to identify as Judaism whatever Jews past or present may have happened to believe, there is practical value, as well as theoretical validity, in the display of an inner logic within Judaism, which dispels anarchy and sets limits.

Let me consider the dichotomy between essence and existence. In an often quoted remark,[12] Rosenzweig states that "He came down" already concludes the Sinaitic revelation, whereas "He spoke" already is the beginning of human interpretation. This admirably affirms, on the one hand, the event of divine revelation against any liberalistic, humanistic dissipation, and on the other, the activity involved in human appropriation against any fundamentalist, passivist, literalism. But would Rosenzweig himself in the end maintain the implied total dichotomy between event and content? On the one hand, "He came down" is already metaphorical: Eastern mystics would require different metaphors. On the other hand—and this is crucial—the event of "descent" makes the interpretation "He spoke" inevitable. Any interpretation other than "He spoke" would be incompatible with the event of descent itself, for the event is a descent because it confirms man in his finite humanity (it is not an ineffable presence which dissipates his humanity), and he is being confirmed by being spoken to—and bidden to hear and respond. Revelation, in short, has a built-in content if only because it is revelation—because it is not an ineffable Presence in man which dissolves him, but rather a Presence speaking to man which singles him out for response. Hence all Jewish believing openness to the future is a structured openness, not an empty one, if only because it is an openness which listens and responds, works and waits. Not all varieties of religious experience are assimilable to Judaism.

But to grant this much structure in Judaism is to be compelled to seek out far more. It is, in fact, to regard Judaism (as doubtless every other profound form of spiritual life) as a dynamic whole, which in its historical career is able simply to absorb some novel events and experiences, is forced to respond to others through an internal restructuring and—this must be considered at least possible—is vulnerable to experiences so radical that the strain may be intolerable.[13]

To an "essence of Judaism" of this kind the historian can have no valid objections. He doubtless protests rightly against the kind of caricature which (mostly apologetically inspired) is a mere empty abstraction, such as an "ethical monotheism" which has lost the living God and which, as a wit once put it, mistakes Jews for members of the *Kant-Gesellschaft*. But without at least the heuristic use of a concept of essence as indicated he cannot, even as historian, indicate how Maimonides falls within Judaism while Spinoza does not. And when he turns theologian he confronts helplessly such contemporary *curiosa* as an atheism which claims to be a valid form of Judaism.

The historical protest is only against caricatures. The existentialist protest shows real limitations in the essence-approach itself. Nineteenth century essentialism identified the quest for religious meaning with that for religious truth. There were "higher" and "lower" religions, and the highest was *ipso facto* the truest religion. But such nineteenth and early twentieth century debates as to which religion was highest, Judaism or Christianity, have now lost all reality. One may still speak of higher and lower religions, but no longer of one which, by some independent standard, is highest. Indeed, even if this were still possible, an objective inquiry into religious meaning would still not settle the question of religious truth. Thus a student of comparative religion could still suspend his judgment, and a Feuerbach and a Marx were able to regard Christianity as the highest religion, and yet reject all religions as false.

The limits of the essence-approach, I think, are most tren-
chantly stated in terms of a critique of Hegel, whom I have come
to regard as the greatest modern religious philosopher. Hegel's
philosophy of religion develops four fundamental affirmations.
(i) Every genuine religion is an actual divine-human relation.
(ii) From the conflict of religious claims none emerges as absolutely true or false, and all as relatively true and false. (iii) The
exception is the Christian religion which, reconciling all partial
religious truth, is absolute religious truth. (iv) This fact, however,
is known only to philosophy. Christianity itself still sets up an
either/or between its own truth and non-Christian religious falsehood. Philosophy alone recognizes the partial truth of all genuine
religions, and the Christian absolute truth as their synthesis.[14]

Hegel (and I think Hegel alone) makes a strong case for identifying the quest for religious meaning with that for religious truth.
But he still calls forth the existentialist protest. This protest would
be decisive enough even if it were directed only against the fourth
Hegelian affirmation. Its rejection alone would suffice to create
a gap between essence and existence, if only because the philosopher is no longer, like Hegel, above all parties, but only neutral
to them. But existence and truth require not neutrality but a
commitment.

An essence of Judaism abstracted from existence abstracts from
three logically though not existentially separable questions. Why
a commitment to *any* religious truth? Why a commitment to Judaism? How respond Jewishly in the here-and-now?

Of the first two questions (which represent external challenges)
I will here only say that the Jewish thinker is deluded when he
begins with essence rather than existence. He is not a man-in-
general, an impartial spectator who may choose between religious
options in an existential vacuum. He already exists as a Jew, and
is already singled out as a Jew, and he cannot make an authentic
religious commitment unless he relates it to his singled-out Jewish
condition. Hence he is deluded when he seeks an authentic third

possibility between accepting and rejecting his singled-out Jewish condition—recourse to an unreal humanity-in-general, or an unreal religion-in-general. He is further deluded when he accepts the value of Jewish survival and his own Jewishness, but rejects Judaism, and does not face up to, and come to terms with, the absurdity that the Jewish faith is the cause of Jewish survival, and yet a four-thousand-year-old mistake. Finally, he deludes himself when he thinks he can abandon Judaism for a non-Jewish religion and yet remain a Jew.[15]

The third question represents an internal challenge. It exists because the God of Israel speaks *into* the historical here-and-now, and hence, potentially, into *any* here-and-now. Hence Jewish theological thought, however firmly rooted in past revelatory events, has always remained open to present and future, and this openness includes vulnerability to radical surprise.[16]

This is best seen in the greatest theology ever produced within Judaism—the Midrash of the Talmudic rabbis. Midrash is dialectical, and it is a whole, and it is an open whole.[17]

Midrash is dialectical because it must hold fast to contradictory affirmations which thought can hold together only in the form of symbol and metaphor. Divine Power transcends all things human —yet divine Love becomes involved with things human, and man, made a partner of God, can "as it were" augment or diminish divine power. Israel's election is a divinely imposed fate—and a free human choice. Man must wait for redemption as though all depended on God—and work for it as though all depended on man. The Messiah will come when all men are just—or all wicked. These affirmations must be held together unless thought is to lose either divine infinity or finite humanity, or the relation between them. Yet they cannot be held together except in stories, parables, and metaphors.

But Midrash, lacking system, is yet a whole, with a logic of its own. There is what may be called a Midrashic framework, which systematically resists philosophical or religious dissipation of its central affirmations. Midrashic thought resists a fatalism which dissipates human freedom in divine Power, and a paganism which limits divine Power literally, for the sake of human freedom. It opposes a mysticism which denies the reality of evil, and a skepticism which despairs on account of it. It rejects a particularism which denies the universal significance of the divine-Jewish covenant, and a universalism which either denies the reality of that covenant, or else affirms that it has come to an end.

The Midrashic framework is an open framework. The Torah was given at Sinai, yet it is given whenever a man receives it, and a man must often hear the old commandments in new ways. There are times in history when evil can be explained as deserved punishment, others when no such explanation is possible—when divine Power is, "as it were," suspended, and God Himself suffers in exile. Such openness is necessary if history is to be serious.

Until this century the Midrashic framework, while subject to external challenges,[18] has remained internally unbroken. But because it is open, and open not to fancied occurrences but to actual events, this framework is not wholly invulnerable. Today, vulnerability is no mere theoretical possibility. For the Jewish theologian of today cannot continue to believe, or continue to engage in theological thought, as though the events associated with the dread name of Auschwitz had not occurred.

V

Men shun the scandal of the particularity of Auschwitz. Germans link it with Dresden, American liberals, with Hiroshima. Christians deplore antisemitism-in-general, while communists erect monuments to victims-of-fascism-in-general—depriving the dead of Auschwitz of their Jewish identity even in death. Gentiles shun Auschwitz because of their real or imagined implication in its guilt.

Jews shun Auschwitz as well. Only after many years did significant Jewish responses begin to appear. Little is and can be said
even now. Perhaps there should still be silence. Yet one truth is
already totally obvious—that Jews must ever after remember
Auschwitz, and be its witnesses to the world. Not to remember
would be blasphemy. Not to be a witness would be a betrayal.

Yet such is the extent to which the world shrinks from the
truth that once a Jew begins to speak at all he must say even the
obvious. Must he say that the death of a Jewish child at Auschwitz
is no more lamentable than the death of a German child at Dresden? He must say it. Must he distinguish between the mass killing
at Hiroshima and that at Auschwitz? At the risk of being thought
a sacrilegious quibbler, he must make the distinction. He must
point out that Eichmann was moved by no "rational" purpose
such as victory when he diverted trains needed for military purposes in order to dispatch Jews to their death. He must add that
there was no "irrational" purpose either. Torquemada burned
bodies in order to save souls. Eichmann sought to destroy both
bodies and souls. Nor can a Jew fail to stress that Jews were the
singled-out victims. It is true, of course, that Jews were not the
sole victims, and a Jew would much prefer to think that Jews were
merely a species of the genus "inferior race." But the ineluctable
truth is that Jews were the prototype by which "inferior race" was
defined. Auschwitz is the scandal of evil for evil's sake, and Jews
were the singled-out victims. This is the rock on which in all
eternity all rational explanations—whatever their value and legitimacy—will break apart.

Resisting rational explanation, Auschwitz will forever after resist religious explanations as well. No religious meaning will ever
be found in Auschwitz, for the very attempt to find it is blasphemy. There remains only the possibility of a religious response;
this, however, is inescapable. To find such a response may as yet
wholly transcend any Jew's power. Yet his faith, his destiny, his
very survival will depend on whether, in the end, he finds it.

How can a Jew begin to seek a response? Looking for precedents, he finds none either in Jewish or in non-Jewish religious history. Jewish (like Christian) martyrs died for their faith, believing that God needs martyrs. Job suffered despite his faith, able to protest within the sphere of faith. Negro Christians died for their race, unshaken in a faith which was not at issue. The one million Jewish children murdered in the Nazi holocaust died not because of their faith, nor in spite of their faith, nor for reasons unrelated to faith. They were murdered because of the faith of their great-grandparents. Had these great-grandparents abandoned their Jewish faith, and failed to bring up Jewish children, then their fourth-generation descendants might have been among the Nazi executioners, but not among their Jewish victims. Like Abraham of old, European Jews sometime in the mid-nineteenth century offered a human sacrifice, by the mere minimal commitment to the Jewish faith of bringing up Jewish children. But unlike Abraham they did not know what they were doing, and there was no reprieve. This is the brute fact which makes all comparisons odious or irrelevant. This is the scandal of the particularity of Auschwitz which, once faced by the Jewish believer, threatens total despair.

Not until I faced this scandal did I make what to me was, and still is, a momentous discovery. Jews throughout the world—rich and poor, learned and ignorant, believer and unbeliever—were already responding to Auschwitz, and in some measure had been doing so all along. Faced with the radical threat of extinction, they were stubbornly defying it, committing themselves, if to nothing more, to the survival of themselves and their children as Jews. In ordinary times, such a commitment may be a mere mixture of nostalgia and vague loyalties. In the age of Auschwitz it is in itself a monumental act of faithfulness, as well as a monumental, albeit fragmentary, act of faith. To be a Jew after Auschwitz is to confront the demons of Auschwitz, and to bear witness against them in all their guises. It is to believe that they will not prevail, and to stake on that belief one's life and those of one's children's children.

Why is there this response when there might have been, and by all logic should have been, total disarray? I believe that whereas no redeeming voice is heard at Auschwitz a commanding voice is heard, and that it is being heard with increasing clarity. *Jews are not permitted to hand Hitler posthumous victories.* Jews are commanded to survive as Jews, lest their people perish. They are commanded to remember the victims of Auschwitz, lest their memory perish. They are forbidden to despair of God, lest Judaism perish. They are forbidden to despair of the world as the domain of God, lest the world be handed over to the forces of Auschwitz. For a Jew to break this commandment would be to do the unthinkable—to respond to Hitler by doing his work.[19]

Does the commanding voice of Auschwitz save the Midrashic framework from destruction? It is too soon to say. In the Midrash God is only "as it were" powerless, for the Messiah is still expected. In Elie Wiesel's *Night*[20] God hangs on the gallows, and for the hero of *The Gates of the Forest* a Messiah who is able to come, and yet did not come at Auschwitz, has become unthinkable. Yet in the end this hero says the *Kaddish*, whereby man returns to God His crown and His sceptre.[21] But how the Jews after Auschwitz can return these to God is not yet known. Nor is it yet known how God can receive them.

VI

The Nazi holocaust has brought Jews and Christians closer—and set them further apart. I was always aware of the first. Only gradually and painfully did I face up to the second.

A sense of great Jewish-Christian closeness explains, strangely enough, why there is little on Christianity in my earlier essays, what little there is being devoted to the secondary task of dispelling time-honored Christian misconceptions of Judaism. In the age of Hitler what separated Jew and Christian seemed dwarfed by what united them. I was not unaware of phenomena such as the Nazi "German-Christian" church, nor of the fact that outstanding theologians were enlisted in it. But what mattered to me personally were not Christian Nazis in Germany but rather Christian anti-Nazis, however small their number. And what mattered to me theologically were those Christian thinkers who could recognize Nazism as idolatry, and resisted it. I have always revered Kierkegaard, the first Christian to recognize the nature and extent of modern idolatry, to whom Jewish as well as Christian theologians are indebted. I have always needed the support of Christian fellow-believers, and indeed wonder whether, had there not been a Christian renewal initiated by such men as Barth, Tillich, and Niebuhr, the Jewish renewal initiated by Buber and Rosenzweig would have been possible. And when a new generation of Christian theologians rejects its neoorthodox fathers and announces the death of God I feel, as a Jew, abandoned and betrayed.[22]

A sense of Jewish-Christian closeness explains why what Jews and Christians share is said by implication in my earlier essays, and why there is no sense of urgency to discuss Jewish-Christian differences—at a time when both Judaism and Christianity were threatened by neopagan forces. If no such discussion is found even in my later essays, it is because I always stood in need of what may be called a Jewish theology of Christianity, but am unable to supply this need to this day.

The ancient rabbis recognized "righteous Gentiles" as being equal to the high priest in the sight of God; but they had no real acquaintance with Christianity and, of course, none with Islam. Medieval Jewish thinkers recognized Christian and Muhammadan monotheism and, considering the state of medieval Jewish-Christian and Jewish-Muhammadan relations, it is astonishing that they did as much. But it has always seemed to me that in the modern world there was need for more—for a Jewish recognition that the Christian (and Muslim), rather than merely affirming One God, stand in a living relation to Him. Thus I always was and still am dissatisfied on this point with traditional Jewish teaching. At the same time, I was never able to accept Rosenzweig's famous "double covenant" theory, according to which all except Jews (who are "with the Father") need the Son in order to find Him. How can a modern Jew pray for the conversion of the non-Jewish world to Christianity, when even premodern Jews could pay homage to Muslim monotheism? Rosenzweig's doctrine is overrun by events at a time when Christians themselves are beginning to replace missionary efforts with interreligious dialogue. And I now wonder whether even for Rosenzweig himself it was more than a stage in his self-emancipation from modern paganism.

I am thus left with no doctrine, but only with openness to Jewish-Christian dialogue. But what is a religious recognition which does not recognize the other in the terms of his own self-understanding? The heart of dialogue, it seems to me, is to refuse to give an abstract answer to this question, and instead risk self-exposure. If Jew and Christian are both witnesses, they must speak from where they are. But unless they presume to be on the throne of divine judgment, they must listen as well as speak, risking self-exposure just because they are witnesses.

For many years I believed that the long age of Christian triumphalism over Judaism had ended and the age of Jewish-Christian dialogue had arrived. Today I am less sanguine. In view of recent Christian developments, such as ecclesiastical declarations deploring antisemitism and absolving Jews of the charge of deicide, this may seem a strange, even perverse, personal development. But I think that insofar as this development has indeed been personal it reflects more than idiosyncrasies. Moreover, recent events have shown that it is merely a growing realism.

To most observers it has always been a plain fact that, ever since the Age of Enlightenment, it was secularists who spearheaded the struggle for Jewish emancipation, and that the organized Christian forces sometimes accepted it, often opposed it, but rarely if ever led the fight. This plain fact it took me many years to accept.[23] I saw the distinction between Nazi and Christian antisemitism, but could not bear to admit their relation. Least of all could I face the fact that few even among anti-Nazi German Christians had opposed Nazi antisemitism.[24] As I put it in one very recent essay, in the grim years of Nazism and after, it was a simple human impossibility to see enemies on every side.[25]

But America has always been different, and the churches in the 1960s differ everywhere from those of the 1940s. There are historic changes in Christian attitudes toward Jews. Why does a Jew find it hard to rejoice? The situation is similar to that between the American Negro and his erstwhile white oppressor. It is precisely when the latter begins to examine his soul that the former realizes the extent of his former oppression—and how great that oppression still is. As a white man I need a James Baldwin to tell me the truth. Just so, the Christian needs to hear the truth from Jews. And the truth is that the organized Christian forces will find it easiest to drop the ancient charge of deicide, harder to recognize roots of Christian antisemitism in the New Testament, and hardest of all to admit that both Jews and Judaism are alive. Faced with the fact of Jewish survival after the advent of Christianity, Christians have looked upon Jews and Judaism as a fossil, an anachronism, a shadow. It is not easy to reverse a doctrine which has persisted for nearly two thousand years, assuming secular as well as religious forms, and to recognize that both Jews and Judaism have had an unbroken life throughout the Christian era.

That this is a realistic judgment is shown nowhere more clearly than in Christian attitudes to the most incontestable contemporary proof of Jewish survival—the first Jewish state in two thousand years. During the momentous events in May and June 1967 the secular Western press understood that Israel was fighting for its life. Few Christian spokesmen showed a similar understanding. Why were they neutral between Israel's claim to the right to live and Arab claims to the right to destroy her—except because of old, theologically-inspired doubts as to whether Israel had the right to live? Why has there been all along much concern for Arab refugees from Israel, but none for Jewish refugees from Arab lands—if not because of old doctrines that Jews had to be landless, and landless people were rightless? Why were ecclesiastical authorities untroubled by two decades of Muslim control of the Christian holy places (and of Arab desecration of the Jewish holy places), but seemed to find Jewish control unbearable?

But another still deeper and far more troubling question is raised by the recent events in Israel. For two long weeks in May 1967 the world-wide Jewish community perceived the spectre of a second Jewish holocaust in a single generation. For two weeks it listened to the same words emanating from Cairo and Damascus which had once emanated from Berlin. For two weeks it longed for Christian words of apprehension and concern. But whereas some such words came from secular sources, from the churches there was little but silence. Once again, Jews were alone.

The question is deeper and more troubling because what is at issue is not an old Christian antisemitism but rather a new Jewish-Christian problem—the fearful fact that Hitler, against his will bringing Jews and Christians closer, also had his will in setting them further apart.

A Jew at Auschwitz was murdered because he was a Jew; a Christian was murdered only if he was a saint: but there are few saints among either Jews or Christians. Hitler tried to create a veritable gulf between Jews and Christians, and the horror is that he has still posthumous successes. For whereas the Jew after Auschwitz exists with a sense of abandonment, the Christian cannot bear to face this Jewish abandonment. Knowing that, as a Christian, he should have been with the abandoned, he is racked by a sense of guilt the more deep the less he has cause for it. In May 1967 Jews heard the commanding voice of Auschwitz. As for the Christian community, it did not consciously commit the sin of abandoning Jews to a second holocaust. It failed to recognize the danger of a second holocaust, for it still cannot face the fact of the first.

Few things are more important than to bridge this Jewish-Christian gulf, and at a Jewish-Christian colloquium prior to the events of May 1967, I made an attempt. I said that had every Christian in Hitler's Europe followed the example of the king of Denmark and decided to put on the yellow star, there would be today neither despair in the church nor talk of the death of God. I said with every emphasis that I spoke as a witness, not as a judge. To remove every trace of ambiguity or doubt I stated that I had been sixteen years of age when Hitler came to power, and had not known then, nor knew now, whether I would have become a Nazi had I been born a Gentile. Yet a leading Christian thinker, himself a lifelong anti-Nazi, mistook my remarks for Jewish triumphalism. So wide is the gulf between Jews and Christians which Hitler succeeded in creating. So close are we all to handing him further, posthumous victories.

VII

On a public occasion in March 1967 I asked the following question: "Would we [like Job] be able to say that the question of Auschwitz will be answered in any sense whatever in case the eclipse of God were ended and He appeared to us? An impossible and intolerable question."[26] Less than three months later this purely hypothetical question had become actual, when at Jerusalem the threat of total annihilation gave way to sudden salvation,

atheists spoke of miracles, and hard-boiled Western reporters resorted to Biblical language.

The question *is* impossible and intolerable. Even Job's question
is not answered by God's presence, and to him children are restored. The children of Auschwitz will not be restored, and the
question of Auschwitz will not be answered by a saving divine
Presence. Indeed, could there be a Jewish acceptance of such a
Presence if it were to manifest itself, and a rejoicing in it?

And yet, may a Jew despair of salvation after Auschwitz on
account of Auschwitz? May he cast out all hope and all joy? Or
could he retain hope and joy, and yet fail to relate them to
Auschwitz? Any of these responses would be further victories to
Hitler, and are thus impossible.

Into precisely this impossible and intolerable contradiction
believing Jews were placed by the events of Jerusalem in May
and June 1967. For precisely and only because of their connection with Auschwitz was there a radical astonishment which
gave a military victory (rarely applauded in Judaism, and never
for its own sake) an inescapable religious dimension. And it is
precisely because of this connection that a Jew must both tremble
and rejoice. He must tremble lest he permit any light after
Auschwitz to relieve the darkness of Auschwitz. He must rejoice,
lest he add to the darkness of Auschwitz. Rejoicing after
Auschwitz and because of Auschwitz, the Jew must be a witness
to the world, preparing a way for God.

2

Self-Realization and
the Search for God

*A Critique of Modern Humanism
and a Defence of Jewish Supernaturalism*

> Therefore shall a man first take upon himself the yoke of
> the Kingdom of Heaven, and then take upon himself the
> yoke of the commandments.
>
> M. Berakot 2.2

I

Man will at all times seek ultimate integration. It is intolerable
to him that his life as a whole should not have a unity through
which he can assess meaning to all its aspects.

It is significant that the criterion governing most modern attempts at such a synthesis can be expressed by the term "self-
realization." Idealists and romanticists mean by this term the
realization of an ideal self slumbering within every person; prag-
matists and naturalists refer rather to the whole realm of human
living, physical as well as spiritual. They agree that to give ultimate meaning to his life man must turn on himself, arousing
those powers in himself which represent his highest opportunity.

Underlying this view is the faith that what is contradictory and

Reprinted from *Judaism* (Fall 1952), pp. 291-306.

evil in human nature is merely a lack of something; that it is "unreal" or "unnatural"; and that the individual can master it and aspire to perfection by realizing what is positive, his "real" or "natural" self. Thus, "self-realization" means to the idealist the realization or approximation of an envisaged ideal self. And it is taken for granted, first, that the individual is able to form the right conception of his ideal self, and secondly, that to realize or approximate it is a task which is obstructed by no basic obstacle. In the naturalist frame of reference, the prime criterion of self-realization is health. Evil is "the unnatural," which health automatically eliminates. Health produces social harmony because it balances pleasure and duty—a healthy egoism and a healthy altruism; it produces inner harmony because the healthy man concentrates on such of his problems as are solvable, ignoring those which are not. Health also gives freedom to the individual's creative powers while providing harmless outlets for his destructive urges—and creativity is fulness of life. Harmony eliminates evil; creativity eliminates emptiness.

Religion also is interpreted in terms of self-realization. The fact that many modern definitions of religion do not even include God indicates what has happened: religion has been transformed from a total integration of life through relation to a supernatural God into total integration through self-realization. The convictions leading to this transformation are again the same: all meaning that the individual can find in his life is inherent in his own nature; and any meaning that he cannot find in himself is both unattainable and practically irrelevant, therefore properly to be ignored.

Other interpretations of religion do include God. But, again, in many of these, He appears as an *idea* only, His *existence* being acknowledged with embarrassment if acknowledged at all. Afterlife, salvation, eternal judgment are here meaningless words; nature and history are interpreted in terms of science. An existing God, if affirmed at all, is at best permitted to retain the function of a First Cause, required perhaps for cosmological interpretation but of little if any significance for the life of the individual. *Ideas* of God, however, are here regarded as of utmost importance for the individual's life. For the kind of idea he has of God will determine his scale of values and, thus, indirectly, the kind of life he is motivated to live. Individual life, as well as human history, can become

> a battle for the pure idea of God and man, which is not to end until the principle of divine holiness has done away with every form of life that tends to degrade and disunite mankind, and until Israel's Only One has become the unifying power and the highest ideal of all humanity.[1]

Here man undoubtedly creates God in his own image, ideas of God deriving not from an existing God who reveals Himself, but from human conception and evaluation. Again, the actual faith behind this religion is a faith in the "true" or "real" self which enables man both to form adequate ideas of God and to live without basic difficulty in *imitatio Dei*.

What becomes of prayer when God is understood as an idea only? Where every trace of even unconscious belief in the being of God is lost, prayer is no longer an appeal to the Other for help and guidance; it is an activity designed to arouse and inspire the better, the true self. The individual no longer seeks help from God, but from himself.

Whatever may be the lasting value of this ideal of self-realization or the partial truth in it, as a principle of ultimate integration it is totally inadequate. The reason for its inadequacy is the error of the faith on which it is based. If an ultimate self, harmonious, perfect, and unambiguous, were realizable, "self-realization" could perhaps serve as the principle of ultimate integration. A man's ideals might not, then, be absolute, but they would be the best he could know or be expected to know. As to his realization of the ideals, he might be far from complacent; but he could be confident at least that the degree of perfection he would achieve would depend only on his knowledge of the ideals and on the energy he was ready to devote to their realization. He would definitely not need the guidance or mercy of an existing God. His unconcern with his own ultimate destiny could be understood as the heroic attitude of a good soldier who is concerned to do his duty, but gives no thought to his own fate.

But this kind of self-confidence and heroic self-sufficiency rest on a tragic illusion. There is no such thing as a single, unambiguous, perfect self, the source and end of ultimate integration. On the contrary, the more deeply the individual searches his soul, the more clearly does he come to understand the irreducible tensions which lie in his nature. Biological necessity and spiritual freedom are not merely mutually irreducible, which would still make possible a division of authority, as it were, between these two parts of human nature; they are also inextricably intertwined. Face these tensions in their sharpness and profundity, and you at once recognize that the one potential self is an illusion; you can no longer discover the unambiguous self you can and ought to be—and to give it adjectives such as "ideal," "creative," "natural," or "healthy," is no help at all.

The unprejudiced man soon senses that there is something wrong with self-realization as the principle of ultimate integration. If he attempts self-realization in the naturalist terms of health, he himself transcends this attempt sufficiently to feel that health does not exhaust his ultimate obligation. Health, with all its happy implications, seems to be merely what makes him fit to face that obligation. At times, it even seems necessary to sacrifice health in the service of ultimate responsibility. Health comes to seem something like an ultimate criterion only when sickness renders him unable to be genuinely responsible.[2] If he attempts self-realization in idealist terms, setting up an ideal and striving to reach it, he transcends this attempt sufficiently to marvel at his presumptuousness. Knowing his ideal to stem from himself, he suspects it of being tainted with hidden self-interest. And even while striving to reach that ideal, he knows his effort to be vitiated by motives which are anything but pure. Nor can he ever free himself entirely from the fetters of this impurity. For every effort designed to achieve that effect has its own admixture of impure motives.

That these misgivings are not empty scruples, the twentieth century illustrates with abundant clarity. It demonstrates the fact that destructiveness is not merely something "unnatural," the product of sickness, and it demonstrates that an idealistic attitude is not in itself a sufficient guarantee of moral goodness. "Normal" men beyond suspicion of sickness, morbidity, and frustration "express themselves" in war, destruction, and wholesale murder. "Idealistic" youths serve evil tyrants in noble devotion, committing nameless crimes out of a sincere sense of duty, and sacrificing their lives to the kingdom of evil. This is the stark fact: when health becomes the ultimate law, the "blond beast" is set free for breaking the fetters of morality; when the spirit is its own unqualified measure, Satan, the perverted spirit, is free also, transforming a mere urge for security into a metaphysical lust for power, a mere desire for survival and perpetuation into a mystic yearning for eternal glory gained through terror and destruction.

To recoil from these criminal manifestations is not to free oneself of the roots of the evil. Who does not know the ruthlessness and hardness of heart that sometimes go with health, or the difficulty of controlling the destructive urges stemming from vitality? And as for man's spiritual life, what of envy masquerading as righteousness, cruelty as justice, selfishness called freedom, avarice called equality? Happily, in most cases, such perversions only partly corrupt the ideal into which they enter; but, tragically, the perversion is only partly conscious, and only partly corrigible. The individual who understands this situation and still has the courage to attempt the realization of a pure and ideal self will do so in profound humility. But this humility, too, if conceived in terms of self-realization, becomes tainted with self-righteousness.

Ultimate integration is inaccessible through self-realization: it is equally inaccessible through religion defined in terms of self-realization. As a historical and psychological phenomenon, religion may, and perhaps even must, be defined in terms of self-realization; but as a way of life claiming to be a *valid* synthesis, it cannot be defined in these terms. Characteristically, liberalism sees no need to distinguish radically between religion considered from the standpoint of history or psychology, and religion considered from the standpoint of its validity. For its whole faith rests on the hypothesis of one normative self, progressively revealed in personal and human history. But once this illusion is destroyed, a religion defined in terms of self-realization is revealed as pure nihilism.

The weakness inherent in a religion defined in terms of self-realization cannot be overcome by merely choosing another aspect or activity of the self as the source of certainty. In Schleiermacher's celebrated definition, religion is held to be, "a feeling of unqualified dependence."[3] But "feeling," too, is a kind of self-realization, and a religion defined in such terms suffers from the same weakness. Thus, if "feeling of unqualified dependence" refers to such feelings as are actual, religion will include sacrificial devotion to dictators and charlatans, and blind obedience to nation or race exalted as the manifestation of the Absolute.[4] If, on the other hand, we mean by this "feeling" an emotion men *ought* to have, we either set up arbitrarily someone's actual feeling as absolute standard, or we seek this standard through the conception of an ideal feeling. But then religion—the actual feeling of unqualified dependence—becomes secondary to the philosophy defining that ideal feeling, and dependent on its fate. Religion is no longer the ultimate source of total integration.

No religion, of course, can dispense with ideas man forms of

God. What we are discussing here is the view that holds God to be an idea *only*, or else to be known and relevant only as such. Such God-ideas serve here as an ultimate principle of integration by making an absolute claim on man's allegiance. Now, it is plain that God-ideas have undergone a vast development in the history of civilization, and the claim of the liberal era that this development has the form of inevitable progress toward one fixed aim can hardly be sustained. On what basis, then, does a man give *absolute* allegiance to an idea which is relative to his civilization and to the caprices of his own nature? But let us suppose we could assume that the God-idea is steadily progressing toward absolute purity. If we believe that our God-idea is not altogether pure yet, by what standards do we know how high we have risen in the scale of purity? And by what right do we give *absolute* allegiance to an idea whose degree of relativity we do not know? If, on the other hand, we claim to have reached the final degree of purity in our idea of God, will not a later age smile at our presumptuousness? And again, by what standards do we measure its finality?

But the main objection to the religion of self-realization is not relativism; quite possibly an adequate philosophy of religion could overcome it. Let us assume, therefore, that we could conceive a God-idea sufficiently free from relative admixture to claim our absolute allegiance. This God, who is an idea only, can perhaps persuade and inspire; but He surely cannot succor, love, and forgive. To speak of the succor, love, and forgiveness of a God who is an idea only is to employ a misleading metaphor. There are, of course, those who find their lives totally integrated through divine commandment and inspiration, and who calmly do without succor and forgiveness. But these are people who are caught in the idealist illusion about their nature and power which we have already analyzed. To know of the inextricable togetherness of freedom and bondage which is our state, is to know that no total unity comes from a God-idea "enthroned on high," but unable to "look down low" (Ps. 113:5-6). While the Absolute Ideal may perhaps inspire to imitation, it at the same time paralyzes because of its very absoluteness. A God, then, who is an idea only, or relevant only as such, still fails to integrate our lives; and *this* failure is more critical than any we have yet considered. Indeed, it is the crucial failure of the religion of self-realization.

If life is to find total integration, we must seek it in a Reality transcending our contradictory self and the ideals and standards relative to it.

II

Though he may perceive the futility of attempting ultimate integration through self-realization, modern man feels that somehow he cannot escape that futility. Religious tradition once believed that it had found access to a Reality transcending the relativity of the self through divine *revelation* or else through *rational proof* of God's existence. Modern man seems to find both these paths closed to him.

Modern man has no reason to doubt the sincerity of those who have taken their own experience or the experience of others to be divine revelation. But his own intellectual conscience compels him to interpret "revelation" in terms of "experience-of-revelation." To him the authority of revelation depends on the authority of human experience.[5] This is still a form of self-realization, afflicted with all the weakness inherent in it. Thus, modern man feels himself confronted with the dilemma between a flight to a supernatural revealed authority which he can no longer accept, on the one hand, and a flight to an authoritativeness of human experience as little acceptable to him, on the other. Morally, this seems to be a dilemma between the sins of intellectual dishonesty and spiritual pride.

Nor does modern man find himself any better off when he tries to establish God's existence by rational proof. He may presuppose that his reason is equipped for the task and that, though it is part of mere relative man, its axioms and laws are those which govern ultimate reality. If so, he presupposes rather than proves the existence of a God who gave him reason so that he might know Him. This kind of faith appears to be implied in the traditional proofs of God. If modern man refuses to make that *apriori* assumption, the certainty of God becomes dependent on the capricious and relative "certainties" acquired by a relative reason; for by these God is to be proven. Such a God is never really certain; He is always a mere hypothesis, living in dependence on precarious certainties. Nor is He really God. It has often been pointed out that a God who is proved without being presupposed in this proof is both too "far" and too "near" to be God: He is too "far" because there is something nearer and more certain by which He is proved; He is too "near" because man's finite reason can pass judgment on Him. Again man is faced with a dilemma. To ascertain God's existence by rational proof he must presuppose either a God who fashioned his reason, or the capacity of his reason to prove a God whom he has not fashioned. To attempt rational proof of God in awareness of this situation seems either self-deception or outright insolence.

III

An iron logic, it seems, has led man from a synthesis found in God, to a synthesis found in an autonomous self, to the surrender of all aspiration toward ultimate standards and ultimate meaning. A self revealed as caught in relativity cannot be the source of ultimate integration, nor does it seem able to recover any access to an absolute God. But we should be reluctant to accept this development as inexorable. This would be to dismiss lightly and *in toto* what seemed unquestionable reality to so many religious generations. We must, then, probe a little more deeply

into man's ultimate situation. To make this difficult task somewhat easier, let us first try to understand the meaning of God and
of life with God as reflected in biblical and rabbinic tradition. For
modernity has unconsciously tended to misinterpret these, in
accordance with its own very different ideas.[6]

The biblical and rabbinic tradition is pervaded by the conviction that it is impossible to doubt or deny the existence of God.

The modern mind will at once attribute this conviction to philosophical naiveté and the inability to deal critically with evidence.
But this notion hardly goes beyond the surface. It is true, of
course, that the evidence presented for divine revelation is not
examined as critically as it might be. Nature is too simply taken
as evidence of a God who guides it. History is too naively
assumed to prove divine retribution. The certainty stemming
from personal experience is not subjected to adequate criticism.
But, this kind of naive acceptance of evidence is only incidental
to the certainty of the existence of God. For it is realized that the
evidence frequently fails. Nature harbors evil as well as good.
Human nature appears afflicted with shortcomings such as cannot
be attributed to man's own fault. History, above all, shows conditions which impel a Jeremiah to contend: "Wherefore doth the
way of the wicked prosper? Wherefore are all they secure that
deal very treacherously?" (Jer. 12:1), and a rabbi must admit: "It
is not in our power to explain either the prosperity of the wicked
or the afflictions of the righteous."[7] "Times of wrath" occur,
when "all people cry and weep, but their voice is not heard, even
though they decree fast-days, roll themselves in dust, cover
themselves with sackcloth and shed tears."[8] And often man finds
no evidence in his heart of the presence of God.

But while the evidence can become doubtful, God cannot. If
nature reveals evil, then God "form[s] light and create[s] darkness, make[s] peace and create[s] evil" (Isa. 45:7). The fact that
men cannot see divine purpose evidenced in history merely

proves that: "My thoughts are not your thoughts, neither are My ways your ways" (Isa. 55:8). If inner experience is dead, it is because God "hides His face" (Ps. 13:2; 44:35; 69:18), "stands off" (Ps. 10:1), "forgets" (Ps. 13:2), "forsakes" (Ps. 22:2), or "sleeps" (Ps. 44:24); but the failure of inner evidence never suggests that God does not exist. Even the great skeptic of the Bible, Kohelet, who regards life as a whole as vanity, concludes from this conviction: "This is the end of the matter, all having been heard: fear God, and keep His commandments; for this is the whole man" (Eccl. 12:13). No objective evidence to the contrary, and no feeling of being deserted, can affect the certainty of God. As Job puts it: "Though He slay me, yet will I trust in Him" (Job 13:15).

We cannot fairly dismiss this absolute and fact-defying certainty of God as the mental habit of a religious civilization. How then can we understand it? We shall be totally unable to do so unless we rid ourselves of the modern prejudice that all religious life is an evolution of religious *feelings* or *ideas*. In accordance with this prejudice, man forms notions of God with the assistance of external and internal evidence, and the more he becomes conscious of this activity of his, the more thoroughly does he arrive at a state of objective detachment in which he judges the merits of the God-idea, and weighs the evidence for the existence of God. However, when in Jewish tradition God's existence is nowhere doubted nor made dependent on evidence, this is not because man is here at too primitive a level to have reached the stage of objective and critical detachment; it is because of a profound certainty that such a detachment is impossible. *God's existence is man's existential apriori.*

> Whither shall I go from Try spirit? Or whither shall I flee from
>   Thy presence?
> If I ascend up into heaven, Thou art there;
> If I make my bed in the netherworld, behold, Thou art there.

> If I take the wings of the morning,
> And dwell in the uttermost parts of the sea;
> Even there would Thy hand lead me,
> And Thy right hand would hold me (Ps. 139:7—10).[9]

This is not a rather primitive and unscientific statement of a universal God-idea. From a God-idea one could "flee" at least to the extent of viewing it in an attitude of objective detachment. The God of the Bible is not an ultimate object; He is *the* Subject, each man's living, personal God. Any attempt to subject God's existence to critical judgment is, therefore, held to be insolence, because it means to judge the Judge. To deny His existence is more than insolence: it is "folly" (Ps. 14:1; 53:2), since it is the rejection by man of his own "light and salvation" (Ps. 27:1); it is rebellion, since it is the attempt to replace God's authority by man's (Ps. 10:4; also Ezek. 28:9). The denial of God is self-destruction or rebellion; it is never merely an erroneous objective statement. In his ultimate relation to Reality, man must be *participant;* he cannot remain *spectator.*

Attempts to describe the nature of this God in biblical and rabbinic tradition must be understood as part of this fundamental situation. The avowed task here is not to describe consistently and adequately an infinite God as He is in Himself, a task that could be undertaken only by an objective spectator. The task is to describe the living relation between this infinite God and finite man, and to do so as an inevitable participant.

God is infinite and yet directly related to each finite person. This is the inexplicable, yet indubitable, basic fact about God. He is "enthroned on high and looketh down low" (Ps. 113:5-6). He is both "far and near":

> God is far, for is He not in the heaven of heavens? And yet He is near, . . . for a man enters a synagogue, and stands behind a pillar, and prays in a whisper, and God hears his prayer, and so it is with all His creatures. He is as near to His creatures as the ear to the mouth.[10]

The direct relation between the infinite God and the finite human person is by its very nature paradoxical. If this relation were one-sided, it would destroy itself; for then the infinite God would devour the finite person's freedom and his very identity. It is a mutual relation. "Everything is in the hands of Heaven except the fear of Heaven,"[11] is the word of a rabbi to whom human freedom is real yet limited by Divine Presence. But if this relation is a mutual one, then paradoxically the free actions and reactions of finite men make a difference to the infinite God. Biblical and rabbinic tradition express the reality of this paradoxical relation in a well-nigh infinite variety of metaphors. These metaphors, which are mostly anthropomorphisms, cannot be regarded as "impure" philosophical notions; they are *symbolic* terms designed to describe a relation which cannot be grasped in any terms other than symbolic. Occasionally the rabbis are fully conscious of this, especially when in their stress on human responsibility they even make the omnipotent God dependent on impotent man.

> *Ye are My witnesses, saith the Lord, and I am God* (Isa. 43:12).
> That is, when ye are My witnesses, I am God, and when ye are not My witnesses, I am, as it were, not God.[12]
>
> When the Israelites do God's will, they add to the power of God on high. When the Israelites do not do God's will, they, as it were, weaken the great power of God.[13]

The paradox in these statements is fully intended, and the term *"as it were"* has the full rank of a technical term in rabbinic theology, indicating the symbolic character of the statement it qualifies.[14]

God's nature, as revealed in His relation to man, reflects the paradox inherent in this relation. In rabbinic theology, the concepts of divine *justice* and divine *mercy* are striking in their prominence.[15] Philosophically, absolute justice and absolute mercy are mutually exclusive; but in rabbinic theology, they remain mutually irreducible. God's mercy, to the exclusion of His justice, would wipe out the difference betweeen the righteous and the wicked. His justice, without His mercy, would destroy all men; and even if it be conceived that God tempers His justice to finite man, "demanding according to man's power," infinite divine retribution would still be totally incommensurable with finite human sin.

> *The Lord made heaven and earth.* This may be compared to a king who had some empty glasses. Said the king: "If I pour hot water into them, they will burst; if cold, they will contract and snap." What then did the king do? He mixed hot and cold water and poured it into them, and so they remained unbroken. Even so, said the Holy One, blessed be He: "If I create the world on the basis of mercy alone, its sins will be great; on the basis of justice alone, the world cannot exist. Hence I will create it on the basis of justice and mercy, and may it then stand."[16]

This togetherness of justice and mercy is not a harmonious compromise. In a mutual limitation through compromise, both justice and mercy would lose their meaning. Thus R. Akiba insists on the absolute and unqualified justice of God's judgment,[17] and in the Midrash God is made to say:

> All I do, I do in justice. If I sought to pass beyond justice but once, the world could not endure.[18]

Consequently, men are warned not to make light of their responsibility before the bar of divine justice:

> He who says, God is indulgent, his life shall be outlawed.[19]
> If the evil inclination says to you, "Sin, and God will forgive you," believe it not.[20]

But on the other hand, divine mercy is likewise absolute and unqualified. For whatever their relative merits, before God all men need mercy absolutely. Even Moses and David asked that their sins be forgiven, by reason not of their merits, but of God's grace.[21] Nor did they pray thus only because of their humility.

> All men need grace, including Abraham, for whose sake grace came plenteously into the world.[22]

The Midrash expresses the principle of mercy:

> He said, 'I owe no creature anything, but I give to them gratuitously.'[23]

Justice and mercy coexist:

> If we have merit, and if we possess good deeds, He gives us of what is ours; if not, then He acts charitably and lovingly toward us from what is His.[24]

But do not then both justice and mercy become meaningless? They may become so in philosophical theory, but not in the religious life. The ultimate unity of mercy and justice in God is indeed an ineffable mystery.[25] Man not only can, but must live in the double certainty of his responsibility before the bar of divine justice and of his security in divine mercy. For radically speaking, man can, and cannot, do the will of God. Insofar as he can do His will, it is only by reason of God's help;[26] yet insofar as he cannot do it, his contrition is a spontaneous and acceptable offering.[27] Man must pray, not only for forgiveness of sins already committed, but also for divine help against future temptations.[28] Yet a man who acts has full freedom, and no sin is preordained.[29]

The sins of the past, of which no man is free, do not destroy the freedom of present and future. For man is at all times free to repent, whatever the sins of the past.[30] In contrast with the gates of prayer which, tragically, are often closed, the gates of repentance are always open.[31] But again, even for the ability to repent man must pray for divine assistance.[32]

Thus the religious life is a tension between two certainties: responsibility before God, and safety in Him. There is no *apriori* limitation to either of these.

> The Israelites say to God, "Lord of the world, Thou knowest how hard is the strength of the evil inclination." God says, "Remove it a little in this world, and I will rid you of it altogether in the world-to-come."[33]

How much is "a little"? That cannot be known. That is why man must both tremble and rejoice: he trembles because, before the throne of divine justice, what he does is nothing compared with what he ought to do; he rejoices because, nevertheless, it is something, and because through the mercy of God it is everything. Therefore it has been said: "Love and fear God; tremble and rejoice when you perform the commandments."[34]

I V

Guided by the insights of biblical and rabbinic tradition, we may penetrate the problem of man's ultimate integration sufficiently to grasp this basic fact: the way in which modern man has arrived at the situation we have tried to describe is not, as he has habitually assumed, necessary and unquestionable; on the contrary, it is rather founded on subjective and dubious assumptions. Modern man has dogmatically assumed the same approach in his search for ultimate integration as he has adopted in his scientific inquiries—an attitude of objective, critical detachment.

This attitude is quite proper in the case of scientific inquiry, because scientific inquiry deals with the realm of *objects*. We know objects by detaching ourselves from involvement in them, and by simultaneously subjecting them to our critical judgment. The exercise of autonomous judgment is possible because man is, in principle, able to view the world as object. It is necessary because he requires objectivity to plan both his biological and his moral life.

However, if modern man claims objective detachment and the autonomy of his critical judgment to be basic to the problem of his ultimate integration, he commits a plain fallacy. For man's *existence* cannot become an object for him, neither can he assume toward it an attitude of objectivity, detachment, and autonomy. While he thinks in "detachment," he is in fact involved in existence. Thus, an attitude of objective detachment and objective judgment toward the problem of ultimate integration is a form of self-deception, due to our inability to free ourselves from the habits we form in relation to the world of objects. Or it is a hidden dogma, a subjective decision taken in relation to his own existence. In the very act of assuming an attitude of detachment, and of subjecting it to his autonomous judgment, man is already deciding to be his own judge and the master of his own life. Little wonder that the results at which he arrives on this basis confirm the hidden initial dogma.

In the same manner, we must consider the question of God's existence. If there is a God, and if He is *God*, He embraces man's existence with such totality as to make objective detachment altogether impossible. If a man can pass judgment on God and His existence, it is not God on whom he passes judgment. A God who can be an *object* is not God. Because a God who is subjected to man's objective judgment is not God, *God can neither be proven nor disproven*. If God is God, He is not an object, but *the* Subject. He is man's absolute existential *apriori*.

Insight into the impossibility of assuming an attitude of detachment and autonomous judgment would, in itself, lead merely to an infinite suspension of judgment. But if man becomes fully aware of his position, he realizes too that he must go further. For he cannot remain neutral here. Thought can be suspended, but not existence. Suspension of judgment itself is here an impermissible judgment. Man exists by compulsion; he is therefore compelled to make a *decision*. For to refuse to make a decision is also to decide.

Thus, because man cannot detach himself from his existence, he is compelled to meet it with decision. And if he is in search of

ultimate integration, he must seek it in ultimate decision. Ultimate decision must be made in the perspective constituting his
existence: the togetherness of, and conflict between, dependence
and transcendence, and the inherent necessity to integrate these
into ultimate unity.

What, basically, are the choices possible in this situation?

Man can make an effort to recover the blissful pagan ignorance
which he has lost. He can tell himself that his transcendence is
reducible to his dependence or his dependence to his transcendence; that his responsibility is merely the function of his needs,
or that it can easily rule them. But as we have seen, history sooner
or later shocks man out of such ignorance or self-deception.

Man can face his conflict but belittle the need for its ultimate
integration. He may claim to be satisfied with transforming his
one problem into many problems, and with solving these merely
pragmatically. But he transcends the relativity of his life sufficiently to remain profoundly disturbed by a wholly relative
existence.

Man can face his conflict and accept it as inexorable fate, realizing that ultimate integration cannot come through himself, and
deciding to live in that knowledge. This is tragic existence. For if
he lives his unreconciled conflict absolutely, his vitality and his
search for happiness become tragic futility, his responsibility and
sacrifice become tragic quixotism.

Man can, and in this situation often will, rise in rebellion.
Aware of the inexorability of the conflict, he may yet strive to
transcend it and to become his own measure. But this is the counsel of despair; it makes man say:

> I shall persist in utter metaphysical defiance, infinitely lonely,
> supported only by my moral insight. I shall offer absolute resist-
> ance to the ultimate principle and shall despise it.[35]

Were man's weakness only biological, he might well take this
heroic attitude. He might despise pain, unhappiness, and death

because of the autonomy of his moral insight. But his weakness is not only biological; it is also spiritual, because it is spiritually that he is sinful. Therefore, this attempt at self-redemption amounts to rebellion, and is tragically futile.

But man can make yet another decision, the decision of faith. He can submit to God as his existential *apriori*; he can accept the "yoke of the Kingdom of Heaven."

V

The decision of faith differs from other decisions as radically as these do from objective detachment. Decision stems from the insight that existence is inescapable. The decision of faith stems from the insight that God is inescapable. Man surrenders his neutrality in the realization that he cannot be neutral; he surrenders authority over his existence in the realization that he cannot be his own authority. In the state of existential decision, he knows that he cannot refute God; in the decision of faith, he knows that he cannot reject or escape Him. He knows that whatever he decides, he is under the authority of God: Nebuchadnezzar does the will of God as fully as do Moses or David. Indeed, the very agony in which man tries to reject God, testifies to Him. And in rebellion, man harms not God, but himself.

We must understand clearly the specific nature of the decision of faith. A modern writer properly warns:

> If we believe in . . . a . . God not because He is the truth, but assume His truth only because we believe in Him, then there are as many gods and as many truths and values as there are beliefs.[36]

If the decision of faith is on the same level as other possible decisions, man makes God's sovereignty or even His existence depend on his belief in, or acceptance of, Him. This is the final heresy. The distinctive nature of the decision of faith is that it is at the same time no decision at all, because in accepting God's sovereignty man realizes that he accepts that to which he is subject regardless of his decision.

We are here at the crucial point in man's religious situation. *Before* he makes the decision of faith, he is free not to make it. He may thereby lose all hope of ultimate integration; he may live a life of self-contradiction; he may arrive at self-destruction: all the same, he is free not to accept the "yoke of the Kingdom of Heaven." *After* the decision of faith, there is no freedom to reject God; there is merely freedom to rebel against Him. But in rebellion as well as in submission, man now testifies to God. Even the non-believer testifies to Him, through his tragic ignorance.

Here, then, we have the fundamental tension in the religious life: the decision of faith in which man expresses the irrelevance of all his deciding to the sovereignty of God is, nevertheless, the greatest of all decisions. Total submission to God is not only the ultimate in humility; it is also the extreme in self-confidence: "Everything is in the hands of Heaven except the fear of Heaven."[37] If God exists, He is the *absolute existential apriori;* yet man dares to leap from a position in which he is free not to accept Him to total acceptance of His sovereignty. Whence this momentous audacity?

Man finds the grounds for both his humility and his self-confidence in himself. He is in a state of dependence; yet he transcends it in that he knows it. It is because he knows of his sin that he cannot escape his obligation. Sin would not be sin if man could not know of it. Knowing it, he must face the responsibility to combat it. What is man's ultimate attitude to be? If humility leads him to surrender his obligation, he escapes from what he knows to be his responsibility. If awareness of his responsibility leads him to battle his weakness entirely by himself, he becomes involved in sinful pride.

From this contradictory situation the decision of faith derives both its audacity and its humility, which become an ineffable unity. Realizing the audacity implied in the decision of faith, man knows that to let his humility destroy *this* audacity is to escape from his responsibility. If there is a God, He does not wipe out man's responsibility; He makes it inescapable. He is each man's own personal God—"near," not "far."

But, all the same, man could not venture the decision of faith were it not for the fact that this daring is at the same time no daring at all, and that therefore man's supreme self-confidence is at the same time his supreme humility. For if there is a God, man's total dependence on Him includes both his dependence and his transcendence, both his acceptance and his rejection of Him. Man's faith, his own *decision*, is then at the same time *given*. Revelation, which becomes revelation only through man's decision to accept it as such, is then at the same time absolutely given, because God's sovereignty includes man's decision. For if there is a God, He is the sovereign of each man's personal destiny— "near," not "far."

The decision of faith, then, is the only decision which man can make without qualification. To accept the yoke of the Kingdom of Heaven is the only ultimate integration man can realize, because here it is not he alone who realizes it. But this ultimate integration does not imply an infallible security. On the contrary, because it transcends all evidence, proofs, and refutations, faith is the greatest of all risks. Even the ancients, who felt so secure in their faith, sensed this. "Even though He slay me, yet will I trust in Him," are the words of Job. The Mishnah says: " 'Thou shalt love the Lord thy God with . . . all thy soul' (Deut. 6:5),—that is to say, even if He takes thy soul from thee."[38]

Modern man knows that the risk is vastly greater even than this. For he understands what the ancients in their faith were not always conscious of: the position of man before the decision of faith. In a paradoxical paraphrase of the passage of the Mishnah, modern man might tell himself: " 'Thou shalt love the Lord thy God with . . . all thy soul'—that is to say: thou shalt love abso-

lutely Him of whom thou hast certainty only by reason of thy
love. And thou shalt rejoice in this thy unique opportunity for
absolute love."

VI

"A man must first take upon himself the yoke of the Kingdom
of Heaven, and then take upon himself the yoke of the commandments."[39] To accept direct and absolute responsibility is to the
man facing God—the decision of faith having been made—not
only a possibility, but a necessity.

Before God, man becomes free. For at last, he is redeemed from
his tragic dilemma. No longer must he accept his responsibility
with an implicit claim to moral autonomy—obvious presumptuousness, in the light of his confused insight and sinful actions—
or live in an action-paralyzing humility which betrays his responsibility. To accept total responsibility is now no longer an act
vitiated by hidden pride or self-assertion: it is a glorification of
God. For it is God who "gave the Law," and along with it "all the
implements by which it is carried out."[40] It is His grace which
makes Him "demand according to *our* power"[41]—a power which
stems from Him. The self-confidence required for the assumption
of responsibility is here identical with total humility. Of course,
there is still, as there always is, danger of self-perversion through
sinful pride; but man may risk this danger now for the sake
of God.

Man's *decision for* responsibility is here redeemed from its inherent enigma; his *life in* responsibility is freed from the stifling
influence of human failure. Environment, which often reveals individuals and their consciences as products rather than agents,
bedevils their sense of responsibility. Tantalizing evidence of so-
called "inexorable" "waves of the future" saps the strength of
conscience. But such spells have no power over the man who lives
before God. For he knows that, fundamentally, he finds his law

not in looking forward, but in looking upward. And he knows: "It is not given in thy hand to complete the work, but thou art not free to desist from it."[42]

Even more dangerous to life in responsibility is the failure of the individual himself. Nothing ordinarily threatens a man's sense of responsibility more than the seeming inevitability of failure and defeat. But upon the individual living before God the effect is very different. For the tension between ideal responsibility and actual sinfulness becomes a source of ever-renewed spiritual energy, drawn from the certainty that through the mercy of God the discrepancy is not after all catastrophic.

To the man who lives before God the *possibility* of taking upon himself the "yoke of the commandments" is a *necessity*. God is man's own, personal God: he cannot elude or escape Him; he is personally responsible to Him; he cannot evade the directness of this claim by seeking shelter in "circumstances"—at least in principle he is always responsible. Nor can he escape it through referring to his own past habits: the doors of repentance are always open.

But how can man know the commandments of God so that he may do them? What is it that he is to do? The man who lives under the "yoke of the Kingdom of Heaven" need never be in a state of total ignorance. His knowledge of himself before God involves solid principles of social conduct. If men are directly responsible, then they possess a dignity requiring that they never treat one another "as means only."[43] If God makes men responsible, this requirement is the law of God.

But man can never hope to possess the law of God in a set of general norms to which he need only subordinate his individuality. Even in the realm of social conduct, the need for its application involves a leap from the security of the general norm into hazardous individual decision. And the individual's responsibility before God is not confined to the realm of social conduct. How then is man to gain knowledge? Is he to determine the law of God in his heart? Is not "the heart . . . deceitful above all things, and

exceedingly weak" (Jer. 17:9)? In this conflict man turns to God,
calling upon Him to be his God *here and now,* even as he himself
must be His servant here and now. His general fate and freedom
are given to him by God in His "farness"; he now calls upon
God's "nearness" to give him specific guidance. "Give me understanding that I may keep Thy law" (Ps. 119:34). "Teach me Thy
statutes" (Ps. 119:26). Sometimes, his plea is answered. Sometimes, he can say: "Thy word is a lamp unto my feet, and a light
unto my path" (Ps. 119:105). But sometimes, too, he learns the
law of God only in his affliction, and at other times no answer
comes at all. For God hides His face and answers not.

This is tragic affliction: man's life as a whole is in God's hands,
but he does not know its meaning here and now; he has accepted
the "yoke of the commandments," but he is not told the unique
laws which pertain to his unique situation. Yet even this affliction
need not be catastrophic. If God is not "near," He is at least "far."
Where God fails to speak, man both can and must dare attempt
to fathom His law. He *must* do so because of his responsibility
before God's judgment. He *can* do so because of the ultimate
security of all he does and plans in God's mercy.

VII

"Do His will as if it were thy will, and He will do thy will as
if it were His will."[44] Man cannot ultimately make himself the
measure of his life. "Self-realization" cannot be his standard of
ultimate integration; rather must he surrender his self to the
"yoke of the Kingdom of God" and to the "yoke of His commandments." But strangely, he who thus loses his self gains it; he who
surrenders the aim of self-realization to God arrives at the fulness
of self-realization.

To accept the law of God is to accept the limitations of human
existence. For this law is given to *men;* it is given neither to
angels, who have no natural urges, nor to animals, who do not

possess the direct responsibility of freedom. Therefore, to accept the law of God is neither to mortify vitality nor to stupefy moral responsibility; it is to find redemptive reconciliation between the joy of living and the burden of responsibility.

Once, when he had caught a glimpse of the radical contradictions inherent in his condition, man's vitality was paralyzed. The joy of his every breath was withered by an inescapable sense of guilt. For while he enjoyed even a single breath of life, he knew that others were crying to heaven in mortal pain. To give his joy precarious survival, he had to try to escape from his moral self. But now it is different. Having surrendered to God's commandment his self-assertive joy of living, he receives it back as a gift from God. Accepting humbly God's law to men, he accepts as part of it the life of nature. What was before egoistic self-assertion set up against duty is now glorification of God through acceptance of the human lot. At least in principle, man's vital and moral selves have found reconciliation.

In the last analysis, to attempt ultimate integration through self-realization is to attempt to escape human nature. In seeking unity in himself in spite of the contradictions inherent within him, man cannot but strive to become either an angel or a beast. Both of these attempts end in a hopeless loss of self. Man finds his self only when he surrenders himself to God, because thus only does he come to accept the contradictions of his state. He no longer runs away from, but lives, his human existence. He can live thus, and do so serenely, because of his confidence that ultimately all contradictions rest in the mercy and justice of God.

Man continues to live in pain and anguish. He continues to be troubled by the question of where the expression of his vitality begins to conflict with his moral responsibility. But after his humble and serene acceptance of his human lot as a whole, this question is no longer paralyzing, this conflict no longer catastrophic. And even his pain and anguish are now a praise of God.[45]

3

In Praise of Abraham, Our Father

Rightly or wrongly, I have always thought highly of Abraham, the first Jew. It was not the condescending esteem we feel, say for an ancient Greek scientist who apparently furthered scientific thought but whose ideas would appear naive today to any college senior. The greatness of Abraham, to my mind, surpassed any "contribution" to the "progress of ideas": it was a greatness equally great at any time. The relationship I had thought it permissible to have to Abraham was a *direct* one, conceiving Abraham not as separate from us by many links in the chain of progress, but as the here-and-now guide and father of every mere Jew aspiring to be a good Jew. In taking Abraham with such live seriousness, I readily admit that I was influenced by Kierkegaard's magnificent *Fear and Trembling*. But I also believed it to have the backing of Jewish tradition.

RECENTLY, however, I suffered a sad loss. Rabbi Joseph H. Gumbiner's essay "Existentialism and Father Abraham" (COMMENTARY, February 1948), discovered for me that Abraham is a pure illustration of "ethical monotheism," as distinguished from Kierkegaard's Abraham, who experienced an agonized conflict between the ethical and the religious.

Alas, I am now deprived of Abraham. I can take small comfort

Reprinted from *Commentary* (December 1948), pp. 521-27.

in the assurance that I need not be ashamed of him; that, on the contrary, he was further advanced in his moral ideas than his contemporaries, being the first to hit upon the truth that child-sacrifice is unacceptable to God. Abraham has been put in his place . . . and it is a relatively low one.

To Rabbi Gumbiner (and, he claims, to Judaism) Abraham represents no more than a step in the moral progress of mankind, and this progress is necessarily measured by standards which are universal, and superior to the specific example of Abraham. Thus is destroyed any direct relation we might have to Abraham as a guide and father; for every Tom, Dick, and Harry now knows what it took Abraham such a long struggle to realize: that Judaism is "ethical monotheism." And if we imagined him alive today we should be compelled to instruct him in all the refinements and further progress that have been made since his important—but by now banal—discovery.

LET us for the moment resign ourselves to the loss of Abraham. Another question quickly presents itself as even more important: whether the criteria which Rabbi Gumbiner applies to Abraham are to be applied to Jewish tradition as a whole. If what is good and bad or living and dead in Abraham is to be measured by outside standards of moral progress, why not follow the same procedure with Moses, the prophets, the rabbis? By what right can we exempt any part of the Jewish past from this kind of valuation? *On this question depends the fate of Jewish theology.*

That may sound like a grandiose assertion, but it is inescapable. What is more, it explains why we can rightly speak of the non-existence of a modern Jewish theology. *For it has not been asserted in modern times in any self-consistent or tenable form that Jewish tradition (or any part of it) supplies truths or authoritative standards directly obligatory for modern man or modern Jew—truths or standards that transcend the social and cultural norms of our day.*

The question "What is Judaism?" may be posed in two forms. One of these, the purely historical one, does not interest us here. What concerns us is the question "What is *valid* or *true* Judaism?"—the Judaism to which we are obligated and which defines what is a good Jew, here and now. To Rabbi Gumbiner it is "ethical monotheism," to others it is ethical nationalism, to others again it is something else—potentially if not in actuality. What happens in these cases is that some external principle and ideal is employed, with whose help is selected the "essence" of Judaism. Rabbi Gumbiner may deny that his principle is extraneous to Judaism, but the mere fact that he singles out "ethical monotheism" from a tradition which is, to say the least, also a lot of other things, presupposes a previous, superior yardstick as to what is living and dead, or important and unimportant in Judaism.

This procedure is typical of modern Jewish "theology." Jewish tradition is approached as something considered vaguely as either "inspired," in some sense "true," or "morally progressive." The question immediately arises whether, as Jews, we are obligated to this tradition because of these attributes or merely because it is Jewish. Obviously it cannot be the latter—or at least in that case this obligation has nothing to do with theology: it is pure nationalism. We are, then, obligated to the "truths" and "inspired teachings" in our tradition. But how do we measure them? We can only measure them by criteria of *general* reason, *general* ethics, and *general* philosophy: monotheism is the "purest form of religious thought," the "prophetic ethic" is "most advanced," "up-to-date" and so forth.

But if we follow this procedure (and it is difficult to see how any type of "modern" Jewish thought can do otherwise), two fatal implications immediately follow:

(1) The whole of Jewish tradition becomes at once superfluous, for the simple reason that we are certain of our basic moral and religious criteria prior (logically prior) to our judgment as to what is living and dead in Judaism. We could as easily deduce

"ethical monotheism" from pure reason, or derive it from pragmatic criteria—whichever our philosophic preference. I do not mean, of course, that the Jewish tradition becomes practically valueless; it may continue to be necessary for the inspiration of individuals and a people. But from a strictly theoretical viewpoint the conclusion is inescapable that if I am to read that tradition with the notion that what is authoritative in it depends on my judgment, and not on the intrinsic religious truth and authority of that tradition itself, then the perusal of this tradition is no different from that of any other valuable literature. I am then a Jew as I may be a Platonist or Kantian or pragmatist. And my religion is *essentially* a religion of reason, intuition, or ecstasy; it is not *essentially* Jewish religion.

Some of the Reconstructionists understand this implication when they admit that the basic ideas of Judaism are to be derived from reason, and are therefore, at least potentially, basic to *any* (and all) highly developed religions; their defense of Jewishness lies in the no doubt correct insight that in practical life no abstract religion is possible, and that it must crystallize itself in definite patterns, forms of civilization. Hence, a Jew may find good grounds for carrying on the stream of Jewish tradition if he is convinced to begin with that he ought to live the universal truth in the particular Jewish pattern. But that he should so live it cannot be shown *theologically*. At best we can adduce only practical (social, national, etc.) reasons why he could not just as well become a follower of Unitarianism, Bahai, or Ethical Culture.

(2) This brings us to our second difficulty. If Jewish tradition (or any part of it) is true or obligatory not because it is Jewish or tradition but simply because it is, as a body of thought, convincing, then it must be equally true and obligatory for all men. There is not the slightest theological justification, in that case, for the separateness of the Jewish people. Our obligation is no longer to Jewishness but to truth and goodness, and, while in a world full of falseness and evil there are good grounds for continuing Jewish

tradition as a convenient force against them, this is only a tactical consideration; essentially, we should be obligated to truth itself—the truth which is the object of all men of good will.

In other words, modern Jewish theology has not really succeeded in showing—in theologically valid terms—that Jews should continue to be Jews, and that to be a good Jew may include, but must necessarily transcend, the obligation to be a good man.

Now it may very well be that we can philosophically demonstrate what Hermann Cohen called a "religion of reason" and show that, in actual fact, Judaism alone of all the historical religions conforms to it. In that case we might be well satisfied with giving loyalty to our Jewish tradition only until such time as there would evolve a more universal religion embodying the "religion of reason." Many of the early modernists certainly believed this, and could therefore be satisfied with understanding the Jewish "mission" as a relative one—a temporary, special, historical obligation to the "religion of reason." It is the contention of this essay, however, that a "religion of reason" cannot be fully satisfactory to modern man and that Judaism is not identifiable with it—unless it be a Judaism distorted to fit the requirements of modern rationalism.

But we must first ask another question: is Jewish theology possible at all? Is it possible to have a discipline which claims to attain truth and validity, and *ipso facto* universality — for what is true is universally true, and what is valid is valid for all men — and yet is particularly Jewish — that is, assigns a special position to a specific tradition, and a special task to a specific people?

Our answer is, for the present, that *classical* Jewish theology (i.e. the theology of ancient and medieval times) has demonstrated this possibility. Classical Jewish theology starts out with the concept of *revelation* which is by definition *supernatural*. By reason of this single concept, classical Jewish theology differs radically from anything so called in modern times: it really is Jewish theology. *For it finds its justification in the formal assertion that the criteria of its validity lie in the revelation itself—in the fact of its being revealed.*

Traditional Torah and what the moderns with vast equivocation call "Torah" differ radically in that the former is, in principle, absolute instruction, whereas the latter is merely random confirmation of the values to which the pupil subscribes to begin with. The fact that the traditional Jew may have been arbitrary in his interpretations of the Torah is not of primary importance; the important thing is the assertion of the absolute authority of the revelation as such. (That he was aware of the dangers of subjectivism or "humanism" as regards interpretation is evident from his belief in the necessity of a *Torah she-b'al-peh* in addition to the *Torah she-bikh'tav*—a revealed interpretation over and above the revelation itself.)

This conception, we say, really *was* Jewish theology: (1) It entailed a direct obligation to the Jewish tradition instead of encouraging a selection capable of confirming one's presupposed values. Abraham, Moses, or the prophets were not men exemplifying the view of progress current at the time; they were, at least in theory, direct authority. (2) Reason and human capacity were of inestimable importance, but they were not entirely sufficient—at least not sufficient for being a good Jew; for in that case the revelation would have been superfluous. (3) The obligation to be a good Jew over and above being a good man was theologically demonstrable: for whatever reasons, there was a Law of Moses which, unlike the Law of Noah, was obligatory not for all mankind but for Israel alone.

LET us assume for the rest of this essay that medieval Judaism is unacceptable to the modern Jew, and that the concept of revelation, at least in the sense of a written code of law and doctrine, has been destroyed beyond recovery by historical criticism.

Can we fall back on the "religion of reason"—"ethical mono-theism"?

Twentieth century insight finds the "religion of reason" pro-foundly unsatisfactory. The difficulty is not so much whether we can philosophically justify its basic notions; for the present pur-pose we may disregard the fact that many present-day philoso-phies deny, in the name of reason, the very meaning of a concept of God and moral value. We may disregard the assertions that the "religion of reason" is untrue; but we must face the fact that it is inadequate to meet the human needs that it presumably serves. Irving Kristol, in his incisive criticism of Milton Steinberg's *Basic Judaism* (COMMENTARY, January 1948), has shown precisely this. A religion which lives by the ideals of reason *alone* (i.e. without an existing God in addition to an idea of God—an existing God who reveals himself supernaturally) can be satisfactory only where it is believed that the gap between the envisaged ideal and the lived reality is not crucial; that it is a matter of degree only, and that it will be progressively bridged.

A "religion of reason" requires the conviction that there are few human ills which more effort will not heal. But what reli-giously sensitive persons of the 20th century have come to realize is that moral progress in degree, important though it be, does not span the gap in kind: there are conflicts in existence which can never be solved by a little more effort. Modern men have become aware of the tragic element in life.

As Kristol puts it: "The horror that breathes into our faces is the realization that evil may come by doing good—not merely *in-tending* to do good, but *doing* it." This the "religion of reason" cannot understand. Nor is it equipped to face the fact that in the 20th century, men—all of us—find themselves compelled to com-mit or condone evil for the sake of preventing an evil believed to be greater. And the tragedy is that we do not know whether the evil we condone will not in the end be greater than the evil we seek to avert—or be identical with it.

The "religion of reason," we increasingly recognize, is the illu-

sion of an expanding bourgeois civilization. It is compelled, especially in a time of crisis, to discourage ultimate questions as to
good and evil, as to the ultimate consequences of one's moral
action. It is compelled to become the religion of the philistine, "a
comfortable religion for an uncomfortable world."

FORTUNATELY, Judaism is not identifiable with the bourgeois "religion of reason." True, it is a religion of reason *also*, but
it is more than that. And one of the first requirements for a *real*
reconstruction of Jewish theology is to protest against the falsifi-
cation and banalization Judaism has suffered by most, if not all,
of its liberal interpreters. The rationalists of the 19th century
(and many of the 20th) saw in Judaism the assertions that man
is free, though morally obligated; that God represents moral law;
that the messianic age is to be brought about by human effort.
But they conveniently forgot the rabbinic assertions concerning
the *yetzer ha-ra'* (the evil inclination), an inclination so strong
that only God in the world-to-come can uproot it. They forgot
that God is represented not only as moral law (which may be
understood in naturalistic terms), but also as love, forgiving to
just and unjust alike (which cannot be so understood). They forgot that while on the one hand the Messiah is said to arrive when
men repent—when the world has become good enough to make
his coming *possible*—he is on the other hand said to come when
the world will be so wicked as to make it *necessary*. They stressed
the midrashim asserting Israel's election as the result of its free
choice, but ignored those that saw it as a supernaturally imposed fate.

Our naturalists and rationalists thought to improve Judaism;
they made it more "systematic" and "scientific." As becomes ever
clearer today, they sucked the life out of it, and transformed profound insights of religious existence into platitudes.

ASSUMING that the medievalist interpretation of Judaism is unacceptable to modern man, the first task of a new theol-

ogy is to understand Judaism as it actually was in terms truer and more adequate than the prejudices of liberal rationalism. We can here merely assert a general conclusion which we intend fully to corroborate elsewhere: *Judaism is to be understood, not as an evolution of ideas in the direction of a pure rationalism, but as confrontation of finite human existence with the Infinite.* Jewish "ideas" are to be understood not in themselves (in their systematic-philosophic coherence), but as the reflection of this confrontation, in historic and personal existence. This accounts for the fact that the profoundest statements made on sin and freedom, reason and revelation, God's justice and mercy, this world and the world-to-come, are not scientific or systematic but (if I may use Existentialist terminology) *dialectical,* that is, they express profound and irreducible tensions, struggles, conflicts—and resolutions—arising in and from the basic relationship of finite to Infinite.

TRADITIONAL sources abound in such a dialectical vision. The tension in the relationship between finite man and infinite God is made irreducible by its *immediacy* and its *mutuality.* In its *immediacy,* it differs sharply from the philosophic relationship to the first cause. "God is far—for is He not in the heaven of heavens?—and yet He is near. . . . For a man enters a synagogue, and stands behind a pillar, and prays in a whisper, and God hears his prayer. . . . He is as near to His creatures as the ear to the mouth." The infinite God, paradoxically, is yet ever-present to finite man.

That it is a *mutual* relation (in contrast with mysticism) is another vast paradox: the action of finite man cannot, and yet does, make a difference to the infinite God. " 'Ye are My witnesses, saith the Lord, and I am God.' That is, when ye are My witnesses, I am God, and when ye are not My witnesses, I am, *as it were,* not God." Statements such as this reflect fully and consciously the two-way, mutually-dependent, dialectical character of the God-man relationship. It is reflected no less in the descriptions of the *nature* of God, especially of His qualities of justice and mercy. Insofar as man is free and responsible, God is absolutely just, "never passing beyond justice but once"; yet insofar as man is finite, God is absolutely merciful: "If we have merit, and if we possess good deeds, He gives us what is ours; if not, then He acts charitably . . . toward us from what is His." Absolute mercy and absolute justice are mutually exclusive; yet on the basis of either alone, the world (and the relationship between finite and Infinite) is not possible: "If I create the world on the basis of mercy alone, its sins will be great; on the basis of justice alone, the world cannot exist. Hence I will create it on the basis of justice and mercy, and may it then stand."

In the rabbinic interpretation, man can only understand himself as both finite and yet transcending finitude. Insofar as he *ought* to combat the evil inclination (the *yetzer ha-ra'*), he *can* do so, especially with the help of the God-given "remedy" against the "disease"—the Torah. But while man can and must combat evil in degree, only God can root it out in kind: "The Israelites say to God, 'Lord of the world, Thou knowest how hard is the strength of the evil inclination.' God says, 'Remove it a little in this world, and I will rid you of it altogether in the world to come.' " Again, insofar as the evil inclination is traceable to God it is potentially good and necessary for human life: yet it at the same time causes a contradiction in human life: "Woe to me from my *Yotzer* (Creator) if I follow my *yetzer* (evil inclination); and woe to me from my *yetzer* if I follow my *Yotzer!*"

The human situation involves a dialectical tension between a host of other notions which cannot even be mentioned here. Among them are the ethics of motive and the ethics of consequence, the relationship between the individual and the world, history and the trans-historical, this world and the world-to-come. To this last relationship R. Jacob refers in his profound statement in *Pirkei Avot:* "Better is one hour of repentance and good deeds in this world than the whole life of the world-to-come; yet better is one hour of blissfulness of spirit in the world-to-come than the whole life of this world." L. Feuer, in his *Jewish Literature Since the Bible*, omits the last half of this statement. This is a nice illustration of the sort of modern "improvement" of classical Judaism which transforms religious profundity into moralistic platitudes.

SUPPOSING our historical interpretation of Judaism to be correct, how does it lead to theology? We are confronted, to begin with, with an alternative: we may dissolve the "confrontation" we spoke of in terms of "experience," that is, interpret what was subjectively to Abraham and the rest of Jewish tradition a direct relationship to the Absolute as a mere *feeling* whose objective correlate, the "outside," is denied or left in suspense. But then we escape the real question—the religious question—which is not directed to "experience" but to "existence." "Existence" inescapably concerns *me*, and, being part of *me*, it at the same time resists complete rational penetration. It cannot be dissolved into a theoretical system, even if it is a system of "feeling" or "experience." That is to say, *I escape the question of religious living until I face the real choice: whether this "outside" is Nothing or Absolute Transcendence—the choice between nihilism and faith*. This choice cannot be left in "scientific" suspense—for *my* existence cannot be left in suspense: it must be *lived*.

As regards Jewish history (which we say is a confrontation between finite existence and the infinite), we can take three attitudes: we may consider it a psychological curiosity and ignore the religious question; we may call the "outside" the Nothing—in which case we deny the very basis of Jewish theology and break away from a tradition which lived by an erroneous assumption; or we may make the decision of faith, in which case we find a new (and, this writer believes, the only possible besides the classical) basis for Jewish theology.

LET us briefly indicate the feasibility of this basis in some crucial points:

(1) A religious existence differs from a religious idea in the fol-

lowing: an idea, once thought, becomes the permanent possession of mankind; but existence must always be lived anew. As we have said, anyone can subscribe to "ethical monotheism": but to live in direct relationship to God by virtue of faith (if there is such a thing—which depends on the decision of faith itself) is no less difficult because it has been done a thousand times before. While we may learn no "religious ideas" from Abraham, we may learn from him (probably we are not great enough to do this) religious *existence*. In other words, the existential approach provides the sole possibility (aside from the classic one) of finding a direct religious and theological guidance in Jewish tradition. And this in no way conflicts with what is really scientific in the contribution of the historian of ideas. One may well use one's reason and yet turn to tradition and search for the ultimate possibilities of an existence lived in confrontation with the Absolute.

(2) Judaism is not alone in searching out the deepest strains of existence: we have no monopoly on profound living. Nor is Judaism alone in the decision that the "outside" is the Absolute rather than the Nothing: we have no monopoly on faith. But Judaism is alone in asserting that *its people,* for no other and better reason than that they are Jews, are forced by their destiny to live in that confrontation with the Absolute which, for others, is a matter of individual inclination or individual fate. Once we have shared the first decision with Judaism (the decision that the "outside" we must face is the Absolute), we are confronted with the question whether we shall share the second decision with Judaism as well: that Jewish history is to be understood as *a fate urging to faith.* Nothing in the science of history either compels us to make this decision or prevents us from making it. But one thing is clear: if we do not make this decision, and cannot accept the classical interpretation of Jewish existence, there is no theological basis for Judaism.

The approach here suggested would not only solve the perplexities noted above, but also solve the time-honored problem: "What is a Jew?" To tradition the answer was clear: *a Jew is a person who by reason of his descent is obligated to the divine covenant,* which obligation is not altered by the fact that he may reject it. It is modernism which is full of difficulties. Is Jewishness a matter of race? Then it includes him who is not even aware of his Jewish descent, and excludes the Jewish convert! Is it a matter of religious belief? Then it excludes the Jewish atheist!

The new interpretation resolves the problem in a manner not unlike the classical one: a Jew is anyone who by his descent is subject to Jewish fate ("the covenant"); whether he responds to Jewish fate with Jewish faith (whether he is "obedient" or "stiff-necked") does not affect, though it is related to, his Jewishness.

Is it meaningless chance to be forced to this type of existence? Or is it meaningful destiny? To answer this last question affirmatively is a decision of faith. Only if we shed the banalities of a philistine optimism which is really a fear both of the tragic and the Absolute, and make this decision of faith in order to "prepare the world for the Kingdom of God"—only then has the time come for a reconstruction of Jewish faith and theology.

To RETURN to Father Abraham—for at last I have regained him as father and guide. And I have regained him not without the help of Kierkegaard. To be sure, I will, as a Jew, subscribe to "ethical monotheism." But I am not so much concerned with the purity of Abraham's philosophic ideas: I am concerned with him as the awe-inspiring representative of an *existence* not essentially different from the existence in which all men live. This existence has fearful strains—which Abraham lived in an extreme form—and which we inevitably share. All of us today have in many things the alternative only between evils; and if "ethical monotheism" were all we had, we tremble to think of ourselves in eternal judgment. For we would have absolutely nothing with which to face up to the moral paradox that some of the evil we do or condone is both unavoidable and inexcusable.

Thus I revere Abraham who lived the human paradox to the extreme and yet had faith that it was not fatal. . . . Abraham waits for us, as the potential father of every Jew aspiring to be a good Jew: for he teaches us to live courageously the ethical under the moral law, in an existence which requires divine love superseding the ethical if it is to be healed of its tragic tensions. Hence we can confess with Kierkegaard: "No one is so great as Abraham! Who is capable of understanding him?"

4

Can There Be Judaism Without Revelation?

Israel's Relation to the Divine Is Central

"Now Mt. Sinai was altogether on smoke, because the Lord descended upon it in fire; and the smoke thereof ascended as the smoke of a furnace, and the whole mount quaked greatly . . . and the Lord descended upon Mt. Sinai. . . ." (Exodus 19:18-20)

The Bible reader who comes upon this passage cannot but feel its majesty. His imagination is fired, he is prepared for what is perhaps the greatest chapter in the Bible: the Ten Commandments. Indeed, it is not likely that he will give much thought to these lines, eager as he is to pass on to the Decalogue itself. Perhaps this is fortunate: the curious reader who does pause to reflect is no longer able to pass on so quickly—or even to pass on at all. For what is asserted here baffles the understanding. We are told of a revelation, of a real incursion of eternity into time, God into history.

Now there is no obvious reason why anyone should implicitly accept, as a fact, that a revelation did actually occur, or that such a thing is possible. There are even serious and obvious reasons against it. But it is, conceivably, no wasted effort to find out whether we can comprehend what so hallowed a text clearly as-

Reprinted from *Commentary* (December 1951), pp. 564-72.

serts; such an effort might be useful even if it should end in failure.

THE assertion itself is simple: God "descends" in order to make manifest to man either His nature or His will.

But it is one thing to state the assertion, and quite another to understand it. How can God "descend"? If—as is commonly held in Jewish tradition—His being is in eternity, He cannot descend, at least not in the sense of being transmuted into time, for if He did, He would cease to be God. Fittingly the Midrash comments: "One might think that the Glory actually descended from Heaven, and was transferred to Mount Sinai; but Scripture says: 'I have talked with you from Heaven.' " The Midrash thus makes God use the heavens as intermediaries; but this is a poetic way of stating the difficulty, rather than a solution.

But if God cannot cease to be eternal, perhaps time can cease to be temporal? Perhaps in revelation a moment of time is transmuted into eternity? Again this is impossible. In the Biblical act of revelation God descends *into* time; far from destroying time, revelation serves to make it meaningful even in the sight of eternity. What are the Ten Commandments if not commandments designed for time, for fulfilment within history? If revelation changed time into eternity, it would not be revelation but the Messianic "end of days."

Time, then, must remain temporal, and eternity, eternal; how is it possible that the two should meet?

Perhaps if, in our ignorance of how God could possibly reveal himself, we could at least understand how it is possible for a man to receive a revelation, we might be satisfied. It turns out, however, that here too we are confronted with difficulties which seem insuperable. These may be stated in the form of a dilemma: either revelation discloses what man may discover by means lying within his own powers—but then it is superfluous; or else it discloses what lies beyond human means of discovery—but then it would seem to lie beyond human comprehension too, and the recipient of a revelation could not understand it. Revelation is apparently either superfluous or senseless; either we know the will of God by our own ability, potentially if not actually—in which case we require only a philosopher such as Socrates but not a prophet; or else we are unable to learn it, even through the mouth of a prophet.

And here, it would seem, the whole matter must be left; from every angle revelation appears unintelligible.

To be sure, it is always possible to resort to equivocations. For example, we might speak of revelation as if it were something akin to poetic inspiration. But let us not be deceived. Poetic inspiration is not supernatural; it is the natural product of man, and a product of God only in the sense in which every natural event may be so. To liken revelation to poetry is to make it something which it is not—that is to say, to admit defeat in facing the question of supernatural revelation.

THERE is nothing wrong with an admission of defeat, provided it is frank and unequivocal. It is the mark of wisdom, not ineptitude, to admit one's helplessness in the face of the unintelligible. We might put an end to the whole matter by concluding that revelation is in principle impossible, and that wherever the Bible asserts it, it cannot be taken seriously. In which case the question of the actual occurrence of a revelation, on Mt. Sinai or anywhere else, would not even arise.

The 20th century is inclined toward this view not only by the difficulties inherent in the Biblical doctrine but also by our whole modern outlook. The modern historian has applied himself successfully to what may be termed the naturalization of Biblical history. A historian such as Graetz, writing more than seventy-five years ago, still insists that the events at Mt. Sinai are unique, inexplicable in terms of natural causes; yet even he shows distinct traces of the modern outlook. He refers to the revelation at Mt. Sinai as an "overwhelming experience"—an ambiguous expression. More significantly, he speaks of a "discovery of conscience" at Sinai; but a discovery is made by man, not given by God. Most significant perhaps is his comment on another supernatural event, the division of the Red Sea—"an escape which they [i.e. the Israelites] were forced to regard as a miracle." The task of the new historian, then, became not to record supernatural events, but to explain them away plausibly.

DEVELOPMENTS in the writing of history since Graetz demonstrate the fruitfulness of the new method. Such a work as Salo Baron's *Social and Religious History of the Jews* wishes to leave the reader in no doubt that the evolution of the Mosaic religion is as natural a phenomenon as any other the historian may treat. This approach undermines what for a brief time was the last—and very weak—stronghold of the faithful: the supposed qualitative uniqueness and novelty of the ideas expressed in the Jewish religion, which, it was argued, required a supernatural explanation. The Mosaic religion has been shown to have emerged harmoniously and naturally from previous religions, and its novel aspects have been explained as the result of physical and political forces, or the genius of the man Moses.

The modern historian has thus shown that historical facts can be explained without the hypothesis of revelation. He has, moreover, also explained why Biblical man resorted to such a hypothesis: belief in supernatural agencies was quite common in an era which knew or cared little about natural causation, or was even unaware of the concept. Add to this what psychology teaches about dreams, visions, and the like, and the explanation of the Biblical belief in revelation is complete.

In short, the logical problems make it difficult for us to take revelation seriously, and the modern genetic-evolutionary explanation of religious history absolves us of the duty to do so. Which is the reason why, in modern Jewish theology, the concept of revelation lies dead and buried.

BUT perhaps revelation has been buried prematurely, after all. It is possible that this burial proves, not the demise of the interred, but an indecent haste on the part of the undertakers.

If the modern historian believes himself to have refuted the possibility of revelation, this belief is doubtless fostered by what he has done to one particular account of revelation: the Orthodox account. This he has refuted, at least in principle. "Judaism," wrote the late Joseph H. Hertz, Chief Rabbi of Great Britain, "stands and falls with its belief in the historic actuality of the Revelation at Sinai." True to Orthodox tradition, the rabbi regards revelation as a source of information concerning empirical facts; a view which implies that these facts are to be exempted from critical examination. The critical historian rejects this demand as running counter to all scientific method. He has already proven that much supposedly Sinaitic material is of different origin, and quite possibly he will prove one day that Israel never was at Sinai. Hence a battle ensues, and—in view of the achievements of Biblical criticism and archeological research—there is no doubt as to who will be the eventual victor. Orthodoxy escapes an immediate rout only to the extent that the relevant facts are sufficiently remote in history to elude precise verification.

Has modern rationalism, in its refutation of Orthodoxy, also refuted the entire Jewish tradition? For it is a fact that revelation is accepted by this tradition. Moreover, it is a central doctrine: the Mishnah considers the denial of *Torah min hashamayim* ("Torah from Heaven") so serious an offence as to deny the one who commits it a share in the world to come. If we wish, we may explain this insistence as a mere tactical device, designed as a prop for the tradition itself; but if we do this, we take a low view indeed of Talmudic Judaism. No religion of integrity regards its central doctrines as mere useful fictions, and it is difficult to picture a man suffering martyrdom for the sake of an illusion created by himself for his own benefit.

Was the traditional insistence on revelation perhaps the result of a lack of sophistication about natural causation, as in the Bible itself? It does not appear so. Judah Halevi writes: "Moses held direct communication with God . . . his words were not creations of his own mind. . . . He had not seen a vision in his sleep; nor had someone spoken with him between sleeping and waking, so that he only heard the words in fancy, but not with his ears, so that he saw a phantom, and afterwards pretended that God had spoken with Him." Halevi is not a primitive believer in miracles, unaware of natural causation: he fully faces the contemporary doctrine of natural causation, and maintains supernatural revelation in spite of it. Even more impressive is the case of Maimonides. Supreme Jewish rationalist of the Middle Ages, he rejects any unnecessary recourse to the supernatural. Yet the chief theme of his *Guide for the Perplexed* is a defense of the world's creation which he regards as a "fundamental principle of the Torah . . . next in importance to the principle of God's unity"; and he takes this view because, to him, only if the world has been created is revelation possible. Even in post-Enlightenment Jewish theology, from Moses Mendelssohn on, the doctrine of revelation survives, albeit precariously. But with the decline in the quality of theological thinking, there is little effort to meet head on the challenge of the modern outlook, and the modern reassertions of revelation sound often like mere pious repetitions; nevertheless, even as such they reflect an uneasy, though ill-defined, reluctance to surrender the concept to the triumphant anti-supernaturalism of the age.

At least in one respect this uneasiness is justified: if revelation must go, with it must go any possible *religious* justification for the existence of the Jewish people. In the absence of a binding commandment supernaturally revealed to a particular people, it makes as little sense to have a Mosaic religion for the Jewish people today, as, say, a Platonic religion for the modern Greek nation. A person is a Platonist because he accepts the truth of Platonism, not the authority of its author—much less because he shares his national origin. The truth of Platonism, if true it is, is universal; whether one wishes to be a Platonist or not is a matter of individual choice. Similarly, the values of Judaism, if valid, are universally so; Judaism becomes a matter merely of rational individual subscription to a particular doctrine or school of thought, and any religious basis for the existence of the Jewish people lies in shambles.

To BE sure, it is always possible to seek refuge from this dilemma in evasive rhetoric. So, in these days of strong Jewish feeling, much is heard about "Jewish values" created by the "religious genius" of our forefathers; to these, it is asserted, modern Jews have a unique obligation. This is no doubt an attempt to save Jewish religious particularism on non-supernatural grounds; but it succeeds only at the cost of moral and religious ruin. There are no more "Jewish" than German or Russian values, or, for that matter, Communist or capitalist. Values are universal and are either valid or invalid; and their source is significant only to the historian, not to the people who live by them. To assert a special Jewish obligation to special Jewish values is to subscribe, wittingly or unwittingly, to a doctrine vicious in its implications. An outgrowth of modern nationalism, it exalts the particularity of national or cultural expression at the expense of the universalism that values inherently require. If we Jews have indeed produced religious genius, we have given it, long ago, to the world; we cannot and dare not keep its insights to ourselves. We try in vain to save Jewish religious particularism on non-supernatural grounds; in the end, we are led to a perversion of classical Jewish doctrine: the substitution, for the worship of God, of the worship of the "Jewish vision" of God.

Moreover, the uniqueness of Jewish genius is a fiction. How can it be maintained in the face of modern scholarship? We cannot have it both ways: either Judaism is unique as a divine revelation to the Jewish people, or Judaism emerges as gradually evolving from, and in interpenetration with, surrounding cultures, making its contribution, no doubt, but a contribution which has, at least in good part, been absorbed by non-Jews. We Jews are not alone in erecting fictions to escape this dilemma. Certain liberal Protestant theologians, having abandoned Christian supernaturalism, nevertheless find early Christianity unique on natural evidence, i.e., its moral superiority over contemporaneous Judaism; this superiority, needless to say, is wholly fictitious.

IF, THEN, revelation is impossible for all the reasons mentioned, only one religion remains tenable in the end: the religion of humanity, expressed in what one might call a "bible of mankind," a compendium of what is best in world literature and art. There are, indeed, important thinkers who have come to exactly this conclusion. But our situation would be quite different should we be able to save the principle of revelation after all. Should there be a direct interference of God with time, it would not only be possible but necessary that this act address itself, not to mankind in general—an abstraction—but to concrete individuals and peoples. All of which leads to the inescapable conclusion that Judaism stands or falls, if not—as Rabbi Hertz maintains—with the revelation at Sinai, then at least with the possibility of revelation in principle.

But it is, of course, possible that Judaism falls rather than stands, and that more than three thousand years of Jewish existence were lived by a fundamental illusion. Hence we must, with unremitting insistence, return to our original question: is revelation possible? Can there be a direct incursion of God into history?

THE question is: "Is revelation possible?" But wherever we may have to look for an answer, it *cannot* be in science or metaphysics.

Science deals with empirical facts, in categories which exclude the miraculous. But revelation is miraculous by definition and thus cannot be an empirical fact. If there is to be such a thing as revelation, it will have to take place, not in time, but in the timeless moment in which eternity passes into time. That which has already happened in time is empirical fact, and this comes under the scrutiny of the scientist. But what has not, or not yet, taken on a temporal extension is outside scientific proof as well as refutation. Hence revelation is by its very nature impossible within the framework of science; and whether it is possible outside that framework, science is unable to decide. Any attempt to do so is doomed from the start.

Metaphysical attempts are similarly doomed. The area of metaphysics, while not necessarily empirical, is yet rational; but the miraculous, if it exists, is extra-rational. Hence if the metaphysician discovers that revelation is rationally impossible, because paradoxical, he only discovers what revelation by definition implies; and if he discovers that it is rationally possible he has discovered not revelation, but something else.

But are not then all our difficulties removed? If science and metaphysics remain neutral in the matter of revelation, what is to prevent us from accepting it simply on faith? Indeed, why worry about its *possibility*, instead of accepting, without further ado, the *actuality*, say, of the historic revelations of Judaism? There are those who are prepared to make such a gesture of acceptance. But there are surely many more for whom such an act adds up to a defense of sheer, blind faith, unmitigated in its blindness by any sort of rational argument, and therefore intolerable.

The truth is that by defining the province of science and metaphysics we have merely cleared the path to the crucial difficulty. Within the categories of the empirical and the rational, reality is too restricted to have room for the miracle of revelation; but with these restrictions removed, it is so wide as to make revelation meaningless—it becomes a wholly unintelligible break into time occurring at the most sublime or most ridiculous moments, which could be the message of God or the devil, or simply a manifestation of the unintelligible. As a wholly unintelligible break into time, revelation would not add one whit of meaning to the time it invades. Indeed, it might destroy such meaning as time possesses when taken in itself; for there would be no reason why revelations should not invade time constantly and anywhere. Formerly, the supernatural seemed to elude us; now, by a swift and somewhat ludicrous reversal, it is the natural which seems to travel toward dissipation. In other words, through blind faith we are in danger of turning back to primitivism.

This surely raises, of all objections, the most formidable. Science and metaphysics do not refute the principle of revelation, but neither do they seem to offer evidence for it. Why not, then, discard this superfluous and troublesome concept? Ockham said wisely: "Principles ought not to be multiplied beyond necessity."

Is the concept of revelation unnecessary? *Or does it solve a problem otherwise insoluble?* This, and this alone, is the correct way of putting our question. Indeed, it is the proper question to ask of any doctrine of faith. For religious faith is neither knowledge nor superstition: not knowledge, because its evidence is subjective and outside public proof; not superstition, because it is outside refutation as well as proof, and because it is not arbitrary. *Faith may be defined as the sole positive answer to questions of ultimate importance, the asking of which is still reason's prerogative but which reason is no longer able to answer.* Questions that reason can answer as well as ask belong to knowledge; statements that are not answers to intelligible questions are superstitions, both arbitrary and meaningless.

Is revelation the solution of a problem implicit in existence, and otherwise insoluble? Unless we can answer this question affirmatively we shall be compelled to discard the concept of revelation as useless and devoid of meaning.

"THE world and the fullness thereof," says Rabbi Banayah in the Midrash, "were created only for the sake of the Torah."

Even after maximum allowance is made for rhetorical extrava-
gance, this statement can only mean: man's existence is incomplete without revelation. Such, indeed, is the consistent traditional
teaching. Largely ignoring the physical universe, Jewish tradition
is chiefly concerned with the existence of man; this it views in
terms of a history moving on from Creation to the Messianic "end
of days"; and the crucial events within that history are a succession of revelations. But creation and redemption are themselves
doctrines of faith; hence one must first consider, however briefly,
their function; only then can Rabbi Banayah's statement become
intelligible.

Creation and redemption are doctrines designed to solve the
riddle of human existence. For man is a riddle unto himself; the
core of the riddle lies in his apparent participation in two worlds,
that of nature and spirit. Like all animals, he is doomed to death;
but to realize this is to be able to form a concept of death—and of
immortality. Like all animals, he is subject to amoral natural
needs; but to judge them amoral is to look to a moral standard.
Man appears to be mere nature; but in order to recognize himself
as "mere" nature he must be spirit also. Perhaps Rabbi Akiba had
the human riddle in mind when he said: "Beloved is man, for he
was created in the image of God; but it was by a special love that
it was made known to him that he was so created."

Attempts to resolve this riddle appear forever doomed to failure. If man interprets himself as an overgrown animal—different
from other animals only in complexity—he finds that his natural
urges may fit into this interpretation, but his moral and spiritual
nature do not; what his interpretation will not explain is the fact
that he is capable of—an interpretation. Yet if he interprets himself as a pure spirit he fares no better: nature in him forever stubbornly refuses to be transcended. Is then man in insoluble contradiction with himself—a "broken vessel"?

History supplies further evidence that this is, indeed, the case.
If man were but a complex animal he would have no history. He

would realize no meaning beyond what already inheres in his essence as a species. His history would be but quantitative variation—in other words, no history at all. Yet if man were an entirely spiritual being, all that is evil and meaningless in history would be mere temporary accident, and he would, properly speaking, have no history either. As Plato implies, whenever a man achieves the perfection potentially in him he has risen above history. As animal, man would exist in time below history, as spirit, in eternity above it. History itself thus appears intelligible only as a composite of time and eternity, nature and spirit; for it is a domain of meaning, indeed, but of a meaning forever partially frustrated. There is equally much—and equally little—truth in those opposite views of history: the eternal, meaningless recurrence of the Greeks, and the necessary moral progress of the moderns. The one finds too little meaning in history, the other too much; the one tries to reduce history to nature, the other to spirit. Both vainly attempt to resolve the human contradiction as reflected in human history.

Religious faith rests on the conviction that this contradiction is a paradox—either insoluble, or else soluble only by virtue of a mystery, to be asserted on faith. Precisely that solution is offered in the doctrine of creation. Says the Zohar: "After all the creatures were made, God said unto them: 'Let us make one more creature in partnership. Each of you shall have a share in him, and I will give him a portion of Myself.' " In contrast with philosophical syntheses, the doctrine of creation holds on to *both* sides of the contradiction, thus making it naturally and rationally insoluble: man has an animal and a divine aspect, the one irreducible to the other. Yet what is naturally irreconcilable is supernaturally reconciled in the mystery of creation.

However, taken by itself, creation raises as many problems as it solves. To make God the author of time and eternity, nature and spirit, light and darkness, good and evil, must mean, if it means anything, that these contradictions are not ultimate. But, as we know them, they do seem ultimate: evil is still evil, and darkness, dark, their divine origin notwithstanding. Hence the idea of creation must be complemented by the idea of redemption: not one, but both sides of the human contradiction will be redeemed, and nothing will be lost. The creator of all is also the redeemer of all.

CREATION and redemption thus form a religious solution of the human problem, a problem which reason can state but not solve. God will redeem man, but not by making him either less or more than human; either assertion would make human existence meaningless—a tragic contradiction to no purpose. God redeems man by preserving the contradictory elements that constitute his humanity, yet by transforming them in such a way as to take the sting out of the contradiction.

Creation establishes time and history, redemption consummates them. But it is only revelation that can establish the significance of the *here* and *now* as unique. Revelation is the religious category of existence as such. If revelation is impossible, there is significance only to the human situation in general, even though God is its creator and redeemer. Man may then know a law and a promise, but both remain in strict universality—individual men, and individual historic moments, are universally interchangeable. God may then be related to man in general; he is only indirectly and accidentally related to myself, my people, my historic situation.

But existence is inexorably particular. The moral law to which I am obligated may be universal, but the situation in which I must realize it is unique; indeed, the tension between universal law and concrete realization is part of the essential human contradiction. Israel is a manifestation of mankind, but what makes her Israel is unrepeatable and uninterchangeable. A historic situation exemplifies what history as such is, but it is nevertheless something all its own. If revelation is impossible, the particular in existence is a meaningless weight upon time and history—from creation until redemption. History then has meaning only at its beginning and its end; nothing meaningful goes on within it.

But such a history is in the end no history at all. The Platonic philosopher, having risen beyond time to the contemplation of the universal, may leave the particular a meaningless weight. But what if the particular is not accidental? What if, as traditional Judaism asserts, man's temporal aspect is as essential as his eternal one? If this be the truth, we cannot, in the Platonic sense, rise above the particular; and it continues to defy us, even in a world that is God's creation. It requires, not a philosopher speaking in terms of the universal, but someone who can speak in the *here* and *now*, and yet give it absolute meaning—in short, a prophet. If man cannot heal his self-division by ascending from time into eternity, then it can be healed only by God, descending from eternity into time.

A history without God is an unmitigated tragedy—a domain of frustrated meaning. A history which is, as a whole, in the hands of God, but in which revelation is impossible, may be, as a whole, beyond tragedy; but the particular in it, as such, remains a dead and sodden weight. A history in which revelation is possible is one in which every event, no matter how trivial and insignificant, may in its stark particularity be lit up with unique meaning; it is a history characterized by the crucial fact that fulfilment is possible *within* history and not only by abolishing history.

In a history in which revelation is impossible, man's ultimate achievement is to wait for redemption. In his moral actions, he is merely an accidental case of the human species, and all his accomplishments are affected by the contradiction inherent in that species. In a history in which revelation is possible the individual is, potentially, singled out; his actions and existence may become a unique fulfilment. To be sure, they cannot become completely redemptive, but neither need they be of a merely repetitive character: they may become unique contributions toward redemption. The Hasidim taught that the deeds of any individual may leave unique traces in the upper world; for a history in which revelation is impossible, such a doctrine would be meaningless.

Revelation is the solution of the religious problem of the here and now. To assert that revelation is possible is to assert faith in the relevance, before God, of this man, at this time, in this place. Only if there is, or at least can be, revelation, does the God of the philosophers become the God of Abraham, Isaac, and Jacob.

A HASIDIC rabbi used to say: "We thank Thee, Source of all Blessing, for being at once revealed and concealed." Revelation at once reveals and conceals. It lights up the particular as such; it must therefore reveal. Yet it remains concealed as well, for if it did not it would dissolve time itself in its glare. Why, the Midrash asks, did God descend in fire? Because revelation is comparable to fire: "If one comes too near it, one gets burned. If one keeps too far from it, one is cold. The only thing for man to do is to seek to warm himself against its fire." Another Midrash puts this perhaps even more profoundly: "On the instant when Israel heard the First Commandment their souls left them. So the Commandment returned to God and said: 'Sovereign of the universe! Thou art life and thy Torah life; yet Thou hast sent me to the dead!' . . . Thereupon God modified the communication so as to make it more palatable. . . ."

Revelation thus remains a mystery even while it is revealed; and every single word spoken by any prophet is inexorably shot through with human interpretation. Franz Rosenzweig observed: "Revelation is not identical with legislation; it is, in itself, nothing but the act of revelation itself. Immediately, it is its own sole content; properly speaking, it is completed with the word *vayyered* ('and He descended'); even *vayyedabber* ('and He spoke') is already human interpretation." This may be a point of extreme subtlety, but theologians ignore it at their peril. Orthodoxy identifies the human—if ancient—interpretation of the revelation with the revelation itself; it is this literalism which lays it open, as we have seen, to fatal attacks. Modernism, too, identifies divine revelation and human interpretation, but commits the opposite error: instead of making the interpretation divine, it makes of revelation a purely human "creation." Hence modernist theology is in the end indistinguishable from a sort of eclectic philosophy, leading a precarious existence by the grace of whatever trends may dominate the age. To this abject condition its present feeble search for props in anthropology, psychiatry, and even quantum physics bears eloquent testimony.

All interpretation of revelation is human; and Orthodoxy errs in its belief that a revelation could be possessed in the form of a body of truths and laws unaffected by human contingencies and hence unchanging in validity. But it would also be an error to depreciate all interpretations because of their human character. Revelation must pass into human interpretation, else it does not become accessible at all. But this gives rise to the question: what is the proper interpretation? Or, if proper interpretations differ with time, circumstance, and perhaps even individual condition, at what point do such interpretations cease to be legitimate? Or again, to put it more concretely: where does the revelation become the religious law of Judaism? What is that law for the modern Jew? And is there but one such law for him?

RELIGIOUS leaders in Reform and Conservative Judaism have recently given increasing attention to the religious laws and ceremonies of Judaism, and there has been growing concern with the problem of "authority." This present attention to Halachah (Law) reflects a highly creditable appreciation of the problem of the concretely human: Jewish existence, it is realized, loses its specific reality and meaning if it expresses itself religiously only in the moral law, which is, after all, binding for all men. But it is extremely important to realize that this problem cannot be solved by committees that simply formulate codes of religious practice. It is a useless, more, a dangerous procedure to ask for a code of practice without at the same time inquiring into the foundation and ultimate significance of such practice. If revelation is in principle impossible, all such practices, no matter how "creative" or "inspiring," become in the end indistinguishable from folklore; and attempts to foster them consciously are a brand of nationalism with too many religious incongruities to mention.

Any fruitful theoretical concern with Halachah must be preceded by an affirmation of revelation. In this essay, it has merely been asked whether revelation is possible and what it would mean were it to happen. A religious concern with Jewish living presupposes the assertion that revelation *actually happened*, touching Jewish history at least at one point—for this is all that is needed—and singling it out forever for a special task and destiny. Only then is it possible to interpret that revelation in its challenge and promise. Only then is it possible for the Jew to seek out the positive content of his Jewish existence.

5

Judaism and the Idea
of Progress

I

It is well for the theologian to use, from time to time, the auto-biographical form of discourse. To be sure, what matters in theology is truth, and this truth must be universal in some sense (though it is not easy to define this sense). But it is doubtful whether any theologian can wholly achieve the ideal of universality. For unlike matters of science, theological matters are of intimate personal concern to us. Our personal experience here inevitably enters into our conclusions, and this experience is necessarily partial and limited. In writing autobiographically the theologian puts, so to speak, his cards on the table. The reader can judge for himself whether the writer's experience has affected the universality of his conclusions; and if he finds this to be the case he can discount them.

The use of the autobiographical form of discourse, then, may amount to a confession of intellectual modesty. Such a modesty is particularly appropriate in the case of the present topic. It is an intellectual and spiritual necessity for us to rise above our particular historical experience, and to attempt to appraise the historical process as a whole. But such an attempt can never be made without misgivings. There is always the danger, which no

Reprinted from *Judaism* (Spring 1955), pp. 124-31.

one can be wholly sure to have escaped, that our interpretations of history, instead of appraising the historical process as a whole, are mere reflections of the historical age in which we live.

II

The spiritual environment in which I grew up was pre-Hitler Germany. Its ideas—at least the ideas which consciously affected me—were those of the enlightenment and romanticism, the ideas of Mendelssohn and Kant, Goethe and Hegel. One of the firmest beliefs conveyed to me was that history had a purpose. This purpose was the realization of the idea of humanity, of universal freedom. This belief seemed independent of any mysterious divine promises; it was demonstrated by history itself. History had followed a path of necessary progress in the past, and the guarantee for its infinite perpetuation was implicit in history itself. History was the self-realization of human freedom, a process which redeemed itself.

The liberal Jew in Germany had absorbed these ideas for a hundred years, and he found in them much that resembled the teachings of Judaism. The prophets, like Kant, had taught that man was morally free and responsible; and their concept of the Messianic Kingdom seemed indistinguishable from the idealistic idea of humanity. Only in one respect had the tradition to be changed, in order to be reconciled with the modern faith in progress; and this change the liberal Jew made willingly. History no longer required irrational incursions of a supernatural God; its purposes were realized by man inspired by the Ideal. The God of Abraham, Isaac and Jacob became an absolute Ideal.

Within this scheme of history the liberal Jew had to discover his place as a Jew. This was necessary because Judaism is at once universal and particular. Its God, and much of its other teaching, is universal; yet it is also tied to the destiny of a particular people. If there is no link between the universal and the particular, then Judaism breaks asunder. This link can be provided only by history.

But what place could the liberal Jew find for himself in history? If history as a whole was human progress, then the Jew's role within it could consist only in a contribution to that progress. Moreover, it could not be merely a contribution Israel had once made. To justify continued Jewish separateness, the liberal Jew had to insist that this contribution was still being made, and that it was still needed. But this could only mean, either that the Jew, by virtue of his religion, had a truer knowledge of mankind's ideals than anyone else, or else that the Jew was more faithful to them in his life. In either case it meant that Israel had a mission, which was to be the spiritual or moral teacher of mankind.

III

My generation had begun to rebel against the liberal concept of necessary progress. So far as I was concerned, three main objections in the end forced me to abandon it.

In the first place, there was a religious objection. If history is necessary progress brought about by men, then there is, so to speak, nothing left for God to do. He is either a Creator who, having created the world, goes into perpetual retirement; or else He is an ideal which can inspire but not act. In neither case is He a God who may be present to a man, even the lowliest of men, when he calls upon Him in a whisper. Yet without such a God there may be morality; but there can be no living religion.

My second objection concerned the concept of a Jewish mission. This I found both factually untrue and morally intolerable. The moral ideals of the liberal Jew seemed no different from those of his liberal Christian neighbor; and so far as moral practice was concerned, Jews as a group seemed no better and no worse than anybody else. Yet the view which made of the Jews the teachers of mankind had to make a claim to superiority which the facts did not warrant; a claim, moreover, which should have been morally intolerable even if it had been based on fact.

But I soon discovered that no liberal Jew seriously believed this doctrine. Nobody seriously thought that the ideals of liberal Judaism were superior to those of liberal Christianity, or, for that matter, to a simple humanism. And nobody suffered from a moral superiority complex as regards the Jewish people. In other words, the liberal idea of a Jewish mission was a mere theological fiction, invented to justify the continued existence of the Jewish people. A genuine justification the liberal view was unable to provide.

My third and most fundamental criticism of the progress view arose from the brutal fact of Nazism. This evil phenomenon, whose very possibility still defies our comprehension, gave the final lie to the view that history is necessary progress. It also re-futed all revised versions of it constructed to meet the fact of Nazism. A view still popular in America holds that history pro-gresses necessarily but intermittently; relapses may occur, but these become ever less serious. But to me Nazism was, and still is, not a relapse less serious than previous relapses, but a total blackout.

It may be argued that my experience with Nazism unduly colored my view of history as a whole; and that, to a more de-tached view, it might appear as a relatively minor episode. But it seems to me that the argument should be turned the other way round. History is regarded as necessary progress only by those who are relatively remote from the evils of history. And in order to maintain that view they must make light of these evils. The liberal Jew of pre-Hitler Germany had to belittle the sufferings of his brethren in Eastern Europe; and the contemporary believer in necessary progress cannot really take seriously Russian con-centration camps.

But the whole question of the quantity of historical evil falls short of the fundamental issue, at least the religious issue. In the end the fundamental point is that it is religiously intolerable to quantify evil where human beings are concerned. Would Nazism have been less evil if it had murdered merely one million Jews instead of six? Or merely a thousand? Or one? The fundamental objection to the progress view is not that it belittles actual evil, but that it justifies the evil and injustice done to some as a means to some supposedly higher end. This objection would hold even if history were necessary progress; for even then all generations would be a mere means to the last.[1] And the real conclusion I derived from the experience of Nazism is that if even a single brave and honest deed is in vain, if a single soul's unjust suffering goes unredeemed, that then history as a whole is meaningless. With this conclusion, the progress view of history, so far as I was concerned, had suffered total shipwreck.

IV

It might seem that these criticisms should have led me to the conclusion that history is simply meaningless. Or, as we may also put it, that it is a mere extension of nature. Nature is full of strife and suffering. But it is meaningless in the sense that it gives us no reason to ask for a meaning. It simply is what it is. History, it may be said, differs from nature only in degree of complexity. Like the animal, man is governed by needs; like nature, history is to be explained in terms of conflicting needs. To look for a deeper meaning may be psychologically understandable, but it is rationally groundless.

I have never been able to take this view wholly seriously. For it has always seemed to me almost beyond dispute that man differs from the animal, and history from nature. The distinguishing character is the fact of spirit. By spirit I mean the awareness of an absolute. Man, no matter how primitive or irrational, has always an awareness of something other than his needs, and this other is experienced as having an absolute claim on him. And along with this experience goes the experience of freedom to accept or reject that claim.

Man can never escape the ideal or absolute; he can merely exchange one absolute for another. He can ignore anything beyond his needs only by making an ideal out of the fulfillment of his needs themselves. In short, man cannot be an animal; he can only be a philosopher or anthropologist who asserts that men are animals and ought to live like them. It is not necessary to point out that this is just to set up another absolute.

We may put this otherwise by saying that the animal is innocent, but man is not. He cannot depart from the ideal without being aware of this fact. Even if he defies the ideal just because it is the ideal—an attitude which we may call demonic—his very defiance presupposes his knowledge. The devil is not an animal but a fallen angel.

This much, I say, has always seemed to me almost beyond dispute. And I further was never in doubt that it is possible for man to know the true ideal. For the ideal—even the confused, biased, perverse ideal—possesses the latent power of universality. Man, if he but wills and thinks, is at least in principle capable of transcending confusion, bias and perversion, and of achieving a universal and objective standard of good and evil.

We had concluded that history is not, in itself, a realm of fulfilled meaning. We must now add that history is not simply meaningless either. For if the analysis just given is correct, it is clearly false to say that history raises no questions. History is constituted by the fact that the ideal enters into it. The ideal enters in two ways. It enters for the observer who, if truly objective, measures historical fact by universal ideal. It also enters for the historical agent himself, though here it enters often confused, biased or even perverse. Thus both the spectator and history itself perpetually pronounce, however strangely or indirectly, what history ought to be. Yet history never wholly is what it ought to be. Fact and ideal are in persistent contradiction. The question raised by history is not answered by history itself.

We must therefore say that history, taken by itself, is a realm of contradiction, of frustrated meaning, or of the tragic. The tragic exists not in the sphere of suffering as such, and nature is not tragic. It exists only where there is a thwarting of meaning which ought to be, an ideal beheld and striven for yet come to naught. The tragic belongs to the human condition; more clearly than any other of its aspects, it raises the question of faith.

V

While I was gradually forced to reject the progress view of history, I at the same time made what was to me a remarkable discovery. The Biblical and Rabbinic view of history was free of precisely those elements which made the progress view untenable. So far as I could see, there was no real difference between the two views as regards human freedom and the moral ideal. But whereas to the liberal, history was a self-redemptive process, Jewish tradition maintained that history, to fulfill its meaning, requires the incursion of God.

To the liberal a God who actively interferes with history is a mere myth. Moreover, this myth is dangerous; for it tends to seduce those who believe in it to moral inactivity. But I was now able to see that, on the contrary, the liberal view contains its myths, whereas the traditional faith implies the most realistic understanding of history. Moreover, properly it does not lead to quietism.

The progress view is mythological to the extent to which it must ignore facts which will not fit into it. But the traditional faith need not ignore any facts. It can, on the one hand, recognize human freedom and its genuine victories. For its God makes demands upon man, and these presuppose that he is free to live up to them. This fact is enough to refute the charge of quietism. But on the other hand, the traditional faith can also recognize radical failure, and the persistence of the tragic. For it is precisely because history is not self-redemptive that the incursion of God is required if it is to be redeemed. Viewed by itself, history is a dialectic of human accomplishment and tragic failure. Viewed in the light of faith, it is a dialectic of the doing of man and the doing of God.

This dialectic is profoundly illustrated by the traditional Jewish concept of the Messiah. Liberalism transformed this concept into a mere symbol of the ideal toward which human progress tended, and it is difficult to see what, of religious significance, it adds to the belief in progress itself. But the traditional concept speaks of both man and God, and it is consequently profoundly dialectical. It expresses two truths, which in their togetherness transcend finite understanding: that man is free and morally responsible; and that he is dependent on the redemptive act of God. Thus the Messiah is represented, on the one hand, as waiting for man to perfect the world; and, on the other hand, as waiting for him to ruin it. He will come when history has become good enough to make his coming possible; or evil enough to make it necessary. The condition of history could be described no more profoundly; nor what is needed if its meaning is to be fulfilled.

It might be objected that the traditional view, while perhaps more realistic, is yet wholly irrational. The progress view has at least some evidence in its support, whereas the Biblical God has none. But this is to misunderstand the nature of religious faith. Faith is not an hypothesis based on empirical evidence, and subject to perpetual revision. Faith is an absolute commitment, without empirical evidence, and beyond proof and refutation alike. What saves faith from being arbitrary is the fact that it corresponds to meaningful questions, and that these questions are inescapable. One of these is meaning in history. This question leaves us with but two alternatives. We may accept as ultimate the tragic, the thwarted meaning, the persistent contradiction between what ought to be and what is. Or we may commit ourselves to a God of History, through whom the tragic is redeemed, all contradictions reconciled, and nothing is lost.

For faith, then, all history is meaningful. But this does not mean that this meaning is wholly disclosed. It must indeed be disclosed in part, for man is to have a share in its accomplishment. The sphere of disclosed meaning corresponds exactly to what the liberal might legitimately call progress. But the meaning of all else is undisclosed. Even the most tragic of events must have a meaning; yet this meaning is past our finding out. Indeed, it would be both morally and religiously intolerable for us to try. There is nothing incongruous in such a faith, which some would call blind. Provided only we can be sure to have reached the limits of human effort, none but such a faith can be adequate. Through it alone we can be sure that history is meaningful, not just in some points, or at its end, but everywhere; that every soul is safe in the hands of God; that every noble thought and brave deed are preserved, and that no tear is shed in vain.

VI

I had found three main difficulties with the progress view of history. At least two of these were removed by a return, in principle, to traditional supernaturalism. Unlike the liberal, the supernaturalist need not deny or belittle the tragic element in history; on the contrary, his faith is its precise correlate. And unlike the view of the liberal, that of the supernaturalist is religiously satisfactory. For it makes it at least possible that each soul should be an end in itself, and have a direct relation to God.

But could the return to supernaturalism also remove my third difficulty? This, it will be remembered, arose from the liberal Jew's inability to justify his continued existence as a Jew. And on this justification Judaism, at least, depends.

It would of course be possible to consider the meaning of history as a whole and leave the particular history of Israel unconsidered. Presumably each man must reflect, not only on the meaning of history as a whole, but also on his own place within it. And he must reflect on this place, I should think, not only insofar as he is a unique individual, but also insofar as he is a Christian, a Muhammadan, a Hindu, and perhaps even an American, Englishman or Frenchman. But it would be presumptuous indeed for me to reflect on the specific destiny of anyone else. And I am not sure to what extent, if any, this is possible.

Yet by the same token, I cannot ignore the question of Jewish destiny. For while logically derivative it is to me, as a Jew, by no means existentially derivative. I confess that in the years in which my views were formed—years of the utmost tragedy for Israel—it was this question on which my thinking centered. And in a personal account I could by no means omit it.

For the liberal history is wholly man-made. Thus Judaism too is man-made; it is, as it is sometimes put, the product of the religious genius of Israel. The liberal Jew maintains that the Jew should continue to exist as Jew. And this commits him to the view that Judaism, though universal in significance, is nevertheless still under the specific care of Israel. And this can only mean that the rest of mankind has as yet failed to achieve the moral stature of Israel. But this conclusion we have found to be intolerable.

But it is a conclusion which does not follow from the traditional view. For according to tradition Judaism is not the product of the Jewish people, but an encounter through history between God and Israel. God has chosen Israel. And He has chosen her for reasons unknowable to man, and certainly not because of any merit on her part. Thus the Jew may devoutly accept the covenant, or he may rebel against it; but he cannot escape it. The liberal view of the Jewish mission may be arrogant. But there is nothing arrogant in the view which makes Israel an instrument in God's plan for the world.

But what is the nature of this plan? The meaning of history, we have seen, must be in part disclosed, for man is to play a responsible part in its realization. The meaning of Jewish history too must be in part disclosed; for a plan for Israel wholly unknown to Israel would preclude the possibility of responsible participation.

This plan, so far as the Jew's participation is concerned, does not consist in the realization of moral law. For the scope of moral law is universal, applying to all men; applying therefore to the Jew, not as Jew, but as man. The specific meaning of Jewish history lies in what the traditional Jew calls Halakhah. This is the realization of a law governing the Jew's life in all its details. It is a law whose meaning does not lie in itself, for in itself it is meaningless. Rather is it the means by which the Jew perennially reiterates his acceptance of the covenant; his faith that all history is a doing of man and a waiting for God; his faith that this waiting is not in vain.

But to say this much about the meaning of Jewish history is to say very little. And it must be little. For like the meaning of history as a whole, the meaning of Jewish history is mostly undisclosed. Man cannot understand the final reasons for the tensions in his existence, nor the infinity of ways in which they manifest themselves in history. The Jew cannot understand why, in ways so often strange and terrible, he was chosen to exemplify these tensions. Hence he is not, in the end, free to decide whether or not the Jewish people should continue to exist. He is, to be sure, free to decide whether to heed or ignore the divine challenge, or even to regard it as a myth. But if it is really true that God has a plan for Israel, she is as little free to alter that plan as to understand its final meaning.

And this leads us to our final question: is the covenant between God and Israel a reality? Is the view of Jewish tradition the true view? Or is the whole long and tragic story of Israel a mere tragicomedy? It would seem that here a second absolute commitment is necessary, a commitment in its way as radical as the commitment to the God of History Himself. In a way it is even a paradoxical commitment, for what could be more paradoxical than a relation of the God of the universe to a handful of people spread through history? It is difficult not to shrink from this commitment in perplexity; and there can surely be no Jew, no matter how committed, who has not sometimes felt this perplexity.

Nevertheless I cannot recall any point at which I made this commitment. I always seemed already to have made it, though perhaps unaware of what the commitment was. And I venture to suggest that many of my fellow Jews may be in a similar position. The example of the liberal may be a case in point. For he somehow knows that he should continue to be a Jew, whether he likes it or not; yet he cannot give good reasons why he should. Jewish theology teaches that God often hides His face. Perhaps ours is one of these times. Perhaps it is a time in which many of us know some of His will, without knowing that it is His will.

VII

In a sense, my entire essay has been a criticism of the belief that history is necessary progress. And it may be asked why, in the mid-twentieth century, I should still take this view so seriously. For there are many who regard it as no longer deserving serious attention, and to whom therefore my argument would amount to beating a dead horse.

I take this view seriously because there is a sense in which I still wish I could accept it. This sense is, to be sure, not religious; but it is moral and practical. I still wish we could be sure of success in our efforts to transform history, if not into the Kingdom of God, so at least into a condition ever more humane, just and peaceful. And I am sure that I am at one in this wish with liberals of every kind.

But I also believe that most liberals share my inability genuinely to believe in necessary progress. None of us, of course, should have any doubts as to where our human duty lies. But I cannot see how any liberal can still believe that his efforts are supported by a guarantee of necessary eventual success. In this condition the liberal would seem to have the choice between two roads. The road chosen by many today is the road of make-believe. One no longer believes in necessary progress, but regards it as harmful to morale to say so aloud; and thus one preserves the belief in necessary progress as a public fiction. In the end it may well come to this, that no one believes the doctrine any more, yet everybody pronounces it, and expects to hear it pronounced, from lecture platform and pulpit.

But surely such collective make-believe, such deliberate whistling in the dark, can only lead to eventual spiritual ruin. The liberal must choose the alternative road, which consists in grounding a moral and political liberalism in a religious supernaturalism; in a faith which does not have to deny the persistence of the tragic, because it is redeemed by virtue of God.

6

An Outline of a Modern
Jewish Theology

Whatever their differences, all present schools of Jewish theology would seem to have a common failing. This is the lack of system. To illustrate this contention, we need only cast a brief glance at the two main schools, the so-called humanists and the so-called existentialists.

The members of the former school tend to draw heavily on the support of the sciences, and it is perfectly logical that they should. For inasmuch as they deny such articles of faith as supernatural revelation, it follows that Jewish religion (as all religion) is based on natural insights closely related to other natural insights, whether they be philosophical, moral, aesthetic or scientific. But one looks in vain in their writings for a systematic account of the relation between Jewish religion (and religion as such), on the one hand, and all the other forms of human insight, on the other. For example, it is fashionable to relate Judaism to the insights of modern psychology. But the attempts to establish such a relation, frequent though they are, content themselves with random illustrations; they never seem to get down to first principles. The thoughtful reader is therefore forever left wondering whether Jewish religious insight is meant to give the standard of what is valuable in modern psychology, or whether psychology is to be the standard of what is valid in Jewish tradition;

Reprinted from *Judaism* (Summer 1954), pp. 241-50.

whether the whole enterprise is a mere apologetic which assures us that Jews knew long ago what psychology discovered only recently, or whether Judaism still gives us something which nothing else can give; and if the latter, what this something is. The Jewish humanist makes analogous attempts to relate Jewish religious insight to pragmatism, sociology, and even modern physics. And in each case the reader is left in a similar state of bewilderment. All this does not prove that the humanist version of Judaism is untenable; but it does prove that the case at present made for it is poor indeed. And what makes it poor is the lack of system.

The existentialists, too, must be criticized in this respect, though (at least in the opinion of this perhaps not unbiased writer) not quite so severely. They tend to emphasize the difference between religious truth (and consequently Judaism), on the one hand, all ordinary forms of knowledge and experience, on the other. Again this is perfectly logical. For it is perhaps the principal tenet of this school that faith constitutes a unique form of commitment; and it asserts realities removed from natural insight, such as revelation. But again, the fact that this commitment is in some sense outside our ordinary system of knowledge does not mean that one cannot give a systematic account of it. And the fact that religious truth must here be set apart from other forms of truth does not absolve us of the theological duty to relate what in some sense is separated. For the moment we are told of the existential commitment we can raise a number of legitimate questions. Is the commitment possible? What is its meaning, in relation to the rest of human knowledge and experience? Why one commitment rather than another? These are questions which can be answered only in systematic form. And while it may be true that the actual act of commitment transcends all system, there can (and for the theologian must) be system both before and after: before, to explain why and where to leap; after, to clarify the consequences of the leap. The existentialists have been the object of many unjust accusations, such as obscurantism, "failure of nerve" and the like. What has lent such accusations a semblance of justice has been the fact that the existentialists, too, have failed wholly to live up to the demands of system.

System in theology is needed for two reasons, one theoretical and one practical. Whatever theology may be, it is thinking. And thinking is systematic. The function of theology is to save religious faith from obscurantism and arbitrariness. And it can fulfil this function only by giving a consistent account of faith, consistent both in itself and in relation to everything else asserted as true. Thus theology without system is a contradiction in terms. This is the theoretical reason for the need of system in theology.

From this follows the practical reason. Theologians, no matter how different their stand, can argue with each other. Untheological believers often cannot. This is because theologians, merely by virtue of being theologians, are all agreed on at least one criterion of truth: consistency. Because this agreement lends them at least a minimum of common ground, they are able to argue with each other. And in this lies the principal practical value of theology. But where theologians fail to give adequate attention to system they can no longer argue with one another. They can only either sermonize or vituperate. And there has been in Jewish theological discussion far too much rhetoric and vituperation, and too little argument. To this writer it seems that the existentialists have been the primary victims; but it is possible that his own leanings have biased his judgment in this matter. At any rate, what concerns us here is the cause of the undue prevalence of vituperation and rhetoric in contemporary Jewish theology, a phenomenon undoubtedly traceable to the insufficient heed paid to system in all quarters.

There are, of course, some excellent reasons for this situation. And if English-speaking Jewry has failed to produce impressive works in systematic theology, this is not entirely due to theological incompetence. The Jewish spiritual situation in the modern world is such as to make it doubtful whether even the most gifted theologian could produce a systematic theology adequate in all details. But this is no excuse for ignoring the idea of system. For we might be able to produce at least fragments of a system, and we certainly could, by keeping the ideas of system and consistency perpetually in mind, reach a level of theological debate at which rhetoric and invective are left behind, and the followers of opposing schools can genuinely argue with one another.

The article which follows these introductory remarks may seem singularly ill-fitted as an illustration of the virtues which we have exalted. For, as a mere outline of a theology, it cannot substantiate any of the doctrines it puts forward by argument. But the idea of system which we have urged means two things: argument of details, and the fitting of all details into a whole. The outline which follows makes no claim to adequation substantiation of detail; but it seeks to offer a conception, however sketchy, of a whole.

I

Theology is the attempt to give a coherent account of religious faith; Jewish theology is the attempt to give a coherent account of Jewish faith. Theology thus differs from religion, which is the life of faith itself; it also differs from philosophy and science, which are either not concerned with religious faith at all, or else cannot accept it as an irreducible source of truth.

As every other religion, Judaism requires a theology. To be sure, in many ages Judaism did not produce a theology; but in such ages the immediacy of faith was strong and unreflected enough to make its intellectual clarification practically superfluous. No such immediacy is to be found today. Hence the disparagement of theology in some quarters merely indicates confusion, or else indifference to the substance of Jewish faith.

Modern theology often fails to distinguish itself sharply from philosophy, or some such science as psychology. This failure is a specifically modern phenomenon. Since the Enlightenment, modern man has questioned or denied the actuality, or even possibility, of supernatural revelation, once regarded as the autonomous source of religious truth, and the basis of theology. Since that denial, a defense of religious truth, if attempted at all, had to be sought elsewhere—in philosophical argument or, more recently, in scientific evidence. But it is more than likely that this sort of defense is futile, and that the attempted fusion of theology with either philosophy or science is a confusion. As regards the specific tasks of Jewish theology, it is apriori evident, not only that this *is* a confusion, but that it is a confusion fatal to the tasks of Jewish theology. For the categories of philosophy and science are, one and all, universal; but from such *universal* categories no conclusions can be derived which might be a theological justification of the *particular* existence of the Jewish people. Hence the ceaseless, but futile, endeavors in modern Jewish thought to explain and justify Jewish existence in universal categories, such as nation, denomination and the like. If we should have to conclude that the only course left open to the modern Jew is to base his thinking exclusively on the grounds of science or philosophy, then this would be tantamount to concluding that, in the modern world, a Jewish theology is impossible.

The substance of Jewish faith is the direct relation, not only of man in general, but also of Israel in particular, to God. Jewish theology must seek to defend this faith. And it can defend it only if it can defend this relation as immediate, unmediated by general categories. In other words, if it can defend a supernatural God, and a relation to such a God. To justify the substance of Jewish faith, theology must turn its back not only on secularism, but also on all attempts to found Judaism on anything less than an irreducible faith in the Supernatural.

But modern Jewish theology may not simply assume that a

defense of Jewish faith is possible. It must not close its eyes to modern criticism which has seriously put this in question. The method of modern Jewish theology must differ from that of classical theology. This latter "worked its way down," i.e., assumed from the start what to modern man is the thing most in question: the actuality of a divine revelation given to man and Israel. Modern theology must "work its way up," i.e., show, by an analysis of the human condition, that man's existence, properly understood, forces him to raise the question of the Supernatural, and the existential problem of the "leap into faith." That human existence is indeed of this sort is implicit, and sometimes explicitly stated, in the whole of Jewish tradition. But whether the traditional view is correct is a question to be considered independently, by unbiased analysis. Only if such an analysis does in fact find this thesis correct can we go a single step further. For if human existence is not such as to raise necessarily the questions to which faith is the answer, then faith is a relic of an unenlightened age which modern man can do without. *From this it follows that the analysis of the human condition constitutes the necessary prolegomenon for all modern Jewish and, indeed, all modern theology.* On the adequacy of this prolegomenon depends the foundation of its sequel, theology proper. For theology is the explication of the faith into which a leap has been made, and the analysis of the human condition alone can justify the leap into faith itself.

Theology proper, in the case of Jewish theology, will fall into two major parts: (1) the explication of the faith by which the Jew lives insofar as he is a man. If this faith is the true answer to the question raised by human existence, it must be true for all men; (2) the faith by which the Jew lives insofar as he is a Jew; this faith, involving the nature and destiny of Israel before God, is confined to Israel alone.

We have said that faith, to be acceptable to modern man, must reveal itself as the sole positive response to questions inherent in the human condition; and we have further asserted that this view is implicit in the Jewish tradition. If this is true, then the task of Jewish theology proper largely consists in trying to understand Jewish tradition in this light: as reflecting a faith which is the response to perennial human problems. If we may assume that Jewish tradition reflects (along with much that is incidental and inauthentic) also the essential and authentic, then modern Jewish theology in no way seeks to alter the essence of Jewish faith; though it may very well alter Jewish theology. For the task of modern Jewish theology is to understand Jewish faith in terms compatible with modern thought.

II

Philosophical analysis reveals that man is, as it were, half-angel, half-brute. Unlike all other beings, he is not all of one piece. If he interprets himself as an overgrown animal—different from other animals only in complexity—he finds that his natural needs and urges fit into this interpretation, but his moral and spiritual nature do not. Yet if he interprets himself as an unfinished angel he fares no better: nature in him forever refuses to be transcended. Every effort to make himself all of one piece is doomed to ultimate failure, and history is littered with philosophies (as well as so-called sciences) reflecting this failure. Man is in perennial contradiction with himself—a "broken vessel." To mitigate this contradiction may be a task set to human prudence and moral wisdom; but to resolve it is possible, if at all, only for a God.

History reflects the human condition. If man were but a complex animal he would have no history. He would realize no meaning beyond what is already inherent in his essence. His history would be but quantitative variation, in other words, not history at all. If, on the other hand, man were an unfinished angel, all that is evil and unmeaning in history would be mere temporary accident.

History would be necessary progress, and man would be wholly competent to bring about its moral perfection. In truth, history is a domain of meaning, but of a meaning forever partially thwarted. Moral progress is exposed to tragic frustration. Man can mitigate the tragic and evil in history but cannot eliminate it: history, like man, is in need of redemption.

The domain of human freedom is defined by moral law. The moral "ought" marks the perennial human ability and task to transcend an "is." The tension between "is" and "ought" not only constitutes freedom in its profoundest sense: it defines man's very humanity. But any "is" is finite whereas the "ought" is infinite. This means that there are no a priori limits to human freedom and responsibility: man must always strive further upward. But it also means that the tension between "is" and "ought" is never resolved: by his own moral judgment, man is always a sinner. Moral knowledge, and perhaps even moral life, need no God. But man's moral situation raises not only moral but also religious questions. The question is not only: what ought I to do? but also: what is the meaning of my sinfulness, which remains no matter what I do? If the religious question is left open, then the demands of the moral law leave life an unsolved riddle; and if God is denied that riddle becomes a tragedy.

The moral tension of human existence is only one of many, though perhaps the most significant. But perhaps others, raised by problems such as death and solitude, are no less significant after all. All these ultimate tensions derive from the fundamental tension of existence, above described. They all, jointly or separately, pose the fundamental religious question: is the contradictoriness of existence as final as it is seen by our finite reason? Reason can still state this question, but it can no longer answer it. To answer this question, affirmatively or negatively, we require a leap, an act of decision and commitment. A commitment to a negative answer is a commitment to tragic existence, to a way of life lived in the conviction that existence is in its core paradoxical.

The affirmative answer is the decision of faith. *Faith may be defined as the positive answer, given by way of personal commitment, to existential questions of ultimate significance, which reason can still raise, but no longer answer.* Faith asserts that the human contradiction is not final but ultimately redeemed; that what naturally cannot come to pass yet does come to pass; that not one, but both sides of the human contradiction are redeemed, and nothing is lost. Faith asserts the existence of a God who is Creator of all, and Redeemer of all.

Faith is thus neither knowledge nor superstition; not knowledge because its evidence is subjective, and outside rational proof; not superstition, because its object transcends refutation as well as proof, and because it is not arbitrary. Faith is a leap into the dark but, again, not an arbitrary leap—one of many possible leaps, each of which is equally meaningful. It is the sole possible positive answer to the fundamental question posed by existence itself.

Because it is faith, faith in God is an absolute risk. Because it is faith in God—Creator of all and Redeemer of all—it is a risk involving existence in its entirety.

III

Theology is the organized statement of religious faith. Faith consists in the commitment to a positive answer to problems of human existence which reason can state but not answer. Thus every doctrine of faith must reflect a contradiction in human existence which it resolves; and it is part of the business of theology to exhibit this reflection. Jewish theology, too, has this business. What marks it as specifically Jewish is that the faith which is its subject is the faith by which the Jew lives, not only as a man, but also as a Jew.

The God whose existence faith asserts is a mystery. Asserting His existence, faith dares not to make any assertion about His nature as it may be in itself. God's nature, if intelligible, is not the subject of faith. Faith is concerned with God only insofar as He is related to human existence: as the God who has made, and will reconcile, a paradox. The language of faith therefore does not include words such as "Substance," "Force," "Cause" etc., but only terms such as "Creator" and "Redeemer." The God of faith must redeem man, but not by making him less than human, or by transforming him into an angel. To assert either would be to assert that human existence as such is meaningless, a contradiction to no purpose. But faith must assert (if it asserts anything) that what is contradictory to finite understanding is yet ultimately not contradictory. The God of faith must redeem man by preserving the contradictory elements which constitute his humanity, but by transforming them in such a way (unintelligible to finite understanding) as to take the sting out of the contradiction. God thus relates Himself to man in ways which appear contradictory to finite understanding. He is at once a God of Justice who makes absolute demands on human freedom, and a God of Mercy who heals absolutely the contradictions which arise from the use of that freedom. Before Him as Judge all men are radically sinful; yet before Him as Father all sins are radically forgiven. For the same reason, man's moral freedom, and the importance of its responsible use, is at once everything and nothing. It is everything because God makes demands upon men, as if He Himself were impotent, and man the sole agent of history; it is nothing because, after all, God is omnipotent, and history is safe in His hands despite the evil done by men.

God is therefore Person. For whenever a person is in *mutual* relation with another, that other is person as well.

Yet when we speak of the justice, mercy, and personality of God we speak symbolically only. God's nature is a mystery, and only insofar as He is related to man may faith speak of God; yet even in relation to man God remains a mystery. For God is infinite and man is finite; and a mutual relation between a God who is infinite and men who are finite passes finite understanding. Nevertheless, faith must assert the reality of this relation. Man is forever tempted to deny such a mutual relation, either by making God a mere ideal which does not act, or by making man a mere plaything of an omnipotent God. But neither doctrine is a genuine doctrine of faith; for both fail to resolve the human contradiction. The latter denies the very fact (i.e., moral freedom) which gives rise to the human paradox; the former fails to resolve that paradox. Faith, then, in asserting a mutual relation between man and God, cannot speak literally. But to be unable to speak literally cannot mean to remain silent: for, to faith, that relation itself is a reality, demanding participation on the part of man. Man addresses God, obeys His law, prays for and trusts in His mercy. He must treat God as if He were literally Person, Judge and Father. Man must speak, but speak symbolically; or (if we wish) anthropomorphically; for he speaks from his finite situation. But anthropomorphic language, not being absolute truth, is not therefore falsehood: it is the truth about the God-man-relation as it appears from the standpoint of man; and that relation is itself a reality. How it appears from the standpoint of God man cannot fathom, nor is it his business to fathom it.

No religious doctrine is more baffling than that of revelation; yet none is more essential.

Two alternative interpretations present themselves of which neither appears intelligible. Either revelation reveals what man may discover by means lying within in his nature: but then revelation is superfluous. Or else revelation reveals what lies beyond human means of discovery: but then it would seem to lie beyond human understanding also, and the recipient of a revelation cannot understand it. This dilemma cannot be avoided by fashionable equivocations. To associate revelation with poetic inspiration is to make it the product of man; but revelation is either the direct gift of God or not revelation at all.

Yet no doctrine is more essential than revelation, unless it be faith in God itself. Creation establishes time and history, whereas redemption consummates and redeems them. Revelation is an incursion of God *into* time and history; eternity here breaks into time without dissolving time's particularity. Creation and redemption establish the significance of time and history in *general.* Revelation establishes the significance of the *here and now* as unique; it is the religious category of existentiality as such.

If revelation is impossible then there is significance only to the human situation in general, even though God is accepted. And the law as well as the promise known to man remain in strict universality. But this makes individual men and historic moments universally interchangeable. God may then be related to man in general: He is only indirectly and accidentally related to myself, my people, my historic situation.

Existence, however, is of inexorable particularity. The moral law to which I am obligated may be universal, but the situation in which I must realize it is unique. A historic situation reflects what history as such is, but it is nevertheless something all its own. Israel is a manifestation of mankind, but what makes her Israel is unrepeatable and uninterchangeable. If there is no revelation, the particular in existence is a meaningless weight upon time and history, from creation until redemption. History in that case has meaning only at its beginning and at its end: nothing essential goes on within it.

But faith must assert that revelation is possible. For only if revelation is possible does the here and now have relevance before God. And if the here and now has no such relevance the human contradiction remains at least partly unresolved. Only if there is, or at least can be, revelation does the God of mankind become my God; only then does the universal God of the philosophers become the God of Abraham, Isaac and Jacob.

This explains the dialectical character of revelation, above described. An incursion of the eternal into the temporal which destroyed either the temporality of the temporal or its own eter-

nity would provide no essential difficulty for the human understanding; but an incursion which preserves both its own eternity
and the particularity of the temporal is a paradox. But faith *must*
hold fast to this paradox if the particular is to have meaning
before God; it *may* hold fast to it because there is no reason why
what is paradoxical to finite understanding should be impossible
to God. Revelation, like all doctrines of faith, reflects in its own
dialectical character the nature of the human problem to which,
as a doctrine of faith, it corresponds.

This character is reflected also in the content of revelation. It
lights up the particular as such, in its obligation and promise: it
must therefore reveal. Yet in passing into time it becomes transformed: hence it must remain concealed as well. That God speaks,
or has spoken, is a simple fact to the man of faith; but what He
has said is expressed in human language; it is inexorably shot
through with interpretation and hence remains, even while revealed, a mystery.

The modernists of all time distort revelation by transforming
it into natural inspiration; the orthodox distort it no less by equat-
ing the human interpretation of and reaction to the Encounter
with the Encounter itself.

A history without God is an unmitigated tragedy, i.e., a domain
of frustrating meaning. A history which is, as a whole, in the
hands of God, but in which no revelation is possible, is as a whole
beyond tragedy; but the particular as such remains a weight without meaning. A history in which revelation is possible is one in
which every event, no matter how insignificant, may in its stark
particularity acquire unique meaning. It is a history characterized
by the all-important possibility of Fulfilment *within* history; not
merely the ultimate Fulfilment of redemption, which can fulfil
only by abolishing history.

The assertion of faith that revelation as such is possible and, indeed, necessary, is still a universal assertion. It is concerned with
the *category* of the particular, not any special particular. A leap

is therefore required before it is possible to assert the *actuality* of a specific revelation.

Not unnaturally religions divide at this point. While atheist, agnostic and religious believer can agree on the human condition and its need for redemption; while all who have made the leap of faith can agree on the general implications of that leap, and on the general thesis that the contradictions of existence are not final: it is not possible to arrive at the actuality of a particular revelation by means of universal considerations of this sort. Theological reflection, even after the leap into faith, takes us no further than to the establishment of the possibility of revelation as such. The assertion of the actuality of a particular revelation entails a second absolute leap, and a second absolute risk.

There is a second, and perhaps even profounder reason why religions should divide at this point. Only at the point when an actual revelation is asserted do we enter the realm of concrete, unique, unrepeatable existence. Here individuals, peoples, historic situations begin to know of, and live in, their unique condition. And, by the same token, here they begin to be ignorant of the uniqueness of other individuals, peoples and historic situations. Thus, for example, the Jew who asserts a revelation addressed to himself as Jew, speaks of something of which others are necessarily ignorant; at the same time, he is himself ignorant of what may establish the religious significance of the concrete existence of others. The extent to which the adherent of one faith may understand, and pass judgment on, the faith of another is clearly limited. Here, then, religions divide in their claims; but here, also, different claims cease to be mutually exclusive.

Judaism rests on the assertion of the actuality of a series of revelations which have constituted Israel as a historic community destined to serve a specific purpose. Where it speaks of mankind and the God of mankind, Judaism is nothing beyond what might be a universally human religion; only at the point where, leaping into the particular, it is concerned with Israel and the God of

Israel, does Judaism separate off from universal truths of faith.

Jewish existence is established by, and responsible to, divine revelation. Hence it shares the dialectical character of all revelation. That Jewish existence has a meaning is vouchsafed by the faith which accepts the reality of revelation; of a revelation which has established Jewish existence. But the nature of that meaning is involved in the dialectic of the paradox. All revelation both reveals and conceals: thus the meaning of Israel's existence, too, is both revealed and concealed. It must remain concealed: for the divine plan for Israel remains unfathomable. Yet it must also be revealed: for Israel is to play a responsible part in that plan. Since the Jew is to live a consciously Jewish life before God he must have an at least partial grasp of its meaning; but in its fulness that meaning is not disclosed: for his Jewishness is only partly the Jew's own doing. The Jew both makes, and is made by his destiny.

The God-man-relation demands of man a free response, the response through moral law. The God-Israel-relation demands of the Jew, in addition to the moral response, a response expressing his Jewishness in all its particularity. This response is Halachah. Moral law, mediated through the leap of faith, becomes the divine law to man. Halachah is Jewish custom and ceremony mediated through the leap into Jewish faith; and it thereby becomes the divine law to Israel. In themselves, all customs, ceremonies and folklore (including those Jewish, and those contained in the book called Torah) are mere human self-expression, the self-expression of men alone among themselves. But through the leap of faith any one of them (and pre-eminently those of the Torah) have the potency of becoming human reflections of a real God-Israel encounter. And thus each of them has the potency of becoming Halachah, commanded and fulfilled: if fulfilled, not as self-expression but as response on the part of Israel to a divine challenge to Israel; as the gift of the Jewish self to God. Thus no particular set of ceremonies is, as such, divine law: this is an error flowing from the orthodox misunderstanding of the nature of revelation. But, on the other hand, all customs which flow from the concreteness of Jewish life have the potency of becoming divine law, and are a challenge to fulfillment. The denial of the religious significance of any law which is not moral is an error flowing from the modernistic misunderstanding of the nature of the concrete before God.

We have said that, like all revelation, the revelation of God to Israel both reveals and conceals; and that, correspondingly, the Jew both makes, and is made by, his destiny. Thus whether the Jew practices Halachah is, on the one hand, not constitutive of his Jewishness; on the other, it is not indifferent to his Jewishness. If the former were the case, the Jew would wholly make his Jewish destiny; if the latter, he would be wholly made by it.

Thus the meaning of Israel's destiny is in part revealed: it is to respond, ever again, to a divine challenge; to become, of her own free choice, a people of God; to give perpetual realization to this decision in thought and practice. Situations change, and with them the content of the response they require: but the fact of challenge, and the need for response, remain the same.

Yet the meaning of Israel's destiny is also concealed. Man cannot understand the final reasons for the tensions of his existence; the Jew cannot understand the final reasons why he was chosen to exemplify these tensions. Hence the Jew is also unable to decide whether or not Israel will continue to exist. He is, to be sure, free to decide whether to be a devout or stiff-necked Jew, whether to heed or to ignore the divine challenge. But if it is really true that God has a plan for Israel, Israel is as little free to alter that plan as she is able to understand its final meaning.

7

Jewish Existence and the Living God

The Religious Duty of Survival

The modern Jew is an enigma to himself. When he reflects on his existence as a Jew, he cannot but be filled with wonder. Other individuals and peoples may wonder how they have come to be what they are; the Jew must wonder why he should exist at all. For if there are laws of historical change, Jews should, according to these laws, have disappeared long ago. Was there ever another people which continued to exist, under like circumstances, through the centuries? The answer is that there was not. Other peoples require the bond of a common land, or a common language, or a common culture in order to continue in existence. The Jew, for long centuries, has had none of these. Consequently, self-appointed experts in the laws of historical change have been ever quick to predict his impending disappearance. But thus far at least these prophecies have always been confounded. The Jew still exists—a source of wonder both to others and himself.

How is one to account for the continued existence of the Jew? Certainly not in terms of persecution or discrimination. It is true that such forms of hostility may unite their victims, creating in them a group will to survive. They may cling defiantly to the very

Reprinted from *Commentary* (August 1959), pp. 128-36.

trait which singles them out for penalty. But they may also do the very opposite, that is, try to get rid of the fatal trait. In the case of Jews, unlike that of Negroes, this is not impossible. Furthermore, persecution, while frequent, has by no means been constant in Jewish history. There were long periods in which Jews were invited to participate in the life that surrounded them; and they never showed any lack of eagerness to accept this invitation. The conclusion, then, is clear: it is impossible to account for Jewish survival in such negative terms as persecution or discrimination.

Nor do we fare much better with such positive terms as "love of tradition" or "loyalty feelings to the group." To be sure, tradition had a strong hold on the Western Jew until the beginning of the 19th century, and on his East European brother until the beginning of the 20th. But this tradition was, for the most part, not static, fossilized, inert; it was fluid. Also, it was frequently exposed to the threat of disintegration. Yet it did not disintegrate; rather, it preserved itself. Why should Jewish tradition have preserved itself rather than disintegrated? To ask this question is to ask the question of Jewish survival all over again. In short, "love of tradition" does not explain Jewish survival; it is an aspect of the very thing in question.

Precisely the same is true of loyalty feelings to the group. No doubt such feelings are, in some periods of history, a powerful force for cohesion and survival. But in the case of Jews the question is why there should have been such feelings at all among a people which had, for long centuries, neither shared a common land, nor a common language, nor a common external destiny. In the case of Jewish survival, then, "national feeling" or "group loyalty" are not explanations, but again part of the very thing to be explained.

But perhaps collective feelings can exist and survive independently of the experiences which nourish them? Perhaps there are entities such as a "racial will" which are passed on through the blood? We need not waste our time on such fictions. For they exist only in the minds of the demagogues and charlatans of our century.

It becomes abundantly clear, then, that to account for Jewish survival is possible only in terms of the Jewish faith. All the other supposed causes of Jewish survival, such as tradition or feelings of group loyalty, can themselves be explained only in terms of the Jewish faith. It is because of the Jewish faith that the Jew still exists—as we have said, a source of wonder both to others and himself.

This fact places the Jew of our time in a unique position. Like everyone else in the world of today, he is prey to religious doubt. Like everyone else, he is unsure whether, and if so to what extent, he can accept the faith which was handed down to him. But unlike everyone else, he must admit that it is because of that faith that he exists at all.

In current usage, the term "faith" all too often signifies a mere milk-and-water assent to abstract "tenets" and "principles" which are, as a rule, nice, innocuous, and uncontroversial. This is not the kind of faith which can move mountains, or which could be responsible for Jewish survival. The term "faith," when applied to the Jewish past, signifies total commitment. And the commitment was either to an all-consuming experience in the present, or else to memories of such experiences which had taken place in the past.

Whatever one may think of the Biblical account of Jewish origins—whether one takes it to be literally true or merely mythological—two facts are beyond doubt: first, even if the Biblical account is merely mythological there is an element in it which is true; second, countless generations of Jews accepted it as true. The first fact concerns the faith of the Biblical, the second that of the post-Biblical Jew. The first fact serves to explain how the Jewish people was born; the second, why it survived. The Jew of today must contemplate both these facts: if not in order to learn what, as a Jew, he ought to be, at least in order to understand what, as a Jew, he is.

II

It is possible to doubt that Abraham, or even Moses, ever existed. One may advance the hypothesis that Israel never stood at Mount Sinai, and that, consequently, the unique divine revelation by which Israel supposedly was constituted never took place. But it is not possible to doubt that the Biblical account of Jewish origins, however mythological, reflects something which did take place. What took place was a succession of overwhelming religious experiences. The presence of the Nameless was felt in experiences which were themselves nameless.

As such, these experiences were not specifically Jewish. To experience the presence of the Nameless is the core, not merely of Jewish, but of all religious life. What distinguishes forms of religious life is the way in which the Nameless, and the nameless experience, are interpreted.

There are, to be sure, some varieties of mysticism in which all interpretation is rejected. The Nameless, and the nameless experience, both remain nameless. They remain, consequently, utterly divorced from all that is familiar and named. And all existence becomes a striving for an end which, if achieved, transcends all understanding and all utterance.

This, however, is the exception rather than the rule in the religious life of man. The rule is that the Nameless, and the nameless experience, at once relate themselves to something familiar and nameable. In virtue of this relation, they are themselves given names. Thus a religion comes into being.

In the primeval Hebrew experience, there was such an immediate relating of the Nameless to something familiar. But the familiar in this case was not, as it was so often, a part of nature or nature as a whole; nor did the nameless experience utter itself, in this case, in nature-symbols and thus give rise to a form of life which consists in ritualistic imitation of the rhythms of nature. In the primeval Hebrew experience, any attempt at a direct relating of the Nameless to nature was explicitly repudiated. The familiar and nameable which here received religious significance was not nature but human action.

But the nameless experience was not action. It had to interpret itself as a *call* to action. And this call could not be a call unless it was "heard." Nor could there be a "hearing" unless there was a "speaking." The Nameless interpreted itself as a "speaking," and the nameless experience as "hearing." What was heard was a commandment and a promise: the call to action, and the consequences which followed if the call was heeded. Thus in the primeval Hebrew experience, the presence of the Nameless manifested itself in the form of a divine-human covenant.

It must be noted, however, that this experience was not, or at least not primarily, an individual experience. It was a collective experience. It therefore manifested itself, not in a covenant between the Nameless and individuals, but between the Nameless and a people. Indeed, only in this experience did this people *become* a people. This is the secret of the birth of Israel.

It is sometimes said that the Jewish faith has been, since its inception, one of "ethical monotheism." This assertion is true in one sense, but not in another. If by "monotheism" is meant the belief in one universal God, the One God of the universe and mankind, it is more than doubtful that the early Hebrews were monotheists. And if "ethical" refers to codes of conduct universally human in application, it is more than doubtful that their beliefs were ethical. Its God was One, not in being the only God there was, but in demanding a commitment so total as to dwarf all else. And He was ethical in that He challenged to action, and in that this challenge was absolute. Compared to the absoluteness of this challenge its content was, for the time being, secondary in importance; and distinctions such as that between "ethical" and "ritualistic" were not made until a later age.

THESE facts ought to occasion no surprise. Religions begin with committing experiences, not with universal ideas; and where there is no commitment, religions do not begin at all. But if the commitment is radical, it is only a question of time before it becomes universalized. In the Hebrew experience, the only important God became, in due course, the only existing God; and His all-important commandments, commandments addressed and applicable to all men. This development completed itself in the Hebrew prophets.

The prophets universalized the primeval Hebrew experience, but they did not dissipate it into un-committing generalities. The primeval experience persisted. The Nameless had become the God of all men: but He was still immediately challenging, here and now. His commandments had become, at least in part, universally valid, but they had not become abstract "principles." They were addressed by the Nameless, not to "mankind," but to each man. This is why the prophetic God, while universal, could remain in covenant with the people of Israel. He was the God, not of the abstraction "mankind," but of every nation.

There are those in the modern world to whom a religion is the "higher" and "more enlightened" the more it expresses itself in abstractions. The prophets would have been in vigorous disagreement. To them, the use of such terms as "mankind" and "deity" would have indicated, not enlightenment, but a flight from commitment and the divine challenge. The prophetic God, in becoming universal, had not ceased to challenge; nor did He challenge abstractions such as "mankind" which not even a God can challenge. Rather, He now challenged Ethiopians and Philistines as well as Israelites. But the business of a prophet in Israel could hardly be to fathom the challenge addressed to Ethiopians and Philistines.

It was in the experience of the Nameless, then, that the people of Israel was born. This was possible because of three factors: first, this experience interpreted itself as challenge to action; secondly, being a collective experience, it challenged the group; thirdly, it was an experience so profound as to persist even after its universal implications had become manifest.

III

But primeval experiences do not last forever. Presumably they take place, even in primeval times, only intermittently, although this fact is easily concealed from later observers by the clouds of myth. In Jewish history, as in the history of most religions, "revelation" came to be a term referring mainly to events lying in the past. The question therefore arises as to why the Jewish people was preserved, when the collective experience of the Nameless had become what, at first sight, was a dead past recorded in dead documents.

The answer is that neither the past nor the documents were dead. The past lived on, legislating to present and future; and the document which recorded it became the Bible, that is, the Book par excellence. Jewish thinking centered on its exegesis; Jewish living geared itself to its commandments and promises; Jewish experience interpreted itself as derived from the primeval experiences recorded in the Book. From the Biblical to the modern era, the Jews remained a people by virtue of the Book.

But is such a survival of the past, and of its record, proof that both are alive? It may well seem that, if the Book ruled the Jewish spirit for more than two thousand years, it was not because the former was alive, but because the latter was dead; and that Jewish life, during these long centuries, was composed of the monotonous practice of sterile commandments, and of a forlorn hope in a long-lost promise. How can a religious life be anything but barren which springs, not from the immediate experience of the

Nameless, but from slavish submission to the authority of a codi-
fied book? But except for rare periods of religious decline, the
Jew's loyalty to the Book was not one of slavish obedience.
Rather, the Book without kindled the soul within. In rethinking
its thoughts, the Jew thought his own. In imagining its experiences, he relived them. In obeying its commandments, he made
them into a way of life. The past did not kill the present; instead,
reviving itself in the present, it gave life to the present.

The question arises how such an extraordinary relation to the
past was possible. Why was the present, during these long centuries, so rarely at odds with the past? Why did it not claim its
own autonomous rights against the past? How could religious
experience forever regard itself as subordinate to the great religious experiences of the past? There are many partial answers to
these crucial questions, but the decisive answer lies in one element of the Jewish faith—the Messianic element.

The Messianic faith is, of course, Biblical in origin. It was the
prophets who first spoke of an End of Days in which God alone
would rule and all would be fulfilled. Moreover, this faith was
implicit in the primeval experience itself. For once the experience
of the Nameless had interpreted itself as challenge and promise,
it was only a question of time, and religious profundity, until a
new religious dimension had to come into view: that of a future
in which all that was to be done by either God or man would
be fulfilled.

But so long as the primeval experience persisted in Jewish life,
an explicit Messianic faith was, so to speak, not needed. Religious
immediacy could have lived without it. It was when the past, and
its record, took the place of the primeval experience that the
Messianic faith moved into the very center of Jewish religious
life. Had it not done so, no mere hankering after the past could
have saved Jewish life from spiritual—and physical—extinction.
The past could live on in the present only because both present
and past were for the sake of the future. And the Jewish people
could live on, when He who is nameless was not present, only

because the memory of His presence transfigured itself into the hope of His ultimate and all-consummating return.

Our account of Jewish life during these centuries is thus subject to emendation. Jewish thinking was a re-thinking of past thought, but it was *thinking* only because it was directed toward a future consummation. Jewish imagination was a re-living, but it was *living* only because it anticipated the End. Finally, and perhaps most significantly, Jewish obedience to past commandments constituted a way of life, which was possible only because it regarded itself as preparing, and waiting, for Messianic fulfillment. In short, Jewish existence experienced itself as being between Revelation and Redemption. Revelation had been the call for human, and the promise of divine, action: Redemption would be the consummation of all action.

Still, it may seem that the Messianic hope leaves the fact of Jewish survival unexplained. Did this hope not concern the future of a united mankind? Should it not have led those who held it, instead of to group survival, to voluntary self-dissolution—thus anticipating the End? The mystery deepens if one considers that the Jews were, at that time, dispersed among other nations—nations which, for the most part, shared their monotheistic beliefs. Could it be that the hope of the post-Biblical Jew was, after all, not the universal prophetic hope; could it be that, having lost all universalistic fervor, it had become nothing more than a national hope? This, however, is to confuse empty abstractions with religious realities. The truth is the reverse. Had their hope been nothing more than a national hope, the Jews of the Diaspora would have been forced many times to abandon it. It was precisely because it was more than national that they could retain it. Hence, although it may seem paradoxical, it is nevertheless true that it was precisely because of their Messianic sense of kinship with all the nations that the Jews did not lose their identity among the nations; whereas, had they lost that sense of kinship, they would have disappeared among the nations.

Not much reflection is needed to remove the paradox from these assertions. How could a small people live, for any length of time, amid mighty nations and rich cultures without abandoning a merely national hope as both immoral and absurd? Immoral because a moral God could hardly confine His attention to one small and insignificant people; absurd because all the evidence seemed to point, instead, to the fact that this people had been overlooked by history. Clearly, in the centuries of the dispersion, only the most narrow and unthinking could have insisted on Jewish survival on the basis of a solely national hope. But it was the most thoughtful and broadminded who did, in fact, insist on Jewish survival. And this was possible only because their insistence sprang from a hope for something more than national survival. Their hope concerned the relation between the Nameless and all men.

Why, then, did this hope on behalf of mankind not lead to voluntary self-dissolution in mankind? Simply because "mankind" did not exist. There were only actual nations, and some of these did not regard the world as in need of redemption, whereas others believed that it had already arrived. For the Jew to dissolve into either would have meant to him, not to hasten the End, but to betray his post.

We conclude that the Jew of the Diaspora survived because he was able to rise to prayers such as this, uttered by a Hasidic rabbi in an age of fear and hate: "O Lord, send speedily the Messiah, to redeem Thy people Israel! Or, if this be against Thy will, send him to redeem the nations!"

IV

The question now arises as to whether the Jew of today can share the faith of his ancestors, or whether he must consider himself merely as its unwilling product. Can being a Jew today mean

an acceptance of a religious commitment similar to, if not identical with, the commitment of his ancestors? Or is being a Jew,
today, a mere accident of birth?

No doubt, individual Jews have asked this question throughout
the ages. It became universal, however, only when the Jew en-
tered into the modern world. Then it became inescapable. This
was because the modern world cast increasing doubt on the central part both of the Biblical and the post-Biblical Jewish faith—
that is, on the living God. The Biblical Jew had experienced His
presence, and the post-Biblical Jew had hoped for it; but man in
the modern world had come to suspect that all supposed experiences of divine presence were just so many illusions.

This attitude sprang from the modern ideal of scientific and
moral enlightenment. Did not a rational universe preclude the
possibility of irrational divine incursions into it? And did not a
rational way of life consist in reliance, not on revelations and
promises of divine aid, but on the unaided power of human
reason? Ever since the Age of Enlightenment, it has seemed to
the modern-minded—and who is not modern-minded, at least to
a degree?—that the denial of the living God was an essential
aspect of man's scientific and moral self-emancipation. If man
was to be fully free in his world, God had to be expelled from it.

We use the word "expelled" advisedly. The ideal of enlightenment did not compel one to deny that a God existed, but it did
seem to compel one to deny that He could be present here and
now. The living God had to become a mere "Deity," a "Cosmic
Principle"—remote, indifferent, and mute. Time was when the
prophet Elijah contrasted the idols which could not speak with
the living God who could. Ever since the Age of Enlightenment,
it has seemed to the modern-minded that God could speak as little
as the idols.

The religion of the modern-minded came to reflect this conviction. Far from centering on the experience or expectation of a
present God, it on the contrary presupposed His necessary ab-

sence. It became the mere subscription to "ideals," "principles," "tenets," and, in North America, "platforms." Would anyone think of God as a mere ideal who was prepared, so to speak, to meet Him in person?

On entering the modern world, the Jew had no reason to be suspicious of the ideal of enlightenment which ruled it. On the contrary, he had every reason to embrace it with enthusiasm. Who was to be enthusiastic about it if not the Jew, who had just emerged from the confines of the medieval ghetto? Who was to approve of the ideal of universal emancipation if not the Jew, who stood in special need of emancipation? But despite this whole-hearted approval which the Jew very naturally manifested, he soon discovered something of which he was not sure he could approve. The modern expulsion of God from the human world made Jewish existence problematic. The "Jewish problem" appeared on the scene. And it was a problem without solution.

FOR the pre-modern Jew this problem did not exist. He was faced with no serious difficulties of self-interpretation. He believed himself to have once met the living God, and to be committed to this meeting until the Messianic hope would be fulfilled. But what if God did not live, that is, relate Himself to persons and peoples? What if He was a mere cosmic entity dwelling in infinite and impartial remoteness? Or perhaps did not exist at all? What if all the supposed experiences of divine presence had been so many illusions? The moment the living God became questionable Jewish existence became questionable. The Jew had to embark on the weary business of self-definition. This business was weary because no definition would fit.

Was Jewishness a matter of "religion"? Was one a Jew because one subscribed to the "tenets" of ethical monotheism? But while Judaism consisted of ethical monotheism, it could not with impunity be regarded as consisting of mere tenets; and Jewishness could not consist of subscription to them. For there were those who subscribed to ethical monotheism without being Jews, and those who were Jews without subscribing to ethical monotheism. The inescapable fact was that one was born a Jew, and that one was not born subscribing to tenets and principles. The definition omitted the fact that the Jews were a people.

This omission was by no means an accident. A living God could address Himself to a people, but an abstract and lifeless "Deity" could not, for it could not address itself at all. In the case of such a Deity, the best one could do was somehow affirm it. But such affirmations could have no connection with the origin of those who made them. In short, if the living God had to give way to an abstract Deity, the "tenets" of Judaism and the Jewish people fell apart.

But perhaps an alternative definition could heal this defect. Was Judaism not the "culture" of the Jewish people, the product of its "religious genius"? Could Jewishness not be defined in terms of the people which had produced the culture?

But this definition too had a fatal flaw. Perhaps this flaw was not apparent, or did not even exist, for the detached observer. But the Jew was not a detached observer; he was a participant. As such, he had to ask himself a crucial question which the definition could not answer. The question was: why ought he to remain a Jew?

So long as the Jew believed in a living God the question answered itself. To remain a Jew was his duty under the divine-Jewish covenant. But what if God did not live? What if He could not enter into covenants? What if Judaism was not a divine-human encounter, but merely the product of "Jewish genius"? Jewish survival had then to be either an end in itself, or else a means to presumed future "contributions" of "Jewish genius" to the "world." But either view smacked of a chauvinism which no morally sensitive Jew was ever able to swallow. Hence the less forthright accepted the duty to Jewish survival as a mere pious fiction, while the more forthright frankly abandoned it. Jewish survival was merely a right, not a duty; whether or not one chose to remain a Jew was a matter of taste. But if this latter view found general acceptance, how long would the Jews of the Diaspora continue to exist? And how long would the Jews of the State of Israel continue to be Jews? On the other hand, how many Jews are really prepared to advocate, and work toward, Jewish self-dissolution, and to dismiss three thousand years of Jewish existence as a tragi-comic mistake? If a single generalization may safely be made about the contemporary Jew, it is that he still regards Jewish survival as a duty, to be performed whether he likes it or not. He may not have the slightest idea why it should be a duty; he may even consciously reject this duty. Still, he feels it in his bones.

After two hundred years of fruitless probing, the conclusion ought to be obvious. The "Jewish problem," as a problem of self-definition, is insoluble. Jewish existence cannot be understood without reference to a living God. And the Jew of today who persists in regarding Jewish survival as a duty, either persists in something unintelligible, or else he postulates, however unconsciously, the possibility of a return to faith in a living God.

V

But the possibility of such a return must surely be dismissed by the modern-minded without a moment's thought! Can one believe, in this day and age, in a God who reveals Himself? Has this belief not been refuted, once and for all? And must not those who persist in it be dismissed as mere victims of wishful, or fearful, thinking? In the 20th century, faith in a living God may well appear to be a mere relic of bygone ages, and Jewish self-dedication to Jewish survival, a mere part of it.

But the modern world never did refute the belief in a living God. It merely rejected it. One cannot refute the irrefutable; al-

though—if the irrefutable is also unprovable—one is always free
to decide that it does not exist.

To be sure, modern thought refuted many traditional beliefs;
and some of these were once associated with the belief in a living
God. In an age of natural science and critical history, it is hardly
possible to believe in miraculously split seas or documents dictated by God. But to reject revealed documents is not necessarily
to reject revelation. And to be suspicious of miracles is not necessarily to reduce all religious experience to projections of the unconscious mind. One does well indeed to suspect that much that
passes for religious experience is inauthentic, and that it is, not a
meeting with the Nameless, but the mere solitary disport of the
mind with its own conceits. But to regard all religious experience
as such—and hence to dismiss it as merely pseudo-religious—is a
procedure dictated, not by scientific evidence, but by intellectual
prejudice. Or rather, it is to make, under the guise of a scientific
judgment, a religious choice. And the choice is against the living God.

Time was when those who made this choice were imbued with
the spirit of Prometheus. Like that figure of ancient myth, they
wanted total control of their world for the sake of spreading
liberty and light. In the world of today, there are still some left
who are imbued with the Promethean spirit, but their number is
no longer large. Some of those who have decided against the living God are engaged in spreading, not liberty and light, but terror
and utter darkness. Others have made that choice only to shiver
in loneliness and despair. And others again—and these are the
vast majority, at least in the Western world—have lost the assurance of their choice. They are no longer sure whether they have
really made the Promethean choice; they are unsure even of what
it is. Religiously, they are in a state of turmoil.

But perhaps this turmoil is contemporary man's most authentic
religious expression. It would appear to be, at any rate, something
unique in the entire religious history of man. The contemporary

kind of religious turmoil may have existed, in previous ages, among individuals. But never before did it shake a whole age.

All ages prior to the modern were religious ages. They may have disagreed as to the interpretation to be given to the presence of the Nameless, but they agreed that the Nameless *could* be present. In sharp contrast, the modern age—at least in its most typically modern expressions—has been antireligious in spirit. Either by denying its existence or by expelling it into the distance of irrelevance, it denies that the Nameless can be present. What both the pre-modern and the modern ages have in common is that they make their respective religious choices without giving serious attention to the alternative; that is, they choose dogmatically. They make their choice without full awareness that it *is* a choice. Man today is bereft of such dogmatic certainties. Possibly for the first time in human history, he is brought face to face with the most radical of all religious questions. Like man at all times, he must face up to this question. But unlike men at other times, he is compelled to recognize that it *is* a question. Unlike the former, he cannot fail to recognize that the question can be answered only by a decision, and that the decision *is* a decision. And he suffers the turmoil of this recognition. The question is: is human existence closed or open to the Divine? Can the Nameless be present, or are all supposed experiences of such a presence mere illusions? Does God live, or is man inexorably alone?

It is all too human to shrink from great choices. One is tempted to pretend that there is no choice to be made, and to drift in indecision. Or perhaps one will escape from the choice by making it glibly, only to discover later that one has not made it at all. Such flights from choice are readily understandable, because to face up to the choice is to endure turmoil—the turmoil of the conflicting possibilities. One cannot make a genuine choice without first enduring this turmoil, and one must endure it until the time is ripe—for choice, and for action.

If this is true of all great decisions, it is true, above all, of the great religious decision placed before contemporary man. Is choosing for or against the living God a mere matter of scientific hypotheses? Or is it a matter of choosing the path of least resistance? Or of discovering, with the help of reputable psychologists, the most comfortable road to peace of mind? Is it not a choice in which one either commits his whole being or else does not commit himself at all? If this is the case, it is no wonder, then, that man in the present age seems bent on shrinking from this choice. Instead he pretends that there is no decision to be made; and he reinforces this pretense by all kinds of activity, inside and outside church and synagogue, which distract his attention from it. Or, assuming an air of glib resolution, he issues manifestoes which announce that the decision is made, and he reinforces these by repeating them at regular intervals. But the great religious choice placed before contemporary man cannot be evaded indefinitely; nor can its turmoil be circumvented by the proclamation of manifestoes, no matter how often this ritual takes place. The restless flight from the decision must yield to the quiet endurance of its turmoil. Only he who endures the tension of the conflicting possibilities can really know what the decision is about; only he can know when the time is ripe for it to be made. But what will the decision be? And when will the time be ripe for it to be made? This cannot be known in advance.

VI

THE Jew of today is a man of today; he is confronted with the religious question of today; the question is whether or not the Nameless can be present to us. But he is also confronted with the Jewish question of today: whether—and if so why—Jewish survival is a duty. The remarkable thing is that he cannot authentically face up to the religious question without at the same time facing up to the Jewish question.

The Jew of today cannot authentically face up to the religious choice simply as an individual. To do so is, in effect, to evade, if not his Jewishness, then at least the question posed by his Jewishness. And the question demands a religious answer. Hence to evade it is, for the Jew, to evade part of the religious question itself, and thus to fall into inauthenticity. The Jew cannot face up to the religious question "simply as an individual." Whether he likes it or not, he must face up to it as a Jew. To do so is to recognize that the duty to Jewish survival is, for the Jew, part of what is at stake in the religious choice. Man of today must endure the ancient question of whether or not the Nameless can be present. As part and parcel of that question for him, the Jew of today must endure the hardly less ancient question of whether or not Jewish survival is a duty. The religious turmoil is, for him, at the same time a Jewish turmoil. And Jewish religious life today consists in the endurance of this double turmoil.

When the time is ripe for decision, the Jew may well decide that the ancient duty to Jewish survival must be abandoned. Should this be the eventual choice, then the Jewish people, as it has existed for three thousand years, will cease to be. Jewishness will become a mere right, to be made use of only by those with a taste for it. Jews of the State of Israel will become Israelis, and Jews elsewhere will either become members of a denomination like other denominations, or else a minority doomed to eventual extinction.

But the Jew may also, in the end, decide to reaffirm the ancient duty of Jewish survival. This will be possible only if the Jew has remembered, and accepted as authentic, the ancient encounter of his people with the living God. He will then accept himself as part of a people constituted by an encounter with the Nameless, and still extant as a people only because it continues to be committed to that encounter. He will have accepted himself as a Jew because he will have accepted the time-honored Jewish obligation: to prepare and wait for the End in which all that is to be done by either man or God will be fulfilled.

8

The Dilemma of
Liberal Judaism

The Problem of Authority

The liberal Jew of today is in a dilemma. His Jewish conscience urges him to look for an authority which might guide and direct his Jewish life. But his liberal conscience frowns on that desire, as a temptation to be resisted. As a Jew he fears that, unless individuals such as himself accept an authority, there will soon be an end to Judaism. But as a liberal he fears that, should they in fact accept it, there will soon be an end to liberalism. These fears and doubts confront him with the possibility that he might in the end have to choose between his Judaism and his liberalism; that, as critics on both right and left have charged all along, liberal Judaism is a contradiction in terms.

If this dilemma, latently present ever since the rise of liberal Judaism, is becoming open and manifest in our time, it is because of three main conclusions toward which the conscientious liberal Jew is more and more ineluctably driven. Gone are the days when one could arbitrarily pick and choose from the Jewish past and persuade oneself that one's selection was Judaism. The selections have been too many and too varied, and too apt to reflect less the spirit of Judaism than that of those who selected from it, or that

Reprinted from *Commentary* (October 1960), pp. 301-10.

of their age or their class. If the liberal's Jewish life is to have a claim to authenticity, then, there must be a sense in which the Jewish past has authority. This is the first conclusion.

The second is a corollary of the first. Arbitrary picking and choosing may be done by the learned and the unlearned alike. But genuine contact with the past is possible, if at all, only through learning and scholarship. Hence if there is a sense in which the Jewish past has authority for the liberal Jew, there is also a sense in which Jewish learning has such authority. The views of the learned and those of the unlearned cannot carry equal weight; they can approach equality only as the unlearned themselves take steps to become learned.

The third conclusion is the deepest and hardest of all. Indeed, it is so deep and hard that, although it is well-nigh inescapable, the desire to escape from it is stubborn and widespread. If the Jewish past is to have authority for the liberal Jew, then this past cannot be a merely human past, however great. A merely human past could obligate the liberal Jew, if at all, only as a man; and the Jewish part of it, perhaps to a greater degree than other parts, but not differently in kind.[1] If Judaism is to continue to exist, there must be a sense in which the Jewish past has an altogether unique authority for the liberal Jew. But this is possible only if what speaks to him through it is not merely the voice of man but the voice of God. The third conclusion, then, toward which the liberal Jew is more and more ineluctably driven is that Judaism is not a purely human product: that it is, after all, a covenant between Israel and God. Hence he stands under still another authority, and this is the highest, of which indeed the other two are but means and instruments: the authority of God.

These conclusions, we say, are becoming increasingly inescapable for the serious liberal Jew. But because he is a liberal, he also finds them all but unacceptable. For they seem radically incompatible with that intellectual and spiritual freedom the exercise of which he considers both his right and his duty. As he sees his duty, he must criticize the past, not accept its authority; and he must criticize it in the light of standards which are modern and contemporary. It is by virtue of criticism that he sees the present to have progressed beyond the past; and to desist from such criticism and accept past authority would be, in his view, to betray his liberal conscience and lapse into reaction.

Liberal conscience, then, seems to rule out the authority of the past. It also seems to rule out the authority of learning and scholarship. A free believer must think for himself. He cannot be free if another thinks on his behalf. In the sphere of spiritual life, inferior thoughts which are the individual's own are better than superior thoughts which are not—simply because they *are* his own. How then can the authority of learning be acceptable? Hillel maintained that the ignorant cannot be pious.[2] To the liberal, these are hard and indeed intolerable words.

But the hardest authority for the liberal is not that of the past or of learning but that of God. Whether the divine word comes through the mouth of a prophet or a sacred writing or even through his own heart, he cannot, he feels, simply subject his conscience to it. He cannot but weigh that word against his own conscience; and in the end it must be *his* conscience and *his* judgment which are his authority, not a God other than they who legislates to them. If indeed there should be such a thing as revelation, it cannot be a voice *other* than the voice within. It must be identical with it. The voice of conscience, or of free thought, or of religious experience, must be the voice of God.

IN AN attempt to cope with the dilemma of the liberal Jew, our first task must be to consider more closely the concept of freedom which gives rise to it. That concept first achieved prominence in the Age of Enlightenment, and it has pervaded Western consciousness ever since.

It is well defined by Immanuel Kant. "Enlightenment," Kant writes, "is man's release from his self-incurred tutelage. Tutelage is man's inability to make use of his understanding without direction from another. Self-incurred is this tutelage when its cause lies not in lack of reason but in lack of resolution and courage."

In Kant's account, freedom is not the mere ability to choose. This would be altogether compatible with authority, that is, the taking of direction from another, provided only such direction is taken voluntarily. True freedom, for Kant, consists of autonomy. And by autonomy he means the ability to choose in the light of standards approved by one's own thinking, conscience, and experience. Freedom as so defined is radically and completely incompatible with authority, that is, the taking of direction from another. Kant thinks that true enlightenment consists of autonomy, and hence of emancipation from authority; and that autonomy is man's noblest goal. A noble goal: but not a goal that is easy or popular. Kant continues: "It is so easy not to be of age. If I have a book which understands for me, a pastor who has conscience for me, a physician who decides my diet . . . I need not trouble myself. I need not think, if I can only pay."

The modern concept of autonomy has had revolutionary implications for religious thought. The first of these was stated by Kant himself. Holy Writ cannot legislate to moral conscience. Moral conscience must legislate to Holy Writ. We cannot accept a law as moral because it is Biblical. Rather, we can accept a Biblical law only if it is moral; and it *is* moral if approved by moral consciousness. Moses and Jesus are not moral legislators who provide us with moral standards. They merely illustrate moral standards which we already possess.[3]

THE second implication of the concept of autonomy became manifest in the course of the 19th century. Pre-modern historians accept past facts on the authority of reliable documents. And pre-modern Biblical historians accept Biblical facts on the authority of the Bible. But modern historians wholly dispense with authorities. They *reconstruct* the facts of the past, instead of accepting them on authority, and the reconstructing is done in the light of their critical reason. Documents are no longer authoritative statements of what has happened; they are merely one means among others which enable the historian to reconstruct what has happened.

To the modern Biblical historian, the Bible can be no exception. It too is not an authoritative statement of historical facts, but merely one source among others which aid in their reconstruction. Hence the discipline known as Biblical criticism is not a mysterious discipline in its own right. It is but a branch of modern critical history.

But is the Bible merely another book of moral maxims, or another historical record? What of its claim to being the record of a divine revelation? The most momentous of all implications of the concept of autonomy is that revelation is in principle impossible. Revelation is the incursion of a God who is *other* than man into the life of man; and man is receptive to his incursion. But such receptivity is in principle incompatible with autonomy. If indeed man is capable of autonomy, then autonomy is his highest possibility; and if and when he actualizes it, he has transcended all passivity and receptivity in creative self-realization. Only two possibilities therefore remain concerning revelation if man is capable of autonomy. Either God does not contact man at all, being nonexistent or necessarily absent. Or else the God who contacts man is not other than man and present *to* man, but rather present *in* man. Revelation occurs, in that case, in great moments of human self-realization and is identical with it. Religious experience, or moral conscience, are not stimulated or caused by God. They are themselves divine.

It is in this re-interpretation alone, then, that revelation is compatible with autonomy. But if thus re-interpreted, revelation cannot be accessible through acceptance of the Bible. No doubt the Bible is the product of creative religious genius. But if later generations accept it as an authority they do not gain access to revelation but on the contrary bar themselves from it. For revelation consists of spiritual creativity whereas they have lapsed into receptivity and passivity. Only if they themselves achieve spiritual creativity can they penetrate, beyond the product of ancient creative genius, to that genius itself, achieving spiritual sympathy with it. But if they do achieve such creativity, then recourse to either the Bible or the genius which produced it is no longer needed. That bold, iconoclastic reformed clergyman, D. F. Schleiermacher, was able to write: "Not he has true religion who believes in a Holy Scripture, but he who does not require such a Scripture, and indeed could compose one in his own right."

Such, then, are the main implications of the modern concept of autonomy, so far as they are relevant to religion. Whether or not that concept is valid we must in due course inquire. For the present it must be shown that the concept of autonomy has, at any rate, enough validity for the liberal Jew to make pre-modern concepts of religious authority in principle unacceptable. Indeed, it was through recognition of this fact that liberal Judaism first came into being.

Pre-modern Judaism was by no means blindly authoritarian. Tradition stresses that R. Akiba interpreted the Torah so freely that Moses himself could not recognize it; and that what matters in the observance of the 613 commandments is not the letter but the spirit. At the same time, R. Akiba thought that he was merely drawing out what was in the Torah, and tradition insists that the commandments be observed, preferably to be sure in spirit as well as in letter, but in letter in any case. R. Akiba's conviction and the insistence of tradition in the end rest on one single fundamental belief, and this belief is the ultimate basis of pre-modern Jewish authority: the belief, not only in revelation, but in verbal revelation; the conviction that the Torah is not a human product, even one produced under the impact of divine revelation, but quite literally a divine product, dictated by God.

In breaking with the Orthodox view of authority, it is with this belief that, in the final analysis, the liberal Jew broke. Nor can he, even in his most romantic moods, return to that belief today. He broke with it under the impact of the concept of autonomy. But whatever the validity of that concept, it has enough validity to make the break inevitable.

Orthodox apologists often harp on specific blunders or excesses of Biblical criticism. But the true impact of Biblical criticism does not lie in particular radical assertions, such as that Israel never stood at Mt. Sinai. It would be as great even if all the critics agreed that Israel *had* stood at Mt. Sinai. The impact lies, not in specific assertions, but in basic assumptions. A medieval thinker such as Judah Halevi could accept Biblical facts absolutely, on the authority of 600,000 witnesses and an unbroken tradition. A modern historian can accept them, if at all, only tentatively, as a hypothesis capable of being overthrown. In the modern age, to follow the lead of Judah Halevi would be to exempt the Torah, alone among all historical documents, from the methodological requirements of modern history. But this is for the liberal Jew intellectually impossible. He can indeed, as we shall forthwith argue, believe in revelation. But he cannot possibly believe in verbal revelation, that is, in a divinely handed down text.

To do so is not only an intellectual impossibility. It is a moral and spiritual impossibility as well. When confronted with Biblical laws and concepts which seemed offensive to his conscience, the pre-modern Jew had two basic choices. Believing as he did in verbal revelation, he could see himself forced to swallow his scruples. Thus the Orthodox Jew prays for the return of animal sacrifices even today. Or he could interpret what seemed offensive so as to make it acceptable; and believing as he did in verbal revelation, he could believe that his interpretation was faithful to the literal meaning of the Biblical text. For the liberal Jew, both of these escapes are impossible. He is too deeply imbued with the modern historical spirit to be able to believe that modern values are implicit in ancient laws and concepts whose letter contradicts them. Nor can he pray for the return of animal sacrifices. To him, these are ancient but long outmoded ways of worshipping God.

The upshot, then, is clear. Whether or not he can accept revelation, the liberal Jew cannot, at any rate, accept *verbal* revelation. To accept it would be to accept an authority which would silence or fetter his critical reason and his spiritual conscience. But he would cease to be a liberal if he betrayed his duty to give free rein to both.

BUT some liberal Jews have always thought it necessary to go far beyond these negative conclusions. The concept of autonomy was accepted by them completely, with all its implications. Indeed, some have gone so far as to make the concept of autonomy the central positive concept of liberal Judaism. The "Pittsburgh Platform," adopted by a representative group of Reform rabbis in 1885, may be cited as a significant illustration. That platform frankly replaces revelation with "the consciousness of the indwelling of God in man." It openly rejects all traditional laws except moral laws, and what is moral it determines by the standards of modern consciousness. It regards Judaism as "a progressive religion, ever striving to be in accord with the postulates of reason." Not Judaism, not revelation, not the Torah, but reason is the one and only standard of truth and value!

Still, liberal Jews have frequently hedged as regards the concept of autonomy, and they have done so in increasing numbers as time went on. Thus while the Pittsburgh Platform of 1885 is forthright, the "Columbus Platform," adopted by the Central Conference of American Rabbis in 1937, equivocates: speaking of religious experience, but also of revelation; and asserting religious progress, but also that prophetic insight is unique, and hence presumably still unsurpassed. Liberal hedging is epitomized in a prayer which bids us "welcome all truth, whether shining from the annals of ancient revelations or reaching us through the seers of our own time." Whether both truths are revelation or neither is; whether the ancient legislates to the modern, or the modern to the ancient: these are questions which remain unanswered.

Superficially a sign of intellectual cowardice, such liberal hedging in fact reflects a profound Jewish awareness. It springs from the realization that the concept of autonomy, if carried to its logical conclusion, and made the central concept of liberal Judaism, must necessarily destroy Judaism.

To demonstrate this assertion is not difficult: to judge the past by the standards of the present is to presuppose the absolute superiority of the present. It is not merely to reject blind submission to the authority of the past. It is also to deny that we can learn anything whatsoever from the past. The past may approximate or on occasion even reach the level of the present. But it cannot by definition ever and at any point surpass it. Precisely because present standards decide what is true and of value, a Judaism based on the concept of autonomy would therefore have to be a wholly contemporary Judaism, cut loose from all essential ties with the past.

Further, such a Judaism would have to be a wholly man-made product. If based on the concept of autonomy, it could leave no room for revelation, understood as the incursion of a God other than man into the life of man. The voice of God could be present in such a Judaism only if identified with the "religious genius" which had produced it; and the genius would have to be, in essence, contemporary.

How could such a Judaism be related to the modern Jew? It could be understood as a body of universal truths and values. But then there would be no reason why to accept this body one need be a Jew, or why a Jew need accept it *because* he is a Jew. We should be left, not with Judaism but with a "religion of mankind." Or it could be regarded as a body of particular Jewish truths and values, true and valid for Jews alone. But in that case we would save Jewishness and Judaism only at the cost of lapsing into chauvinism and idolatry. In the past, the Jew persisted in his Jew-ishness for the sake of the worship of God. But if God is not other than man but present in human vision, and if He is present for the Jew in his Jewish vision, then the Jew of the future would have to persist in his Jewishness, for the sake of the worship, not of God but of the Jewish vision of God.

This serves to show the most serious and indeed catastrophic implication of the belief in autonomy for Judaism. The God of traditional Judaism can be present *to* man. If man is autonomous then God can be present only *in* man, as "conscience" or "insight" or "creative genius." But to accept this is in the end to fall prey to idolatry. That the voice of the heart is the voice of God is a belief which could seem plausible in ages given to romantic en-thusiasm. But this age cannot but see that the heart, while en-dowed with great spiritual power, is also, as Jeremiah said, deceitful above all things and exceeding weak. And we arrive at this crucial conclusion: God is accessible to man, either as He who is other than man and yet enters into human life; or He is not accessible at all. But this means that we must choose between Judaism and the belief in autonomy. We cannot have both.

THE central problem of the liberal Jew has now be-come clear. Judaism requires a twofold receptivity: a receptivity toward the past, and a receptivity toward a God who speaks through both present and past. The problem is whether this two-fold receptivity is compatible with freedom. And this *is* a problem because the concept of autonomy implies that it is not compatible.

But one may wonder whether true freedom is always auton-omy. Let us first ask: must every free relation to the past assume the absolute superiority of the present over the past? No doubt one's first reaction is to answer in the affirmative. Present science is superior to past science, and present history, to the history of the past. To think otherwise would be to lapse into reaction.

But reflection gives rise to second thoughts. Present science builds on past science, and present history on past history. Is the same necessarily true of religion and morality? Science and history deal with concepts only. Religion and morality are concerned not only with concepts but also with human lives. Concepts can be built on other concepts. But lives cannot be built on other lives. Hence while in science and history there can be steady progress, progress in religion and morality is at best only haphazard and equivocal. Religious and moral truths, even if long discovered, must always be re-discovered; and they are re-discovered, not just by being re-thought but by being re-lived. In short, in religion and morality, the present is not necessarily superior to the past.

This is why one cannot simply subject past religious and moral beliefs to present standards, any more than one can simply submit to their authority. To do the latter would be to avoid the responsibilities of freedom. To do the former would be to remain with a very limited freedom which, by idolizing the present, would become enclosed in its parochial bounds. A truly free spiritual relation to the past is not either of these one-way relations; it is the two-way relation of a genuine *encounter:* a relation in which the past, to be sure, is exposed to the judgment of the present, but in which the present also exposes itself to the judgment of the past. In such a relation there is acceptance from the past. But there is no blind acceptance. For what is unacceptable is not accepted, and what is accepted is appropriated by the recipient and made his own. But this is the crucial point: what the present recipient has accepted from the past is something he has truly learned. It is something new, something which he did not possess before the encounter. This is why, when he accepts it and makes it his own, his very being is transformed.

Such a receptivity, then, far from being incompatible with freedom, on the contrary enlarges and enhances it. It raises the recipient above the narrow dogmas of his time. No doubt a merely passive receptivity is incompatible with freedom. But not every receptivity is simply passive. We must therefore conclude that the problem of freedom and authority, as stated in terms of the concept of autonomy, is a falsely stated problem. And it is falsely stated because the concept of autonomy is itself invalid. Or rather, it is valid for the activities of abstract scientific and historical thought. But it is not valid as a concept of freedom which applies in human life.

This is our first important, positive conclusion, and it frees the liberal Jew from a time-honored but false dilemma. Critics on the right charge that to accept the past must be to accept it entire, and that all selective acceptance is arbitrary. Critics on the left charge that to select from the past is to be committed to present standards of selection, and that to be thus committed is to have no need of the past. Jointly these critics have always charged the liberal Jew with mere compromise.

But such charges have no force for the truly liberal Jew, who meets the Jewish past in a genuine encounter. For in this encounter he learns that not all selecting from the past is arbitrary; and not all acceptance from it a form of blind submission. No doubt his encounter with the past is fraught with danger. He will often project into the past what he believes himself to be discovering in it. And he will often fall prey to blind worship of the past when he believes himself to be freely accepting it. But he must resist the temptation of escaping from the encounter, by a flight either into or from the past. Rather he must cope with the dangers of the encounter in the encounter itself.

WE CONCLUDE, then, that human freedom is compatible with receptivity to the past. But is it compatible also with receptivity to a God who speaks to man through present and past? With this question, we have come upon the crux of our whole inquiry. This question is the crucial question. The difficulties it poses are the crucial difficulties. Indeed, on our ability to answer this question the success of our whole inquiry depends. And in the final analysis, everything thus far said has been said to prepare just for this question: is human freedom compatible with human receptivity to a God other than man—a God under whose authority he therefore stands?[4]

Reception from a human other can appropriate what it receives; the recipient can make what he receives his own. But can he appropriate the gift of a divine Other, and make it his own? Appropriating reception is possible in the first case because giver and recipient are both human. But is it possible if only the recipient is human while the Giver is divine? It may seem that only two possibilities exist in this case. Either the human recipient can indeed appropriate what he receives. But then the divine Giver cannot, after all, be other than the human recipient, and we are led back to the view that the divine voice is in man, rather than being other than the voice of man. Or else the divine Giver is indeed wholly other than the human recipient. But then the latter must receive His gift in radical passivity, and we are led back to premodern authoritarianism. For if the prophet is the mere vessel of the divine revelation, then the words he speaks cannot be a human reflection of an event of divine incursion, but must be quite literally the words of God. In short, we should have landed in Orthodoxy. Thus it seems that the crucial dilemma of liberal Judaism is still unresolved.

As we at long last try to cope with this dilemma we must first turn for guidance to traditional Judaism. For while authoritarian, traditional Judaism is by no means blindly so. And we must never forget that what unites liberal with traditional Judaism is far more than what separates them.

Traditional Judaism is often pictured as a barren legalism, in which the observance of external laws takes the place of a relation with the living God. If this account were correct, then revelation, as understood by traditional Judaism, could reveal laws only, not God along with these laws. And the Jew bound by them would be related only to these laws, giving recognition to their divine origin merely by submitting to them in blind passivity. In fact, however, this legalistic picture is nothing but a gross caricature. Except for rare periods of spiritual decay, traditional Judaism was always a religion, not of *law*, but of *commandment*.

A law discloses only itself. A commandment discloses its giver along with itself. Obedience to a law does not necessarily create a relation to its giver. Obedience to a commandment necessarily creates such a relation. In Judaism, revelation is commandment rather than law. And this means that revelation does not disclose the will of God to the exclusion of God, just as it does not disclose God to the exclusion of His will. It discloses both in indissoluble union. And this disclosure calls for an appropriate response on the part of those to whom it is made: that is, that they should both accept the commandment, and accept it as God's commandment. In prophetic utterances, the words "Thus saith the Lord" are not a mere preamble; they are an essential part of the message. To state the whole point very briefly we may say: traditional Judaism is not the mechanical observance of a system of laws. It is the living covenant between God and Israel.[5]

Where revelation is thus experienced and understood its reception cannot possibly occur in total passivity. Were this the case, the Divine presence would shatter the will of the human recipient, and indeed his very selfhood. The recipient would, as the mystic claims he does, dissolve into ineffable union with the Divine. But revelation which *commands* leaves the human *self* intact, for the commandment is addressed to him. It leaves his free *will* intact, for it is to his will that the commandment appeals. Indeed, the commandment accentuates this will, for it confronts it with a challenge from which there is no escape. Finally and most importantly, in Judaism revelation-as-commandment does not challenge the recipient merely to receive and fulfill the commandment, but to fulfill it with joy—that is, to appropriate it and make it his own.

To the mystic, revelation-as-commandment has always seemed

an impossibility. How can finite man, touched by the Infinite, retain his finite identity? How can this touch even accentuate his will? Finally, how can he appropriate the gift of the Infinite, while himself remaining finite? This may seem an impossibility. Yet it is the innermost secret of Jewish faith and Jewish life that this "impossibility" is actual.

How can it be actual? It is actual by virtue of divine love. In the very moment of touch which threatens to devour finite selfhood, revelation turns into commandment which re-establishes and reassures that selfhood. In the instant in which the commandment confronts man with a radical otherness which threatens to destroy him, it divests itself of enough of its otherness to become capable of enhancing human life instead of destroying it. In Judaism, then, love is not a revelation separate from commandment, let alone an "idea which was evolved only later in religious development." The very disclosure of commandment is also and already a disclosure of love, and would be impossible without it. And the traditional concepts of God as commanding King who inspires fear, and as forgiving Father who inspires love, are not separate, let alone incompatible concepts. The King is Father, and the Father, King. Hence it has well been said: "Love and fear God; tremble and rejoice when you perform the commandments."

Where revelation discloses itself as commandment, later generations which are subject to it cannot be related to it as to a dead past. Were this the case, the commandment would be living commandment only to those who first received it. To all others it would be mere dead law. The past for traditional Judaism is not a dead past. Through it still speaks the God who gave it. He still speaks because He still lives, and because His covenant with Israel is still alive. And the Jew today, as the Jew of old, is enjoined to practice, not arid law, but living commandment. Hence the Midrash well says: "All souls, even those which had still to be created, were present at the revelation of Mt. Sinai."

Our crucial question has thus in part been answered, in terms of Jewish tradition. Is human receptivity to a God other than man compatible with human freedom? If revelation is neither arid law nor mystic union but *commandment*, it is not only compatible with freedom but impossible without it. The human self remains intact even in the moment of touch by the Divine. He is free to choose for or against His commandment. Finally and most importantly, he is free to appropriate His commandment: to observe it, not in blind, slavish fear, but in the kind of love which exists because the recipient has made God's commandment his own, and God's will his. There can be no greater freedom than this. We saw above that free appropriation of the human past raises man above the parochialism of the present. We see now that free appropriation of God's commandment raises him above a human parochialism which is the lot of man when he is divorced from God. The Midrash thus rightly says: "When the Torah came into the world, freedom came into the world."

JEWISH tradition, then, solves most of the liberal's problems. But it leaves one serious problem unsolved, and to solve it, the liberal Jew must crucially depart from tradition. As for tradition, a recipient of the commandment is free to accept or reject it; and if accepting it, to observe it in fear, or in love as well as in fear. But it would appear that human spontaneity does not enter into the act of hearing itself, for the traditionalist holds that what he hears is quite *literally* the word of God. But this belief, as we have seen long ago, is to the liberal unacceptable.

Hence we are compelled to put forward a different doctrine. Human spontaneity enters not merely into the response to the commandment, but already into the *hearing* of it. Hearing does not precede the human response to the divine address. The hearing already contains elements of response. Hence every single word any prophet ever spoke is shot through with human interpretation. Yet had there been no event of divine revelation there would have been no human interpretation. Franz Rosenz-

weig rightly said: " 'He came down' [on Sinai]—this already concludes the revelation; 'He spoke' is the beginning of interpretation, and certainly 'I am.' "

This doctrine, if acceptable, removes all the remaining liberal
difficulties. Regarding the Torah as the human reflection of a divine revelation, rather than as itself literal revelation, the liberal
can regard it as a human book which is the legitimate object of
historical criticism, and whose commandments do not have, in
letter, authority over him. But he may at the same time regard
it as the prime means of access to a divine revelation which addresses him as much as his ancestors. In his quest for the commandment as it applies to him, he does well indeed to take the
ancient human reflection of the revelation with the utmost seriousness. But were he to subject himself blindly to its authority,
as if it were itself the literal word of God, he would not fulfill
God's commandment, but rather bar himself from it. He must
hear with his own ears. He cannot hear with ears of yore.

But is the above doctrine acceptable? If all revealed content is
shot through with human interpretation, must we not conclude
that revelation, apart from this interpretation, is wholly without
content and therefore irrelevant? Do we not, after all, return at
this late point—in practice if not in theory—to the unacceptable
doctrine of autonomy, the doctrine which identifies the word of
God with that of man?

The answer is that revelation and interpretation can be distinguished in abstract thought, but not in the concrete existential
situation in which both occur. To make the distinction between
revelation and interpretation is important, lest we subject ourselves blindly to the authority of the ancient interpretation. But
once we have made it we must ourselves return to the existential
situation, and to its responsibilities. And to do so is to ask: what
does the divine commandment demand of *us*? What can we hear?
What can we do?

In search of an answer, the liberal Jew of today must encounter the ancient reflection of the divine incursion which constituted the covenant under which he still stands. He must also encounter the tradition of those of his ancestors who sought—and received —answers before him. But if and when he himself receives an answer as a result of this encounter, it will be—if the encounter itself is genuine—the answer heard by him with modern ears, and addressed to him in a modern situation. Heard by him, it will no doubt bear the stamp of his human interpretation, just as did the answers heard by earlier generations. But if it is a genuine answer, genuinely heard, his human interpretation will nevertheless be the result of God's address. For He, the God of Israel, still lives; and the liberal Jew, son of the covenant, still stands at Mt. Sinai, as did his fathers.

9

Apologia for a
Confirmation Text

I

In the not so distant past, after lecturing at the university all week, I used to spend Sunday mornings teaching a confirmation class in a Liberal synagogue. My practice invariably was to open the first session of these confirmation courses by asking whether anyone present was prepared to state a Jewish belief to which he subscribed. A lengthy silence was apt to follow, until finally one student might volunteer some such answer as "one God," or "the fatherhood of God and the brotherhood of man," or simply "the brotherhood of man." Upon being asked why he believed as he did, the volunteer would reply, "That's the way I was taught."

"Then how about people who believe differently?" was my next question, and again came the unhesitating reply: "Why, they believe as *they* were taught!" At this point I would raise my voice, in what I hoped was a dramatic manner: "Then who is right?" And the response to that was usually a dead silence.

I confess that I have for many years been deeply disturbed by this disposition of our present-day synagogue-trained adolescents to assume that all religious and moral beliefs are wholly relative

Reprinted from *Commentary* (May 1961), pp. 401-10. This article is a series of reflections on my *Paths to Jewish Belief* (New York, 1960).

to upbringing and environment. What is wrong with a synagogue school if it can impart no substantial conviction to these young people? Nothing is wrong, I may be told; their attitude merely reflects an admirable broad-mindedness—a wholesome self-criticism. Yet it is hard to find anything wholesome in the rest of the standard opening discussion that used to take place in these former confirmation courses of mine.

In trying to challenge the relativism of my students, I would cite extreme and repellent examples of conflicting belief. "What about cannibalism? What about Nazism? Wouldn't you say that at least these are absolutely wrong and false beliefs?" On this, some of the students would surrender. But others were prepared to regard even Nazism with relativistic "impartiality." "*We* may think we are right and they are wrong. But *they* think the exact opposite. So who is to make an impartial decision?"

II

It has frequently been said that relativism springs from an acquaintance with the sciences. If it is true that people in different societies (or with different psychological make-up) believe different things, is it not also "scientific" to conclude that religious belief is entirely a matter of upbringing and environment? But relativism does not logically follow from psychological or anthropological premises. If all members of a given tribe were brought up to believe that two and two make five, we on our part should still regard this belief as simply mistaken. Why should it be denied that in morality and religion, too, one can find *grounds* for choosing between conflicting beliefs—to be sure, very different grounds from the mathematical kind, but grounds all the same? However, the relativism of our adolescents (or, for that matter, of their parents and teachers) is scarcely ever the result of thought—knowledge of the facts and persistent reflection on them. It is, almost invariably, a covenient substitute for thought. For once one has embraced a wholesale relativism on questions of moral or religious truth, one is freed of the necessity to give them any further thought. My impression is, indeed, that it is precisely because relativism provides so easy a solution to difficult problems that the social sciences are seized upon to lend their support to it—the social sciences are not themselves the original source. Nor can the source be regarded as a desire on the part of our adolescents to be broadminded, pluralistic, and tolerant. For tolerance not only does not imply relativism, but is actually incompatible with it.

It is entirely possible to defend everyone's right to his individual beliefs, and even to strain every nerve to understand the beliefs of another, and yet to be passionately convinced of the truth of one's own beliefs. Indeed, to believe in tolerance is to regard at least *one* thing—tolerance itself—as *absolutely* right, and to condemn, as absolutely wrong, at least all beliefs which conflict with it. Had they, for example, merely believed in tolerance, my students should not have hesitated for a moment to condemn Nazism as the worst form of intolerance imaginable. Why, then, should the absurd presupposition that in order to be tolerant one must embrace relativism be so popular in our liberal middle-class society?

The true cause, I am convinced, of the popularity of moral and religious relativism in the "enlightened" sector of our contemporary society lies neither in genuine skepticism born of a hard search for truth, nor in the desire—although doubtless this *is* genuine—to be broadminded, pluralistic, and tolerant. At the base of such relativism lies a desire to avoid facing up to ultimates, or—as a young student of mine, teaching confirmation class this year, puts it—the desire to shrink from a sense of urgency in moral and religious matters.

Facing up to ultimates is a business from which, with at least part of his being, nearly everyone wishes to shrink. For it means facing up to one's ultimate responsibilities, and to ultimate limitations like death. It means being driven toward the making of a commitment, and toward suffering all the doubts and crises which go with such a commitment. Moreover, it is to be compelled to disagree with others, even to have to seem "tactless" enough to voice this disagreement.

Serious and often terrifying as all this always is, in present-day middle-class society it is an awkward business as well. Taking ultimates seriously means "being different"—something to be avoided today at all costs. Being a genuine believer is being odd. (So is being an honest agnostic or atheist.) And who nowadays wants to be odd?[1]

A social science-style relativism is the perfect ideology for avoiding every kind of religious oddness. For this ideology enables one to agree that all religious beliefs are fine as far as they go, while denying that any one of them goes very far. This attitude is bound to be especially attractive to the modern middle-class Jew. The committed Jew, among religious men, always bears a special burden: he must stand up for a minority faith. This burden, easier in America today than it ever was in all other respects, is harder in at least one respect. It means having to be different, in a very special way, at a time when no one wants to be different in any way at all. Considering loyalty to Judaism as a duty, the modern Jew nevertheless shrinks from a genuine commitment to Judaism, which would mark him out as *doubly* different: religiously committed—and to a minority faith.

Here once again social science-style relativism comes to the rescue. If every faith has a relative right, this is surely true of the Jewish faith. And if no faith has an absolute right, this is surely true also of the majority faith. In short, being Jewish is not being different at all. Little wonder, then, that relativism should be so popular an ideology among middle-class Jews, synagogue-goers included. And it is even less wonder that those adolescents who are indoctrinated with it should be loath to give it up.

Yet how long can any form of genuine religious life survive when religious beliefs are taken seriously only "as far as they go"? How long can even the secular life of American democracy continue to exist, when the faith on which it rests is treated as just one belief among others? And how long can Judaism remain alive, as a religion in a non-Jewish majority culture, on the basis of a relativistic ideology? For while such an ideology may demonstrate a person's right to his Jewishness, it must, in due course, destroy every genuine incentive for making use of that right.

III

Whether relativism is, perhaps, a true doctrine, whatever its consequences for religion might be, is a question that need not be raised in our present limited inquiry. This being an essay on religious education in the synagogue, we take a commitment to Judaism for granted. We further take for granted that such a commitment obligates the synagogue school to oppose relativism, and to do so openly and explicitly in the confirmation year. The only remaining question here is just how such opposition should express itself.

Confronted with relativistic and skeptical students, a teacher committed to Judaism will often find it hard to resist the temptation to indoctrinate. Yet attempts at indoctrination, at least at confirmation age, are surely self-defeating. They will be tolerated, if at all, only by the conformist type of student. The bright and skeptical student will regard all such attempts as reflecting the narrow-mindedness of his teacher; and he will be confirmed in his prejudice that broad-mindedness and relativistic skepticism are identical. At the confirmation class level, moreover, the task of the teacher is to stimulate thought, not stifle it; to prepare the adolescent for the intellectual challenges of adult life, not to insulate him from them by indoctrination. What strategy, then, ought to be employed in the assault on relativism?

When I first asked myself this question, I imagined that I would have to cope with it only as a teacher using a suitable confirmation text. I soon found that there seemed to be no suitable texts—all the available ones fell into three categories, and none seemed to me to be adequate.

The old-fashioned liberal text, first, more or less identifies Judaism with liberal humanism, and assumes that all mankind is in progress toward such a humanism. This is the text written before—in spirit if not in time—the revolutionary events of our century: totalitarianism, post-colonial nationalism, social science relativism, and, in the Jewish sphere, Zionism; not to mention the new Jewish and Christian theologies, which endeavor to deal with all these challenges.

It would be overly hasty to assert that liberal humanism is to-day no longer tenable; elements in it are doubtless still valid. At the same time, in the present age liberal humanism is no longer self-evident; and it is even less evident that Judaism is reducible to it. Thus the old-fashioned kind of text (I am of course speaking throughout of Reform texts), which was once regarded as enlightened and rationalistic, but which still talks as if nothing had happened, is, in today's world, a mere indoctrination manual—and ineffectual to boot.

The second kind of text deals with Jewish practice, not in addition to, but in place of Jewish belief, on the grounds that no independent treatment of Jewish belief is in its own right necessary. After all, the author seems to be asking us, has not Judaism always been a "way of life" rather than a "system of beliefs"? And is it not sound progressive practice to induce the pupil to "learn" Judaism by "doing" it?

Much could be said for this approach if it were still true, as it once more or less was, that the study and practice of Jewish rituals and festivals would naturally and inevitably involve the student and practitioner in the beliefs implied by these rituals and festivals. But of course to the modern Jew the beliefs implied by Passover and Yom Kippur are highly problematic, more so than ever before. And the text which refuses to deal with these beliefs in their own right as much as says that new beliefs may at random take the place of the old, so long as the rituals and festivals themselves remain more or less intact; that any kind of new wine may be used, so long as it is poured into the old bottles. This view (curiously antithetical to that of old-style reformers who wanted to preserve the "essence" of the old wine and get rid of the "unessential" old bottles) is nowadays widely popular. Yet if consistently adhered to, its absurdity becomes obvious. Passover would become just another "festival of freedom," the Sabbath just another "socially progressive institution," and Yom Kippur—heaven only knows what; and what is specifically Jewish about these festivals would reduce itself to "folklore," "customs," "ceremonies."

THE third kind of text was, to me personally, the most promising at first, but finally—and by the same token—the most disappointing. Its paramount objective—to induce the student to think for himself—was admirable, and not only because, if successful in its aim, the text would provide the sole genuine antidote against the easy kind of relativism which I had found so prevalent in my classes. A student who has thought for himself believes whatever he does believe on *grounds*. For he himself has questioned the beliefs in which he was reared; and even if he has emerged from the questioning process with his former beliefs pretty much intact, he will no longer believe *as* he was taught merely *because* he was taught it. Such a student has abandoned the kind of relativism which is a substitute for religious thought, and has begun to think instead.

And yet in the year in which I used this highly promising text,[2] I found it a painful failure. Originally I thought its failure stemmed from its asking too many questions and giving too few answers. But gradually it became clear that the real fault of this text lay in its positivistic and pragmatic bias.

Teachers since Socrates have known that if one wishes a student to think for himself, one must ply him with questions, go easy on answers, and refrain from indoctrination altogether. But teachers also have always known that simply to ask questions may, in certain spheres of thought, defeat the original purpose. Perhaps the riskiest of all spheres in this regard is that of religious thought.

IN FORMAL disciplines such as logic, method alone matters. In religious thought, method and conclusion both matter, indeed are inseparable, and the genuine religious believer stakes his life on both. If a religious text confines itself to asking questions only, it must at least convey the idea that the answers are vitally important. But if answers are important, the adolescent wants to know the author's own answers. If these are not given— for whatever reason—the student is almost bound to conclude that answers are either unavailable or else unimportant; that religious thought, in other words, is a mere game.

Some young readers of such a text might nevertheless manage to pursue the search for religious answers by themselves. The danger, however, is that they might then fall into the trap—and for this an "all-questions-and-no-answers" text would bear direct responsibility—of assuming that their own immature thinking was on a par with the thinking of anyone else; and in no sphere could a view of this kind be more mistaken. The material of religious thought has an experiential richness never wholly possessed by any one individual; and that the thinking based on that material is by its nature cumulative is demonstrated in Jewish history from Philo down to Hermann Cohen, Buber, and Rosenzweig. Thus, a Jewish religious text which merely asked questions would deliberately cut the groping student off from the wealth of Jewish religious experience and the cumulative thought which has sprung from it. Superficially, such an approach might seem "impartial" and "objective." In fact, it would only insure that the Jewish faith is judged without having had a proper hearing.

But in fairness to the type of text under discussion, one must acknowledge that it is, on closer inspection, not averse to giving answers. It is averse only to giving "dogmatic" answers. And by these latter it means answers which do not rest on scientific authority.

In this day and age, few will object to scientific answers to religious questions in a Jewish confirmation text. It is always prudent, however, to consider two points more carefully: just how scientific are the answers in the text? And how does the text stand in relation to religious questions admittedly incapable of scientific answers—and to non-scientific answers to them?

The particular text under consideration not only asserts that the theory of evolution and the discoveries of modern Biblical criticism are scientific facts; it also suggests—at least by implication—as facts no less scientific, that (1) revelation is impossible; and that (2) history manifests so thorough an evolutionary trend as to make the best modern thought invariably superior to the best earlier thought, solely and simply because it is modern. But are the latter assertions scientific facts? Are they not, rather, highly controversial modern religious beliefs?

Now in presenting these modern beliefs as having the authority of science, the text does much damage—both to the student's intellect and to his Judaism. Whether the modern Jew can believe in revelation is something the student ought to think about, following the example of the best modern Jewish thinkers. If he listens to the text, however, he will not think; he will accept, on the authority of science, that revelation is impossible. Again, the student ought to consider whether modern is always superior to past Jewish thought; and he ought to examine each individual idea on its own merits. But if he trusts the text we are discussing, he will no longer independently examine past Jewish thought: he will have been taught that Bible and Talmud can at most only confirm insights which modern man finds elsewhere in a better form. (Even the author dimly recognizes this fault, for he gives appendices containing, in addition to modern texts, quotations from traditional Jewish sources. But these latter cannot undo the damage done by the basic indoctrination. They are but marginal and ineffectual decorations.)

What, next, of the text's attitude to religious questions which are admittedly incapable of scientific answers? The text answers these either not at all, or else only pragmatically: for instance, whether prayer is valid, each person must decide for himself; and monotheism is preferable to polytheism because it is more useful in uniting mankind. But the first type of response suggests that one answer is just as good as any other. (For why otherwise should the author not give his own answer, just as he has done in the case of "scientific" questions?) And the second response suggests that concern with religious truth is unnecessary; that what matters is not the truth of religious beliefs but their utility.

Now religious pragmatism is both unpragmatic and religiously perverse. It is unpragmatic because a religious belief "works" only if the believer accepts it by reason of its truth—and not just because it works. And it is religiously perverse because no genuine believer has ever accepted a belief merely on the ground of its utility. Israel has lived through the ages, and indeed still lives today, not because it lived by fictions known to be fictions and accepted on grounds of utility, but because it chose to follow Him whom it passionately believed to be the one true God.

There was, then, in the end, only one fundamental reason why I found the text under consideration thoroughly unacceptable: its failure or refusal—whatever the cause—to go beyond the limits of science, and take a firm stand on behalf of basic Jewish belief.

I V

Reflections such as the above led me to the conclusion that an adequate Jewish confirmation text ought to be informed by two principles. It ought whenever possible to make constructive use of rational argument in support of Jewish belief, considering both the nature of Judaism and the age of the readers. And when the limits of such support are reached it ought to take a straightforward stand on behalf of basic Jewish belief.

I have found that application of the first of these principles fills a crucial need in the religious life of the present-day adolescent. He is, as we have seen, disposed to believe that rationality ends where science ends, and that hence (at least to the extent to which they are scientifically undemonstrable) all religious beliefs are rationally on a par. The metaphysical demonstration that all religious beliefs are not equally rational (or irrational) has therefore a revolutionary and extremely wholesome effect. It furnishes the most telling challenge to the adolescent's easy and thoughtless relativism. Nor should the teacher, frightened off by the term "metaphysical," imagine that such a demonstration is wholly beyond the grasp of adolescents. It is quite possible to make clear that monotheism is more logical than polytheism, because the belief in many gods conflicts with the notions of both divine goodness and divine omnipotence, without which God would not be God at all. And it is not at all impossible to show that a wholesale moral relativism fails to explain how the Golden Rule could have emerged, independently, in many civilizations. Finally (to give one more example), the traditional arguments for the existence of God do not entirely exceed the grasp of adolescents; arguments which, however inconclusive, at any rate show that belief in God is not rationally altogether groundless.

So much for the first principle. What of the second—the text's testimony to Jewish belief when the limits of rational argument are reached? This is a more difficult principle because here theological exigencies easily collide with pedagogic exigencies. Theologically, there is need for testimony to Jewish belief, because while in Judaism reason may corroborate, interpret, and even correct belief, it cannot take its place. Yet as we have seen, pedagogically it is necessary that such testimony should not degenerate into indoctrination.

A possible collision is avoided if the text gives its testimony on behalf of Jewish belief *at the end* of the reasoning process—and only then. The student, having reached the limits of rational argument, will recognize that it can take him no further, and he will, therefore, also recognize what follows *as* belief, and not mistake it for anything else. If the text does its job well, no doubt its testimony on behalf of Jewish belief will impress its young reader. But it will not have induced him to accept this belief on authority. Having made clear that this *is* belief, not a demonstrated doctrine, the text will place the responsibility for acceptance or nonacceptance squarely upon the reader.

Is this still indoctrination? To say so would be to imply that in a world in which all kinds of conflicting causes and values vie for the adolescent's allegiance, the synagogue alone should bow out.

V

Armed with these two principles, and convinced of the inadequacy of existing confirmation texts, I some years ago decided to write such a text myself. I confess that in the actual process of writing it I often came close to regretting my decision, and indeed to abandoning the whole project. The real difficulties of such a text, it became ever clearer, lie not in first principles but rather in execution.

I will refrain from writing about the sort of thing educators usually write about—devices and techniques. These concern all education, not Jewish religious education for adolescents in particular. The specific problems besetting the latter kind of project devolve almost wholly upon issues of philosophical and religious honesty.

What philosophy major does not know that Kant has refuted the traditional arguments for the existence of God? And yet even if the adolescent can understand the arguments themselves, he is certainly as yet unable to understand Kant's refutation. Did this mean that philosophical honesty required that I should tell my young readers the "truth"—that the existence of God is unprovable? But reflection showed that "telling the truth" in philosophy— and religion—is a far more complex affair than is often imagined. For it is one thing to have contemplated the traditional arguments for the existence of God and then, after much struggle and deep thought, to have concluded that they are inconclusive or even invalid. It is another thing entirely to know nothing of these arguments, and simply to be told that God's existence is unprovable.

In the process of contemplation, the "anthropological" argument arouses wonder about man, an imperfect being who yet has a concept of perfection and hence of God. The "cosmological" argument arouses wonder about existence, about the world which, though existing, might not have existed. Finally the "teleological" argument (which even Kant regarded with respect) arouses wonder about the existence of order where there might have been total chaos. To have contemplated these arguments is to have experienced rational wonder. And this wonder will remain even if the arguments are finally found wanting. The person who truly knows the arguments may not end up thinking he has proved the existence of God, or even believing in God. But he can never again regard belief in God as just one irrationality among others.

Yet this precisely must be the attitude of the student who is simply told that the existence of God is unprovable. And this is why, though apparently told "the truth," he is in fact not told it.

How then was I to tell the truth? What I finally did was select the easiest of the arguments to understand (the teleological), state it in a form emphasizing rational wonder rather than rational cogency, and suggest (by emphasizing disorder and evil as well as order and good) that the argument is not wholly conclusive.

And I tried to cope with every philosophical problem that arose in a similar way.

Having reached the limits of rational argument, and finding it necessary to take a simple stand on behalf of Jewish belief, I came face to face with the problem of religious (as distinct from philosophical) honesty. This is a far more universal problem. It exists, not only for a philosophically- and theologically-minded writer trying to produce a text for adolescents, but for any intellectually sophisticated adult who tries to communicate what he himself believes to anyone younger or less sophisticated. Any parent who has ever tried to speak to his child about God recognizes the problem of religious honesty—provided the parent is neither a naive fundamentalist, nor a naive modernist, nor someone satisfied to tell his child lies which are "good for him." And the essence of the problem is that the parent *can* communicate to his child only what the child can understand, and that he *may* communicate to him only what he himself believes.

The naive fundamentalist has no problem because his beliefs are equally intelligible (or unintelligible) to adults and children. If the naive modernist has no problem, it is because he imagines that he can communicate his beliefs to the child without their being altered in the process of communication. But that this is naive is illustrated by a story told by C. S. Lewis. A mother once tried to tell her young son "the truth" about God, anxious above all to avoid the myth about the old man with the white beard. She told him that God was the basic Substance of everything. (One may, wihout altering the moral, substitute "Process" or "the sum total of our ideals.") In trying to imagine something vague, amorphous, and overwhelming enough to qualify as a "basic Substance," the child wound up thinking of God as a huge mountain of tapioca. (To top it all, he didn't even like tapioca!)

How would the more naive kind of "tell-only-the-truth" educator react to Lewis's story—to the fact that the child is an inveterate myth-maker? I imagine he would advise post-poning all talk about God until the child is "old enough to under-stand" the truth, which presumably is that God is "Substance," "Process," the "sum total of ideals"—if indeed He is anything at all.

But one must be profoundly suspicious of any view of religious truth which implies that children are wholly barred from it. No doubt many states—childhood, insufficient intelligence or educa-tion—bar a human being from scientific truths. But these truths concern the abstract intellect. Religious truth, if it is really reli-gious truth, concerns the whole person and his ultimate quest as a whole person. And are children not whole persons? Do they not have an ultimate quest as whole persons? The poet Rilke was able to detect in children a degree of religious awareness which adults have often lost. In this he showed greater sensitivity to and respect for children than the more naive kind of "tell-only-the truth" educator. For the latter is driven to the assertion that children in the myth-making stage are wholly barred from re-ligious truth.

This kind of educator, to be sure, *means* to respect the per-sonality of the child, and this is why he quite rightly refuses to tell him lies. In this he has at least grasped the indispensable start-ing point of any honest student-teacher relationship. If he never-theless fails, it is because he blindly assumes that, by adult stan-dards, all myths must simply be lies. And this assumption in turn is due to his naive belief of being in literal possession of reli-gious truth himself. But can God literally be "Substance," "Proc-ess," or the "sum total of our ideals"? Quite apart from one's re-ligious position, this must radically be denied. For not one of these—or any other—aspects of the known universe or the known self can literally be the object of religious worship, or literally be part of a religious relationship. They can be either only if the known ("Substance," "Process," etc.) is symbolic of the un-known—in short, a myth. To treat these aspects of the known as literally divine is either not to know what one is doing or else to commit idolatry. The mother in Lewis's story, therefore, only got what she deserved. Committing the idolatry of literally identifying God with an aspect of the known universe (it was only an aspect, for "Substance" excludes "self"), she encouraged her son to commit the idolatry of identifying God with an aspect of the universe which *he* knew. What she should have done was tell a story which pointed to the truth as she herself accepted it—in her own symbolic terms. And along with the story she should have made clear to the child that this was only a story, albeit one which had some connection with her own symbolic understanding of the truth.

But *can* such a complicated impression be conveyed to children? I have never been able to believe that children regard all stories as either literally true or else not true at all. And I have always suspected that, whenever the child holds this simple dichotomy, the fault lies with the adult storyteller, who himself subscribes to such a dichotomy. Is it really always true that the child who thinks of God as Father imagines Him as a father exactly like his own, with only the white beard added? I am inclined to think that the communication of symbol and mystery is impossible only to storytellers who are themselves devoid of a sense of both; storytellers, that is, who are either devoid of faith or else reduce God to aspects of nature or self.

But adolescents, after all, are no longer children. How was I to cope with the problem of religious honesty in a book addressed to them? So far as I could see, there was only one way. I had to let them in on the secret. I had to discuss the symbolic status of all images and concepts derived from the known, when applied to God. Is God personal or impersonal? To conceive Him as personal is anthropomorphic. Is God, then, impersonal—a "Substance" or "Process"? But this is physiomorphic (if I may coin the term). If God cannot be defined in terms derived from the human person, neither can He be defined in terms derived from

nature. Physiomorphism is even less adequate than anthropo-
morphism: for while quantitatively more than any man, a
"Process" is qualitatively less even than a man—who can hear,
speak, feel, and think. The upshot is that we can think of God
only in symbolic terms, and that personal are less inadequate
than impersonal terms. Moreover, if one takes one's stand on the
Jewish faith, these personal terms point to a very special truth.
For Judaism believes in the co-workership of God and man, in
the covenant between God and Israel, and in God's availability
in prayer; and the divine-human relationship implied in these beliefs can be thought of only in quasi-personal terms. But while
the Jew must admit that the personal terms are not adequate, he
believes that the relationship itself is real.

HAVE I managed to solve the problems of philosophical
and religious honesty? It is impossible to say. I can only wait
and see. For the answer, while depending in some degree on what
I have put into the book, depends more on what teachers and
students will do with it.

This last is both a disturbing and reassuring reflection. It is disturbing because a book like *Paths to Jewish Belief* is bound to
encourage, through misplaced emphases, unfortunate turns of
phrase, or even downright slips, interpretations at variance with
those intended. And yet the knowledge that both teacher and
adolescent reader will do their own interpreting and criticizing is,
in the long run, far more reassuring than disturbing. For the ultimate, inescapable dilemma before the writer of such a text is
that, on the one hand, he can do no other than present what he
himself believes while yet, on the other hand, he trembles at his
audacity in doing so. The writer may, for the immediate purpose,
de-emphasize his more personal convictions and emphasize "normative" Judaism; but he cannot ever hope wholly to succeed in
"purifying" the text of his private beliefs. What entitles him to
impose them on helpless teachers and students? The answer is

that there is no imposition, for neither teachers nor students are helpless. The writer finds reassurance in the knowledge that the teacher who disagrees with the text in part will voice his disagreement vigorously when teaching it, and that the teacher who disagrees with it *in toto* will not use the text at all. But the greatest reassurance of all lies in the knowledge that adolescents, at this or any other time, are apt to respond to an intellectual and religious challenge not with meek submission, but with an honest inquiry of their own.

10

The Jewish Concept
of Salvation

Judaism is a religion of salvation. It is equally opposed to fatalism, which denies that anything *can* be saved or perfected (the world being meaningless chaos); and to pantheistic mysticism, which denies that anything *needs* to be saved or perfected (the world being already perfect, and evil mere illusion). Unlike pantheistic mysticism, Judaism takes the reality of evil seriously; and unlike fatalism, it believes that evil is destined to redemption.

Salvation, in Judaism, is not a mere abstract assertion. From the earliest Biblical origins, it is a present and compelling experience. Beset by poverty or enemies without, and by sin or uncleanness within, Biblical man, when suddenly freed from these troubles, perceived such liberation to be not a matter of chance, but a revelation of ultimate meaning and reality—a saving act of God.

In due course, the Biblical and post-Biblical Jew became more and more aware of the complexities of history. He was forced to recognize that the moment of salvation did not banish trouble permanently, and that it did not banish it absolutely even while the moment lasted. Men such as Jeremiah and Job saw that salvation often does not come to those most in need of it; and in the

Reprinted by permission of the editors from *Anglican Dialogue* (February 1967), pp. 4-5.

Babylonian exile a whole people waited in vain for salvation, for long decades.

These experiences might have shattered the Jewish faith in salvation. Instead, that faith developed a dimension already implicit in it, by which it met and withstood them—the eschatological dimension. Salvation would be consummated in the future. But since no here-and-now as presently known was wholly free from evil this would be an ultimate future—the Messianic "end of days."

By virtue of this development, Judaism became the first religion to regard all history as endowed with religious meaning. For while meaning in history was as yet only intermittently disclosed, the "end of days" would disclose the meaning of all history—even of that which now seemed unmitigated tragedy and stark horror.

If in this form the Jewish faith was able to survive until today, it was because it developed three further aspects which, jointly, lent it the power to withstand every challenge. First, the Jew came to both work and wait for the "end of days." To wait only would have been to view salvation as a divine incursion wholly unrelated to human action, and hence all history prior to that incursion as meaningless. To work only would have been to regard man as able wholly to complete the work of salvation, and divine action as superfluous. But the one would have been a lapse into inactivity and lassitude; and the other, a lapse into an unrealistic optimism unfit to survive tragedy. If the Jewish faith in salvation had the power to meet every test, it was because it made its followers act as if all depended on them, and pray as if all depended on God.

Secondly, the "end of days" was originally conceived as a messianic age in future time, fulfilling the meaning of history. But out of this grew an additional dimension—the notion of a "world-to-come" beyond all time, fulfilling the meaning of each individual life. The one was the realization of peace, justice and love on earth; the other was an ultimate divine dispensation beyond time and earth, through which each human life would find its ultimate consummation. To be sure, Jewish belief never achieved clarity as to the relation between these two dimensions, and perhaps could not; for the "world-to-come" was thought to be past human understanding. But it seemed clear that tendencies to reduce either of these dimensions to the other had to be resisted. For history could not be a mere "antechamber" of the world-to-come, but had to find fulfillment in its own right. And yet individual lives too had to find fulfillment in their own right; they could not be mere instruments toward a future perfection of history. Salvation had to redeem both the history in which men work and wait, and the individuals who work and wait in it.

Thirdly, though expected to be fulfilled only in the "end of days," salvation never vanished wholly from present Jewish experience. Had it done so the Jew would have found himself cut off from the living God, in possession of the Torah but divorced from its Giver, and wholly geared to future salvation. Yet the Jew remained able to perceive God's salvation in the here-and-now, albeit ambiguously and incompletely. Indeed, the whole Jewish way of life—its working and waiting included—is even now nothing but a celebration of Divine salvation. Thus the "historical" festivals of Judaism are a celebrating re-enactment of the history of salvation insofar as it has already occurred, and an anticipation of the ultimate salvation which is yet to come. And on the "Days of Awe" the Jew stands, even now, before that Judging and Gracious Presence in the sight of which every human life is to find its ultimate consummation.

11

Two Types of Reform:
Reflections Occasioned by Hasidism

I

In 1870 Heinrich Graetz denounced the Hasidic movement as the radical antithesis of the reform required by Judaism in the modern age.[1] In 1907 Martin Buber described Hasidism as itself a reform movement, indeed, as the greatest in all of Diaspora history; and he was bold enough to assert that to find new life in our time Judaism had to assimilate Hasidic elements.[2]

These conflicting judgments illustrate the problem of this paper. Two reforms, we shall argue, are required by modern Judaism; the one if it is to be modern, the other if it is to remain Judaism. But how to reconcile them is our problem, dramatically illustrated by Graetz' and Buber's conflicting views on Hasidism.

In the light of present-day scholarship, no one could still take seriously Graetz' actual judgment on Hasidism, made almost a hundred years ago. On that subject, the great historian was prey to the prejudices of his age, to which all myth, symbol and mysticism were mere superstition.[3] But it would be a romantic blunder simply to dismiss, along with Graetz' judgments, the standards in the light of which they were made. If Graetz repudiated miracles

Reprinted by permission of the Central Conference of American Rabbis from *Central Conference of American Rabbis Yearbook* (Philadelphia, 1961), pp. 208-23.

and magic; if he took a low view of the authoritarianism of the
Zaddik; if he suspected ecstatic experiences of being at worst a
fraud and at best mere self-deception—all this was at least in part
because he saw the need to reform Judaism in the light of modern
scientific rationalism. And this reform, called for and carried out
by men such as Graetz, has remained permanent and irrevocable.

And yet, with the passage of time it has become increasingly
clear that the rationalist kind of criticism would fail to dispose of
Hasidism even if it were suitably brought up to date. This is less
because of developments in Hasidic scholarship than because of
a shift in liberal Jewish life and outlook. At one time, the great
question may have been how to make Judaism modern. Today,
the great question is how to save it as Judaism. The rationalistic
kind of reform, it is now very plain, is largely negative in character; and an additional positive reform is needed if Judaism is
not to be dissipated into generalities and irrelevancies. But those
who seek such a reform have learned to look on Hasidism, not as
a quaint and superseded phenomenon, but rather as a source of
inspiration and hope.

II

We begin with the first of the two reforms, and with the modern, scientific rationalism by which it is inspired. For our present
purpose, this rationalism is sufficiently distinguished from its pre-
modern, medieval predecessor in terms of its methodological
principle of inquiry. Rational inquiry, in the modern view, is the
search for uniformities; and it seeks these throughout the whole
world of empirical fact. To come upon the non-uniform, in this
view, is not to discover an exception to uniformity but merely
one's ignorance; it is, therefore, not an occasion for ceasing to
inquire, but rather a spur to further inquiry.

This seemingly simple and innocuous methodological principle
has proved to be a source of extraordinary power. If modern sci-

ence has advanced with unprecedented swiftness; if it has tossed aside ancient authorities and scientific systems, however reasonable on the surface; if it has achieved an unheard-of measure of control over nature—all this has been far less because of specific scientific discoveries than because of the principle referred to, by which all modern science is inspired. This principle is the true source of the revolution in modern scientific thought.

But this principle caused a revolution in the sphere of religious thought as well. If modern thought had merely advanced new world-views instead of the old it would have called for only minor revisions in religious thought. Because the new world-views sprang from a new principle of inquiry the required change was revolutionary. For whereas pre-modern religious thinkers could confine themselves to the task of reconciling the facts of science with other facts, accepted on Scriptural authority, their modern successors were faced with a rationalism rejecting this authority, by claiming for itself the whole sphere of empirical fact.

Thus Maimonides, for example, was a rationalist in search of uniformities. But his rationalism being pre-modern in kind, he was prepared to accept exceptions to uniformity, even in the domain of empirical fact; and for that reason he could accept the Torah as an authoritative source of empirical facts.[4] Modern rationalists, in contrast, were bound to regard such acceptance as an arbitrary limitation of rational inquiry. Whatever their views on revelation and authority, they could not, at any rate, accept empirical facts on revealed authority. For their methodological principle allowed no exceptions to uniformity but merely the appearance of such exceptions, due to ignorance. But ignorance is not an occasion for submitting to authority. It is, as we have said, a spur to further inquiry.[5]

III

It is to their credit that liberal Jewish spokesmen should have been quick to embrace the spirit of scientific rationalism; and that, in contrast with many other religious spokesmen, they should have embraced it, not as a matter of mere pious proclamation, but in full readiness to accept the consequences. True, there are in our midst, even today, apologists on the right, who busy themselves reconciling archaeology with the Biblical story of the flood; and apologists on the left extolling the Bible for anticipating Einstein and Freud. But on the whole it is clearly seen that the time for reconciliations in the medieval style is long past; and that this is because, whatever our views on religious authority, we can no longer regard the Torah as an authoritative source of empirical facts.

Thus a modern Jew might believe in the splitting of the Red Sea, like his pre-modern ancestor. But unlike that ancestor he would believe it as an hypothetical result of historical reconstruction, not on the categorical authority of the Torah. Or he might share Jehuda Halevi's conviction that Israel once stood on Mount Sinai, hearing not only the thunder but also the voice of God. But whereas Halevi's conviction could rest on the authority of 600,000 witnesses, and on an unbroken tradition reporting their testimony,[6] its modern counterpart had to spring from an inquiry recognizing no factual authorities. Most important of all, the reconstructed events of modern rational inquiry were instances of uniformity, not exceptions to it.

Thus however modern inquiry might explain the splitting of the Red Sea, it would not seek refuge in suspensions of natural law. And whatever the terms in which it might explain the hearing of the voice of God on Mt. Sinai, they would not include an actual voice of God.[7] In short, modern scientific rationalism demanded that all empirical aspects of the Jewish past should become the legitimate object of modern rational inquiry—of an unlimited quest for uniformity. And the moment this demand was accepted modern Jewish scholarship was born.

This was also the birth-moment of the intellectual reform of Judaism presently under discussion. It used to be said that modern liberal differs from pre-modern orthodox Judaism in being open to change. But it has long been recognized that this is no adequate mark of distinction, since orthodoxy—except in its most ossified forms—is itself open to change. The new factor is not openness to change but rather an altered basis for openness. And at least one cause of this alteration was the modern principle of rational inquiry.

A pre-modern rationalist such as Maimonides was forced to alter Jewish belief, as well as seek new "reasons for the commandments," so as to make them rationally acceptable. At the same time he could draw sharp limits to alterations of belief; and while allowing changes in the meaning of the Halacha he could rule out all changes of consequence in the Halacha itself. For his rationalism allowed acceptance of the Torah as containing authoritative disclosures of empirical fact. Maimonides, in short, could be a rationalist and yet an orthodox Jew.

But no modern rationalist could remain an orthodox Jew. For unlike its pre-modern counterparts, modern rationalism claimed all empirical fact as its legitimate domain. And acceptance of this claim, and of its religious implications, is one thing all liberal Jews have in common. They may disagree among themselves as to the degree and direction of change necessary or desirable. They may disagree on the positive basis of such change, battling over revelation and authority. The one point agreed on is a negative principle. This is that no empirical facts, however sacred, may be exempted from the modern search for rational uniformity; that therefore, whatever the place of revelation and authority in liberal Judaism, revelation cannot be verbal revelation; and authority cannot include the authoritative disclosure of empirical facts.

IV

But ever since Mendelssohn, there has been no lack of liberal spokesmen demanding, in the name of scientific rationalism, a far more radical reform of Judaism than that thus far described. The one reform is mainly negative in character; the other would make modern rationalism the positive basis of a transformed Judaism. The one is a matter of common agreement; the other could not be more controversial. For whereas some regard this latter, radical reform of Judaism as necessary if Judaism is to be modern, others regard it as impossible if Judaism is to remain Judaism; and they deny that it is rationally necessary. The proposed reform would transform the God of Israel into a timeless universal principle—a First Cause transcending the universe, or a Process identical with it.

Earlier reformers of this radical kind believed in a Deistic First Cause beyond the universe. Their contemporary successors prefer a Process immanent in the universe and animating it as a whole. What unites both groups is common opposition to the God of Israel who, while transcending Nature and History, was yet capable of entering into both. Both groups dismiss such a God, as incompatible with modern rationalism. A God beyond the universe is in no conflict with the search for rational uniformity; nor is this true of a God somehow identical with the universe as a whole. If the radical rationalist reformers are right, however, such a conflict does exist in the case of a God who, while beyond the universe, yet enters into it. For does not every such entry shatter the system of uniformities? If these reformers are right, then the enlightened modern Jew may believe in a First Cause beyond the universe, or in a Divine Process immanent in it. But he must let go of the God of Israel, as a mere myth of bygone ages. Such, in brief, is the reform which radical rationalists have called for, ever since Mendelssohn.[8] And if accepted, it would be of profound consequence.

The God of Jewish tradition could be present, in the here and now. He could single out persons and peoples, and be sought out by them according to the need of time and place. A transcendent First Cause or immanent Cosmic Process, in contrast, is a timeless principle; and it can inspire to action, not by acts of singling out, but only as an eternal ideal. For a First Cause is indifferent to the particular; and while a Process contains all particulars, it embraces them as a homogenizing Whole. Moreover, neither God can be sought out by men in the here and now. He is accessible, if at all, only by thought rising to timelessness. In short, if the radical rationalist reformers are right, then the here and now, once of the essence of Jewish religious belief and life, reduces itself to a mere unessential accident.

V

The proponents of the radical reform under discussion are prepared to accept this implication. They may even regard it as a purification of a formerly impure Jewish essence. Yet one must say with all bluntness at one's command that this is no purification but rather a distortion. No doubt there is need for eternal verities in Judaism. But the reduction of the God of Israel to such a verity, if it were ever carried out through the length and breadth of Jewish life, would be the end of Judaism.

The very first commandment ever addressed to the first Jew— that Abraham leave his country—is an act of singling out, not an application of a universal ideal, unless a universal peoples' migration were the will of God. The very exodus which constitutes Israel is not an acceptance of timeless verities, but a response to a unique historic challenge. Whatever the facts of early Jewish history, they lived on in Jewish memory as disclosing a God of the here and now.

Moreover, He remained such a God in Jewish experience. The God of Jewish prayer is universal Creator, but He can also be present to each worshipper. His Halacha is law valid in all situations. But it is also commandment, which discloses the Giver along with the commandment; and the Giver wants *this* man to act, not someone else, and now, not at some other time.

Nor is the God of Israel present only to Israel. For in contrast with the God of the Greeks, He is a God of history, and a God caring for personality. But this is the nature of history, that each of its moments differs from every other; and this is the characteristic of persons, that every one of them is unique. Throughout their history, Jews have stubbornly clung to this God, against all doubts and all critics. Even medieval rationalists, enamoured though they were with Greek thought, did not forsake Him.[9] If indeed modern rationalism requires, after all, the transformation of this God into a timeless principle, then the change required is no minor loss, let alone a purifying gain. It is nothing less than unconditional surrender to the Greeks. It is little wonder that liberal spokesmen always had their misgivings about this kind of reform. The astounding fact—indeed, one of the most astounding facts of modern Jewish history—is that their misgivings were so rarely flaming protests. And nothing could testify more eloquently to the power of modern rationalism over the Jewish mind.

VI

Still, liberal spokesmen always *did* have misgivings. Thus they were never quite prepared to reduce historical revelation to a set of timeless verities, or Halacha to a set of universal values. Nor, though inclined to view history as a universal upward movement, did they ever wholly abandon the particular—Israel and the individual human person. And while in philosophizing moments they may have thought of God as universal First Cause or Cosmic Process they were apt, in moments of worship, to pray to the God of Israel. In short, throughout its history liberal Judaism has never wholly forsaken the ancient Jewish belief in the ultimate significance of the here and now in the sight of God.

Moreover, as the nineteenth passed into the twentieth century, and as the latter unfolded its grim and unpredicted aspects, this belief assumed new and unprecedented importance, not only for the modern Jew but for all modern men. Once, perhaps, it could seem that the Jew's Jewishness was a mere accident of his humanity, and his Judaism a set of universal verities. But this time is long gone. Today as always, the Jew must hold fast to his humanity—and hence to any man's humanity—as to a religious ultimate. But if, in an age which has singled the Jew out with unprecedented grimness, this holding-fast sheds no light or meaning on his Jewishness, then it must degenerate into a hollow irrelevancy, if not into a dishonest device for escape.[10]

Again, once, perhaps, it could seem that the human person could live by universal verities alone, such as a Deistic First Cause or a Divine Cosmic Process. But this time too is long gone. For in the present age, the human individual is called into question to a degree which has rarely been equalled and never surpassed. Nature seems ever larger to human consciousness, and the individual person, ever less significant in it. History seems prey, more and more, to anonymous forces, over which even individuals favored by history have little control; hence even those still believing in necessary progress in history tend to regard the individual as a mere means to its impersonal or superpersonal ends.[11] Depersonalization has insinuated itself even into the individual's most intimate relations. For here at least each man is meant to be a unique person; but the impersonal instruments of an industrial mass society threaten to reduce him to a mere instance of the species man. Such a time needs timeless verities and values, which are needed at any time. Its great specific need, however, is for what will give meaning, not to universals such as nature or mankind or history as a whole, but to that most stubborn of all particulars—the individual human person. But such meaning, if ultimate, can be found only with God; and not with the God of the Greeks but only with the God of Israel. Rarely in human history have men—non-Jews as well as Jews—stood in so great a need of the God of Israel. It is not without irony that this need should coincide with a

time of widespread surrender, on the part of Jews, to the God
of the Greeks.[12]

VII

But recent events have not been without effect on liberal Judaism. They have led to a growing stress on the here and now—the
Jewish people, the human person, the particular in its stubborn
concreteness. This stress, however, has not always, or even for
the most part, coincided with a return to the God of Israel. For
while today there is widespread stress on the here and now, the
belief remains no less widespread that a God of the here and now
is no longer acceptable. And those among us who stress the one,
and believe the other, have resorted to a new escape from a new
dilemma. They have surrendered objective truth to universal verities—the First Cause or Cosmic Process—and have withdrawn the
here and now into a sphere of mere human subjectivity.

In consequence of this withdrawal, Jewish prayer, once *between*
a "subjective" self and an "objective" God, is viewed as the self's
disport with its own feelings, conducive to aesthetic or therapeutic
benefit. Halacha, once a way walked *before* God, is reduced to
"custom and ceremony," performed for the sake of warm emo-
tions within or wholesome relations without. Judaism, once a covenant involving a singling-out God and a singled-out Israel, is
seen as a man-made civilization, created by Jewish genius in its
human solitariness. And the human person, who once believed
that he *actually* mattered to God, is now engineered into the mere
feeling that he matters, on the ground that such feeling banishes
anxiety and alienation. All too rarely has our new emphasis on the
here and now amounted to a challenge to the God of the Greeks,
on behalf of the God of Israel. For the most part, it has been a new
form of surrender.

But if this surrender is a rational necessity, then all our attempts to give religious re-assertion to the here and now are foredoomed to failure. For Judaism can be a creative religious civilization only if we forget creativity and civilization, and turn to God. Prayer can bring its benefit only to those directing their heart, away from benefit and toward Heaven. Custom and ceremony can acquire true religious life only if transmuted into commandment—deed done before God. And the individual can conquer anxiety and alienation, not through mere *feelings* that he matters, no matter how skilfully they are aroused and maintained, but only through the *belief* that he matters. But belief is not belief at all unless it lays claim to objective truth.

The events of our age, then, together with the stress on the here and now with which we have tried to meet them, raise one problem surpassing all others in religious significance. This is whether it is possible for the liberal Jew, in the here and now of mid-twentieth century America, to return to the God of Israel.

VIII

It is this question which confronts the liberal Jew, heir to the modern rationalist reform, with that other great reform in modern Judaism, the Hasidic movement.[13] Though worlds apart in space if not in time, the two reforms have much in common, notably the wish to liberate life from forces stifling it. Yet even as regards this aim there is at least one crucial difference. Whereas the Western rationalist reform seeks to free the life of the human intellect, the Eastern Hasidic reform seeks to free the life between man and God. While the one creates something new, the other restores what has always been. And whereas the former reform must break with orthodox authority, the latter must rebel only against orthodox decadence. Orthodoxy, in the decadent form in which Hasidism found it, had clogged up the channels of communication between God and the human here and now. It was the fundamen-

tal aim of Hasidism to reopen these channels, so that the interrupted life between God and Israel might be resumed. It is, therefore, not this aim which makes Hasidism unique. Its uniqueness
lies, rather, in the passion with which it pursued the ancient aim,
seeking, as it were, to storm the Heavens.[14]

No doubt the above is an oversimplification, for Hasidism is a
phenomenon with many facets. Yet at least in the view of this
writer—admittedly no specialist in Hasidic studies—the oversimplification is not a distortion. For it would seem that most of the
facets of Hasidism subserve the fundamental aim just stated, and
that few if any conflict with it.

Thus while Hasidism is a kind of mysticism it is not the kind
which dissolves the human here and now into a conflux with Infinity. Hasidic mysticism is a practical mysticism, one of human
action. But action asserts the human here and now, and the mysticism gives this action ultimate significance, by placing it into re-
ciprocal contact with God. For this reason, Hasidic mysticism is a
truly Jewish mysticism. The Baal Shem Tov uttered good Jewish
doctrine when he claimed that there is no place in which God may
not be found; and that all true actions, performed in the here and
now, leave permanent traces beyond the here and now—in the
"upper world."[15]

Again, Hasidism may seem to speak on behalf of the heart
against the intellect, and on behalf of the common man against the
scholarly aristocrat. It speaks, however, not on behalf of one half
of a dichotomy against the other but on the contrary against all
dichotomies, in the name of a relation between God and the whole
man. Hence Hasidism is, in essence, neither anti-intellectual nor
anti-Halachist. An ignorant boy's playing of a whistle may be a
gift acceptable to God; but so may the prayer of a learned man.
The Zaddik's life includes far more than orthodox Halacha; it
includes Halacha as well.

Hasidism, further, asserts rungs or degrees of human perfection. But this is not to set up ideals beyond ordinary life, surpass-

ing ordinary capacities, and indifferent to the here and now of realization. It is, on the contrary, to lead into ordinary life, and to challenge capacities which are unique and irreplaceable. Said the Baal Shem: "Every man should know that since creation no other man ever was like him. Had there been such another, there would be no need for him to be. Each is called on to perfect his unique qualities. And it is his failure to heed this call which delays the Messiah."[16]

Finally, Hasidism contains elements of pantheistic metaphysics. But metaphysics is only a by-product of its central endeavor, which is not to explain mystery but to live with it. And what metaphysics it has is not pantheism of the Eastern kind, which dissolves the here and now in Infinity; nor of the Spinozistic kind, which makes it an accident of Nature; nor of the Bergsonian kind, which sweeps it along in a cosmic Onward Push. Hasidism asserts divine sparks in nature in order to teach that there is no here and now in which God cannot be met. It asserts such sparks in man in order to teach that man must do the meeting; that the divine sparks in nature are not actualities overwhelming man into passive surrender but potentialities to be redeemed by human action. But such action—whether it be overt action or the inward act of prayer—is commandment performed in the here and now. The pantheistic elements in Hasidism, then, are so reorganized as to focus on the meeting, in the here and now, between man and God. And this raises doubt as to whether they remain pantheistic in any sense at all.

Considered as a whole, then, Hasidism may be viewed as a passionate attempt to reopen, in the here and now, communication between Israel and the God of Israel. When viewed in this light, it confronts the liberal Jew of today with a direct challenge. For while much in Hasidism may be time-bound, alien to us and even odd in itself,[17] its essential aim makes as strong a claim today as it did when Judaism was born. This aim is the search for the God of the here and now—the God of Israel.

IX

But can the Jew of today accept the validity of this search? What of the view of radical rationalist reformers, stated earlier, that the God of Israel is a mere myth of the past? It is now time to show that this view follows not from science but from scientism; not from a critical rationalism which knows what it is doing, but from a rationalism expanded into uncritical dogma. To show this, one requires neither originality nor insights peculiar to believers and theologians. One need but borrow from a philosophical tradition of nearly two centuries' duration, begun by that great rationalist, Immanuel Kant. Kant, it is true, was not essentially concerned with the God of the here and now. But he *was* essentially concerned with the here and now of the human person.[18] And from this concern of his has sprung the greatest tradition in modern philosophy.

As the rational search for uniformity conquered the modern West one implication became quickly obvious. The terms of this search leave no room for human freedom and personal uniqueness. For if explanation is in terms of laws it is without reference to human freedom; and if it seeks uniformity it must aim at explaining personal uniqueness away. For this reason, some thinkers have denied the reality of both freedom and personal uniqueness; and lesser thinkers—notably social scientists—do so even today.

But Kant saw the dogmatism inherent in this denial. He admitted that rational inquiry must *treat* man as an instance of law and uniformity, as much as any natural object. But he denied that this proves that man *is* an object among objects. What if all explanation of man as an object presupposes prior abstraction from man as a subject? What if human freedom and personal uniqueness, instead of being non-existent, merely escape the reach of rational inquiry? A critical rationalism, Kant perceived, must admit this as at least a theoretical possibility.

Kant further perceived that this theoretical possibility is a moral and practical necessity. For while *qua* observer man may view himself as a mere instance of law, *qua* responsible agent he must act as if he were free and unique. Nor can this belief be a mere illusion. If it were, all responsibility would lie in shambles. According to Kant, our freedom and uniqueness is as certain as any scientific knowledge.

It is, however, a certainty of a different kind. Explanation is of objects, in terms of laws. The certainty now referred to is of at least one subject—oneself; and it is not in terms of laws but rather in its unique here and now. And while certainty of the former kind is by a detached observer, who views the world *sub specie aeternitatis,* certainty of the free and unique self is found only *by* the free and unique self, and only *in* the moment of action and involvement. This is Kant's great philosophical discovery, destined to make history.[19]

Kant's discovery gave rise to the problem of interpersonal certainty. If one follows Kant, one cannot assert one's own freedom and uniqueness and yet deny the freedom and uniqueness of others. But can we know others *qua* free and unique persons? Are they accessible to our experience? This has been a grave problem for modern philosophy, from Kant down to Buber's *I and Thou.*

The problem is grave because one cannot reject I-Thou experience, while to admit it is to run the risk of scientific obscurantism. One runs this risk because I-Thou experience forsakes objective detachment for inter-active participation; and because both the self and the other appear in it, not as objects manifesting uniformity, but as subjects shattering it like a miracle. And yet, whatever the limits and dangers of I-Thou experience, it cannot be rejected as in principle vain and illusory. For human action does not take place in solipsistic isolation. It is inter-action with others. Action, therefore, cannot disclose our own freedom and uniqueness without also disclosing that of others; and if the latter disclosure is in principle impossible so is the former. There is a direct line from Kant to Buber's *I and Thou.*[20]

This is not the place for coping with this problem. It is the place, however, for raising the religious question to which it in turn gives rise. If it is necessary to admit inter-human involvement as an authentic form of experience side by side with objective cognition, is it possible to admit human-divine involvement as an experience no less authentic? And if it is necessary to admit the free human other, as a quasi-miraculous break-through of the fixed world of objects governed by laws, is it possible to admit a miracle of miracles—a break-through of a free Divine Other into that world?[21]

In the terms of Kantian and post-Kantian philosophy, the implications of the denial of this possibility achieve unprecedented clarity.[22] Such a denial implies that God must remain an object for us while even another human being can become a subject; that religion must remain confined by the conditions of a spectator-relation whereas even inter-human relations can become forms of participation. But can God be God and yet a mere object? And can religion be religion and yet a mere spectator-relation? Religion is life with mystery. But the denial of the possibility of a divine break through law and uniformity would reduce religion to a mere theory seeking to explain mystery.

But while such a denial follows from a dogmatic rationalism, it does not follow from a critical rationalism of the Kantian kind. For while the former asserts that the world is a fixed system of laws and uniformities, the latter confines itself to the assertion that it must be treated as such a system by the observer who seeks to explain it. And it further recognizes that both the system and the observing attitude are superseded in moments of human interaction. Such a rationalism does not rule out the possibility of a divine break-through into the fixed world of laws and uniformities—provided it is asserted to take place, not by and for the metaphysical observer who seeks to explain mystery, but by and for the religious participant who lives with it.

But while critical rationalism suffices to validate the possibility of inter-human I-Thou experience, it does not suffice to validate the possibility of such experience between the human and the divine. For while the possibility of the former is implied in all responsible action, this is not true of the latter, which presupposes an additional dimension: the faith that man can seek out God in the here and now, and that God can be found in it. At its culminating point, therefore, critical rationalism raises the momentous question whether the world is open to the incursion of God, or a fixed system of laws and uniformities closed to it. But this question it can only raise, not answer.

For this reason, the liberal Jew who faces the Hasidic challenge must at this point turn from a problem of modern thought to a problem of modern life. Philosophical analysis shows that a religious effort to reopen communication with God is no offense to modern critical reason. The question still remains—and it is the vastly more complex and more difficult one—whether such an effort is a concrete possibility of modern life, as well as compatible with the requirements of modern thought.

X

If we wish to face up to this question in all its gravity we must begin with a realistic acceptance of the gulf which separates the modern world from that of the Hasidim. Modern industrial society differs from the society of the *Shtetl;* and, unlike the nature the Hasidim knew, modern nature is subject to unheard-of technological control. In their world, the Hasidim could seek to arouse divine sparks in nature and society, with an enthusiastic directness storming the Heavens. But if there are divine sparks capable of being aroused in modern nature and society, they are more elusive and ambiguous than ever before.

Even more elusive and ambiguous are divine sparks in the inner world of modern man. Living in a world of pre-reflexive immediacy, the Hasidim were capable of direct trust in the self-authenticating power of religious intensity. Modern man, in contrast, if capable of such trust at all, is no longer capable of direct and simple trust. For the inner world of today is dominated by a spirit of reflection and self-consciousness. Moments of religious immediacy are inevitably followed by moments of reflection, in which what immediacy may have taken for the presence of God is suspected of being the self's own production—the projection of wish or fear. Whatever the Hasidic claim on us, therefore, we cannot share the Hasidic style of storming the Heavens. Social conditions without, and a spirit of self-consciousness and reflection within, have ruled this out. And imitation, on our part, of that style would not only be a flight from our own here and now. It might also be a lapse into idolatry. For to know that projections of hope and fear may masquerade as the voice of God, and yet to seek escape from this knowledge in pre-reflexive immediacy, is to run the risk of worshipping false gods.

Aware of this danger, the liberal Jew may seek to avoid it by abandoning, along with Hasidic-style storming of Heavens, the whole search for God in the here and now. For it is all-too-true that if God is made to dwell in safe and infinite distance—as First Cause or Cosmic Process—then there can be no mistaking of a merely human here and now for His presence. And yet, this escape from one form of idolatry is bound to lead to another. For even though God be remote, the human here and now continues to make its religious demands; and, if cut off from God, these turn it into a pseudo-god. Man comes to worship feeling instead of God; the symbol, not what it stands for; Jewish genius, not Him whose presence stimulates it. There is, to be sure, an idolatrous emotionalism which, born of impatient need, mistakes projected desire for God. But there is also an idolatry of pseudo-sophistication which, denying man's actual need of the present God, treats the human as if it were divine. Between these two abysses the liberal Jew of today must walk, in sophisticated simplicity, on a narrow ridge.

Can he walk on this ridge? And can the ridge in due course expand itself, if not into a royal road, at least into a safe pathway? This question will find its answer, not in grand prognostications but only in simple moments of actual walking. Those who walk on the ridge, open to the future, will find strength in the Hasidic example. But they will not attempt to imitate it. For they will walk as the Hasidism walked—not in a world of others but in their own.

Imitation would not only be the wrong way of seeking strength in Hasidism. It would also be a misunderstanding of Hasidism itself. A great Zaddik was asked why he did not follow the example of his teacher in his own way of life. The Zaddik replied: "On the contrary, I do follow his example. For just as he left his teacher, so I leave mine."[23]

12

Religious Responsibility for the Social Order: *A Jewish View*

The following article was part of a Protestant-Catholic-Jewish dialogue, held at the annual board meeting of the National Conference of Christians and Jews in Washington, D. C., on November 20, 1961. The other participants were Prof. J. Pelikan and Father G. Weigel, S.J. I have found the topic not only most important but also—if seriously tackled, and tackled in a brief statement—difficult and full of snares. Among the snares which I sought to avoid and expose are: (a) the mistaking of the separation of church and state for a dualism which makes religion otherworldly, and society, either amoral or else morally concerned in a way which does not only not need religious inspiration but positively rejects it; (b) the belief (found in the various forms of "Biblicism," on the one hand, natural law positions, on the other) that it is the business of religion to offer moral doctrines which are specific and concrete, and yet timelessly valid; (c) the opposite belief that, precisely because religion cannot offer such doctrines, it must confine itself to innocuous generalities, thus leaving the big decisions concerning war and peace, the implementation of social justice etc., entirely in the hands of religiously and morally neutral "experts."

Reprinted by permission of the National Conference of Christians and Jews from *Religious Responsibility for the Social Order: A Symposium by Three Theologians* (New York, n.d.), pp. 12-17.

I

If there is a single religious affirmation which, first coming with Judaism into the world, has remained basic to Jewish belief until today, it is that the God on high loves widows and orphans below; and that He commands men, from on high, to do His will in the social order below. Elsewhere, too, men have had an awareness of the Divine, and a sense of responsibility in the social realm. It was the distinctive contribution of the Hebrew prophets to proclaim that the two cannot be rent apart; that men ought to treat each other as created in the image of a God who challenges them to this task.

II

It is in the light of this basic affirmation that I must seek to answer the question concerning religious responsibility for the social order. And I must begin by opposing all attempts to tear asunder what the prophetic affirmation joins together; that is, on the one hand, a secularism which bids religion mind its business, of which responsibility for the social order is to be no part, and, on the other hand, an otherworldly religion which, accepting this advice, disclaims all responsibility for the social order. Forms of such divorce have existed in all ages. That they may exist in one and the same person has been terribly illustrated in our own time—by those Germans who thought it possible to be Nazis and Christians at once.

I must stress that opposing divorce between the religious and the social realm is by no means equivalent to rejecting the separation between church and state, of which more below. I must stress, too, that secularist social morality has often put to shame

a social morality supposedly religiously inspired; that those rejecting or suspending belief in God have often done His will
toward men more perfectly than those professing belief in Him.
And this fact must give us pause. Even so, one may question
whether secularist morality can, for long, treat men as created in
the image of a God in Whom it does not believe; whether it
can forever resist the temptation to reduce man, from an end
in himself, to a mere means, thus degenerating either into a
merely relativistic morality, or else—and worse—into one resting
on pseudo-absolutes, such as the interests of a deified class, nation or state.

The dangers of divorce between the religious and the social
may seem remote to North Americans, who tend to be practical
in religion and religiously-inspired in their social morality; and
indeed, for the worst examples of divorce we must surely look
elsewhere. Still, we are by no means exempt from danger. For a
religious civilization such as ours invites a secularism assuming a
pseudo-religious garb; and hence religion, meant to be openness
to the divine imperative, may become a device for avoiding it.
Thus, for example, those who begin by responding to the divine
imperative with a dedication to freedom and democracy, may
end up deifying their dedication; and to the extent to which they
in fact do so their actual dedication—as well as what it is dedicated
to—is perverted. Of this danger, there are ominous indications in
our time.

III

So much for the divorce between the religious and the social,
which the prophetic imperative bids us oppose. What of their
relation, which that imperative bids us affirm? This question, unlike the former, is fraught with great difficulty. And its essential
cause is that, while the prophetic imperative is divine the social

world in which it is to find realization is human; and the human world has characteristics which render complex, not only any attempt to *realize* the prophetic imperative, but even any attempt—such as the present—merely to *state* it, in terms concrete enough to be applicable. Three characteristics must here be noted.

(1) All social organization involves power. But power is amoral before it can be made moral, and presumably it always retains aspects of amorality or even immorality. This fact confronts those who would heed the prophetic imperative with a dilemma. They may either forswear all use of power, in order to remain true to the prophetic imperative. But then they condemn their own efforts to ineffectiveness, at least beyond the most private relations and in the social order as a whole; and thus they contribute either to total anarchy or else—more likely—to an amoral order based on naked power. Yet most forms of social order are better than anarchy, and a partly moralized order, better than one not moralized at all. Alternatively, they may seek power, for the sake of the prophetic imperative which demands realization. But then they must recognize that they become compromised in its use; and their religious motivation is no protection against such compromise. Indeed, experience shows that power wielded in the name of God is subject to special perversions.

This is why those who are organized by commitment to the prophetic imperative cannot, on the one hand, escape their responsibility of moralizing power, while on the other hand they must resist all temptations to make a bid for direct power, confining themselves to indirect methods of pressure-by-exhortation. Here lies perhaps the deepest justification for the American principle of the separation of state and church.

(2) What must be the content of such exhortation? May religion advocate specific measures in the name of God, leaving to the state and society the task of their enactment? Here I come upon a second complexity of the human condition, which makes such a neat arrangement impossible. This is that concrete moral

ends are, in the actual human situation, in conflict both with other ends and with the means required to enact them. I cannot think of a single moral and religious end, concrete enough to be directly applicable, and yet valid without exception. Thus believing all human life to be sacred I believe all wars to be evil; and yet I must admit that some wars had justly to be fought. But the concept of "just war" does not supply me with universally applicable criteria. Again, though believing in the Biblical injunction to be fruitful and multiply I cannot deduce from this belief the universal wrongness of artificial birth control. For I must measure the Biblical injunction against the dangers of overpopulation and mass-starvation. In short, I find myself unable to subscribe to what has been called the natural law, supplying us with a knowledge of right and wrong sufficiently concrete to be directly applicable, and yet valid regardless of time and circumstances.

(3) Must religion, then, confine itself to the affirmation of abstract principles, leaving to other forces not merely the task of enactment but also that of specific application? Is religion confined to affirming in general the sacredness of life and liberty, and the evil of exploitation, but barred from taking a specific stand as to when life may be taken and liberty curtailed; and as to what constitutes a just minimum wage? Here we come upon this further characteristic of the human condition, that the moral and religious conscience of a society is manifest, not in an abstract affirmation of liberty or condemnation of exploitation, but in what it protests against, as constituting a case of curtailed liberty, or a case of exploitation. Relevancy lies in the particular. As for the general, this is apt to be invoked not only by the indifferent but even by the enemy; peace has been invoked by the mongers of war, freedom and democracy, by their worst foes. This tendency to hypocrisy is evident throughout human history. But, as George Orwell has shown with such depressing persuasiveness, not until the Twentieth Century have men made it into a system.

Another neat arrangement of the respective responsibilities of religion and society for the social order has thus collapsed. A religion which confines itself to general principles condemns itself to ineffectiveness and innocuousness. The Hebrew prophets, in contrast, were neither innocuous nor ineffective. And this was because they asserted the will of God, not in terms of abstract general principles, but in and for the here and now.

IV

In the light of these reflections, how, then, can I link, positively and concretely, prophetic religion to its responsibilities for the social order? The link is found, I think, not in rules or principles but in a believing attitude.

This believing attitude must, first, stubbornly insist that the will of God is to be done in the social world of man, and that we are responsible for our share in it. It must resist the temptation, born of the frustrations of all ages and especially of our own, of escaping into dualism, whether into a divine world above, unconcerned with man, or into a human world below, unconcerned with God and hence not really human.

This believing attitude must, secondly, face up to the will of God, not in general, or for some other place and time, but here and now. There is no situation which is morally and religiously neutral. There is no power-struggle, however necessarily Macchiavellian, which is not at the same time a situation in which the prophetic imperative speaks to us. And even the thunder of nuclear tests must not be allowed to drown its voice.

Thirdly, the prophetic imperative, being divine, must be taken with radical seriousness, not given mere half-hearted and niggardly concessions. It is one thing to be forced to compromise in the struggle against war, oppression, discrimination and poverty, and to accept such compromises temporarily and with an aching heart. It is another thing entirely to mistake what are at best incomplete achievements finally and self-righteously, as if they were perfect. This believing attitude can never forget that so long as the divine image is violated even in one single human being, the Kingdom of God on earth is incomplete.

Fourthly, this believing attitude knows that while the prophetic imperative is divine even our best efforts to respond to it are only human. And this is true not only of our organized forms of acting but also of our organized forms of belief, doctrine and preaching. Society and religion, even at their best, are under the judgment of God.

Finally and most importantly, this believing attitude knows that while we have our responsible share in the doing of God's will in the social world of man, the fate of that world is not in our hands alone. Throughout the ages, those committed to the prophetic imperative have always been threatened by despair, when faced with the discrepancy between what ought to be and what is. This danger assumes unheard-of proportions in a world confronted with possibilities of total destruction. Today, more than ever, one can heed the prophetic imperative with any kind of confidence only if one heeds it with an ultimate confidence; with the confidence in a God who, while bidding us to work in His world, is also its absolute Sovereign.

13

Human Freedom and Divine Power

Philosophical Reflections on a Religious Issue

The problem of human freedom and divine power may seem to be a mere version of the problem of freedom and determinism (and an outmoded one at that): Is man free to choose? But how can he, a mere part of nature, be exempt from the laws generally believed to govern nature? Is his behavior, then, determined by such laws? If so, how can moral responsibility—which presupposes the freedom of choice—have substance and reality? It may appear that, so far as the reality or unreality of human freedom is concerned, it makes no difference whether the issue is raised by a determination of things due to God or due to natural laws. Moreover, it is widely taken for granted that the modern scientific belief in natural law has replaced the ancient belief in a Deity shaping and ordering all things.

But it goes without saying that religious believers, at any rate, do not regard this latter belief as outmoded. Further, reflection shows that "human freedom and divine power" is not a problem reducible to "freedom and determinism." If it is still a vital problem at all it raises questions which are quite unique.

Conceivably the natural laws of science may not hold universal

Reprinted from *Judaism* (Summer 1963), pp. 338-43.

sway, and not touch human freedom. After all, man is a partly spiritual being, while nature, as far as known to us, is not. Then why should he not, though evolving from nature, be able to rise freely above it? But if there is God man can surely not rise above *Him.* And if there is divine power it surely cannot fail to hold universal sway, and to touch human freedom. This is insisted upon by the religious believer himself, who views himself as owing to God his very being, which cannot but include his capacity for free choice. And yet he also believes that human freedom is a human responsibility as well as a manifestation of divine power. For he knows himself to be responsible before the bar of divine judgment.

Philosophers have not failed to suggest solutions to this problem. But here, as everywhere in philosophy, we shall have to watch with care whether the solutions suggested solve the problem or merely dissolve it. Everyone knows of the mythical surgeon who operated successfully but killed the patient. Philosophers sometimes behave like this surgeon. Faced with a problem about reality, they solve the problem but deny reality. Fortunately this proves not the absurdity of philosophy but merely the absurdity of such philosophical behavior.

Bearing this danger in mind, let us consider two opposite attempts to solve our problem. The first adds up to an outright denial of human freedom, at least insofar as it is freedom over against God. Perhaps man is free over against nature and other men. Over against God he has no freedom. His very being is a manifestation of divine power; and this includes not only the capacity for choice but also whatever use is made of it. Hence there is only an apparent human choosing *over against* God, which in truth is itself a manifestation of divine power. And this is the fundamental truth by which the wise man should live.

BUT can a man live by this wisdom? Certainly not in Judaism and Christianity, which insist on human responsibility even in the sight of God. According to these religions, sin is not a manifestation of God in man; it is a human revolt *against* Him. And from responsibility for this revolt there can be no refuge, even in divine power. In an ancient Jewish legend, Cain, the first murderer, maintains that almighty God has made him a murderer. But God replies that whereas He has created Cain free to choose, and hence free to choose murder, it is Cain, not God, who has in fact chosen it.

But conceivably this Jewish and Christian belief is a false belief, as is in fact implied in some other religious traditions. Thus, some ancients believed that a divine Fate controls all things, human actions included; and that hence whatever a man may seem freely to choose is in fact ordained. Nor is this condition a cause for despondency or despair. Divine Fate which ordains all things ordains them well. And to recognize its working is not only to submit to it but to do so in serenity and love.

But can the fatalistic believer *himself* live by his fatalistic wisdom? Fate may control human action. It cannot control all human thought, feeling and belief. Man may depend on it whether or not he acknowledges his dependence. The acknowledgment itself, at least, must be a free human act. For the whole point of this wisdom is to convert men from ignorance to knowledge, from futile rebellion to serene acceptance. But if Fate controlled man's inner attitude as well as his external actions, then this conversion would be wholly impossible, and fatalistic wisdom quite useless.

This condition ruins every attempt to solve the problem of human freedom and divine power by means of a denial of human freedom. And we therefore turn to the opposite attempt to solve it, which consists of denying the traditional belief in divine omnipotence. There may be divine wisdom, goodness and love. But if power is among the attributes of the Deity at all, it can at most be finite or limited power. For there must be room, so to speak, for human freedom. Such freedom is morally necessary if man is to be responsible. And it is religiously necessary if God is to be a

God Who holds man responsible. The scope of human freedom vis-à-vis divine power may be subject to debate. What is beyond debate is that wherever human freedom holds sway, divine power does not. An ancient Jewish sage asserts that all is in the hands of heaven except the fear of heaven. This sage seems to leave little scope for human freedom. But he also seems to hold that what little scope it has is beyond the power of God.

But if pressed the Jewish sage would insist that limitation of divine power, rather than the literal truth, is only a human manner of speaking and understanding. And a Christian, while accepting divine limitation in the incarnated God, would understand this limitation as divine *self*-limitation, and hence the God so limited as at the same time transcending all limitation. In short, it is not possible to accept, as the literal truth, the limitation of divine power and yet to remain committed to the unfragmented substance of either the Jewish or the Christian faith.

Could one, then, accept this doctrine and remain committed to any vital religion? This too is in the end impossible. Consider these implications. If divine power must be limited, in order to leave room for human freedom, then it must be excluded from the whole domain of human freedom. But this includes all of history and all of man's spiritual life, with its victories and defeats, its joys and suffering, its acts of righteousness and its lapses into sin. Divine power, if a reality at all, would have to lie outside this whole domain, confined to a realm in which there is no human freedom or power; confined, that is, to nature. And even here divine power would recede as there is an advance in the human power to control nature, master disease and postpone death. In the end divine power would reside permanently only in places at which nature sets absolute limits to all human freedom and power, such as in death. But such places constitute not the center and totality of human life but merely its periphery.

The religious man, however, requires God at the center of life as well as at its periphery. And with divine power reduced to the margins, he could find at this center at best only divine wisdom, goodness and love. But what are these without divine power? Only ideals which can inspire man in his strength, goodness and joy; not a reality which can act to support, redirect and redeem him in his weakness, sin and misery. But a mere ideal is not God at all; and a religion left with a mere ideal is not religion but a form of humanism.

It has thus turned out that the first philosophical solution to our problem is altogether untenable, while the second succeeds only at the price of reducing all vital religion to humanism. Does this mean that here philosophy has operated successfully but killed the patient? We have already mentioned that this occasionally happens in philosophy. Thus there are solutions to the problems of time and the external world which deny the reality of time and the external world. Such solutions are manifestly absurd. Is it not equally absurd to solve the religious problem of human freedom and divine omnipotence by denying the reality of either the one or the other, when it seems that every vital religion requires both?

BUT are these cases parallel? That time and the external world are real we know. That human freedom co-exists with divine omnipotence we can at best only believe. And belief, however venerable and sincere, may nevertheless be mistaken. Must one then not say that, in the case under consideration, objective impartial reason, far from misled into absurdity, has exposed a belief which is contradictory and hence untenable? Indeed, this is presumably just what a humanist might say in support of his humanism.

But the case is very far from being so simple. It is true that religious faith lacks objective, rational proof. But it does not follow that objective rationality is the standard by which all things must be judged, religious faith included. The two above theories may prove that human freedom and divine omnipotence cannot

co-exist. But they do so only on an assumption which the knowl-
edgeable religious believer would deny. This assumption concerns
objective reason itself—its capacity to pass judgment on all things.
For *both* the above arguments assume that, whatever the truth
concerning the relationship between man and God—whether there
is such a relation, and if so what it is—it is possible for man to
step outside that relation, to become an impartial bystander, and
thus to discover the truth.

Now it is precisely this assumption which, say, a Hebrew
prophet would deny. He would at once be overwhelmed by the
reality of divine power, and yet be challenged to respond to it in
his human freedom. He would know these two aspects of his relation to God by participating in it, and he would insist that it can
only be understood in the act of participation, to the extent to
which it can be humanly understood at all. He would deny, therefore, that a man can detach himself from participation, become an
impartial, outside observer, and yet understand the human-divine
relation. Hence, he would be far from surprised to learn that attempts to understand that relation should end in failure. For to
him such failure would prove not that the belief in the co-existence
of human freedom and divine power is false, but rather that it
transcends the grasp of impartial reason. In short, he would regard
man, potentially, as an outside spectator of all things—except his
own human relation with God. For man either participates in that
relation, responding to the presence of divine power in his human
freedom, or else he does not know it at all.

With this conclusion, we may seem to have reached a total dead-
lock, so far as our problem is concerned. Philosophy, after all, is
an attempt at objective rational understanding. Yet we now seem
to have reached a radical dilemma. The philosopher must either
accept objective reason as his ultimate standard, by which religious faith as well as all else is to be judged. He will then reject
the religious belief in the co-existence of human freedom and
divine omnipotence as a false belief, but on the grounds of a

belief in the omnipotence of reason. Alternatively, he will respect the religious belief, as the believer himself lives it. But then, he can contribute nothing to its understanding. For reason is detachment. How then can it enter into the life of participation without losing its identity? Vis-à-vis religious faith, then, philosophical reason may seem to have the choice only between two ways of betraying its own proper task—a dogmatic assertion of omnipotence and a skeptical admission of total impotence.

The philosopher, however, can avoid this fatal dilemma. For, first, religious discourse, rather than being impenetrable to all logic, has a logic of its own. Secondly, the philosopher, rather than compelled to remain an external observer, can sympathetically enter into this logic and take long steps toward understanding it. Too often the philosopher is pictured as a man in possession of some absolute and self-sufficient wisdom, proudly sitting in judgment upon life. At his best, he often appears in a quite different role. Recognizing that truth and wisdom already exist in *life,* he seeks to illuminate them in the light of *thought.* Nowhere is this role more appropriate than in the sphere of religious belief.

How could a philosopher who assumes this role illuminate the issue under discussion? We shall confine ourselves to the single but crucial example of prayer. Within traditions such as Judaism and Christianity, every genuine prayer affirms divine omnipotence. And every such prayer affirms human freedom. Deny either element, and the prayer becomes religiously absurd. This is illustrated by two prayers of opposite emphasis:

"Teach me, O Lord, how to pray." External criticism can make no sense of this prayer. For either man is free to direct his heart to God, in which case he may need to pray for health, success and wisdom but not, at any rate, for the ability to pray. Or else he is even without this latter ability until God Himself gives it, in which case he cannot pray at all until God has in fact given it. And then *this* prayer is no longer necessary.

But the philosopher who enters into the logic of religious discourse recognizes that it is these criticisms of the prayer which are absurd, not the prayer itself. Is the worshipper to pray in the presumptuousness that he stands in no need of God for genuine prayer? Or, if recoiling from this, to refrain from all prayer, on the grounds of human incapacity? Both alternatives would destroy all prayer. Recognizing this, the philosopher can recognize also what gives rise to this prayer. He sees the worshipper confronted with a God Who is infinite Power, leaving room for no sphere of human freedom into which it cannot enter. And he sees the worshipper turning—or attempting to turn—to this God, in order that His Power may in fact enter. There is a tension between this all-encompassing divine power and this human turning. But in moments of grace the tension is overcome.

Consider next a prayer with an opposite emphasis: "All glory and power are Thine, O Lord." Once again external criticism is baffled. If all glory and power are God's, how can they be augmented by human prayers of glorification? And if they *can* be so augmented, how can they be complete without such prayers? But once again the philosopher who understands religious discourse can perceive the religious absurdity of such criticisms. What could one make of a prayer, inspired by these, such as *"Almost all glory is Thine"*? Or, alternatively, of the refusal to glorify God, on the grounds that His glory is already complete without prayer? Religiously, both alternatives would be absurd. And the philosopher can recognize what makes them absurd. For he sees the worshipper confronted with a Glory so complete as to be incapable of all human augmenting, and yet waiting, as it were, for spontaneous human recognition. There is a tension between this completeness and this waiting. But in moments in which the recognition becomes in fact spontaneous the tension is overcome. For human glorification becomes then, itself, a gift of divine glory.

The philosopher, then, rather than remaining an external critic, can enter into the logic of religious discourse. But in so doing, must he betray his philosophical duty to impartial objectivity? By no means. He remains true to this duty if he enters into religious discourse of the most varied and even conflicting types; and, if while trying to understand some of its *meaning*, he remains, *qua* philosopher, neutral as to its *truth*. One must add, of course, that the philosopher is a man as well as a philosopher. If it is true that no man can remain neutral on questions of religious truth, then philosophers can do so no more than other men.

14

The Revealed Morality of Judaism and Modern Thought

A Confrontation with Kant

Preface: On Jewish Philosophy Today

This preface is in the nature of an afterthought, written after the essay itself. Its purpose is to state the method which the essay itself uses, and to clarify the reasons for the use of this method, a clarification which will show that this essay means to fall into the discipline of modern Jewish philosophy.

First, while the essay is throughout concerned with the revealed morality of Judaism, it nowhere categorically affirms the reality of revelation. This is not because I am not prepared to make such an affirmation but rather because, in my view, to do so would transcend the scope of philosophy, Jewish philosophy included. For I hold the affirmation of revelation to presuppose a commitment, which in turn permeates the religious thinking which springs from it. Philosophical thinking, however, both presupposes, and stays with, objective detachment, which is why both a religious commitment and the religious thinking flowing from it

Reprinted by permission of the publisher from *Rediscovering Judaism*, ed. Arnold Wolf (Chicago: Quadrangle Press, 1965), pp. 51-76. A shorter version of this article, entitled "Kant and Judaism," was published in *Commentary* (December 1963), pp. 460-67.

are, as such, extraphilosophical. I hasten to add that they are not for that reason antiphilosophical.

This is enough to indicate that the very concept of a Jewish philosophy is gravely problematical. How can thinking be at once truly philosophical and yet essentially Jewish? To say that it must be *essentially* Jewish is to dismiss, as deserving no further thought, that a philosophy might become Jewish by virtue of the accidental Jewish origin of its author. How then can it at once have the objectivity and universality which is required of it as philosophy, and yet be essentially committed to a content which has Jewish particularity? To judge by many contemporary samples of Jewish philosophizing, it must sacrifice either one or the other. If it is a rational endorsement of "values" found in Jewish history and literature, the very endorsement—which, being rational, is universal—makes these values essentially human, because universally valid, thus reducing their Jewishness to a historical accident. But if it remains bound to specifically Jewish goals, such as the survival of Jewish life, this limitation deprives it of the radical detachment and the radical universality required of philosophy. This is not to say, incidentally, that either of these pursuits is useless or illegitimate.

Can there be a Jewish philosophy, then, which is at once genuinely philosophical and yet essentially Jewish? This was possible at least under the special intellectual conditions which prevailed in the Jewish Middle Ages. Jewish philosophy then was the *confrontation between philosophy and Judaism*. This confrontation presupposed that philosophy and Judaism were different from each other and irreducible to each other; that it was necessary to confront them; and that it was possible to confront them in a manner which would compromise neither.

In the Middle Ages, all these conditions were accepted by those who engaged in Jewish philosophy. They accepted, first, the existence of two independent sources of truth, of which one was human reason, and the other a divine revelation embodied in the sacred Jewish Scriptures. On the basis of this fundamental assumption, they accepted these additional ones: that reason and revelation cover at least in part the same ground; that there is at least some apparent conflict between them; and that the conflict is apparent only—that it can be resolved without violence to either reason or Judaism. Without the first and third of these additional assumptions, there would have been no possibility of a Jewish philosophy, and without the second, no necessity for it.

It is noteworthy that, although there was a continuous tradition of Jewish philosophy in the Middle Ages, Jewish philosophy has appeared only sporadically in the modern age, and then unsure of its status. This is no accident. First, it has not been easy—to put it mildly—for modern philosophers to accept revelation as a source of truth, over and above reason itself. Reason, in the modern world, is apt to take itself as autonomous and all-encompassing. It is evident that, on such an assumption, philosophy cannot *confront* Judaism. If taking note of Judaism at all, it can only *absorb* it. Judaism then turns out to be, essentially, a "religion of reason," which is Jewish only by accident.

But even when philosophic reason does not make such radical claims a modern philosophic confrontation with Judaism is beset with difficulties unknown in the Middle Ages. At that time, it was assumed that there was at least one common basis for argument, in principle acceptable to both philosophers and religious believers. Revelation at Sinai—or revelation anywhere else—if actual, was an objective historical fact exactly like any other historical fact. If its acceptance as fact depended on the acceptance of authorities, this was true of *any* historical fact. Judah Halevi could argue, *both* as a philosopher and a believing Jew, that the testimony of the six hundred thousand present at Mt. Sinai could not have been mistaken.

But this view concerning revelation and authority is no longer acceptable either to modern philosophers or to thoughtful modern believers. Modern analysis has disclosed that it is not authority which is the source of faith but rather faith which is the source of acceptance—if any—of authority. An agnostic, had he been present at Mount Sinai, would have heard only the thunder and no voice of God. Revelation, as an objective event of communication, is hearable only to those already listening; and the listening is a listening in faith. This is a view accepted alike by modern philosophers and the best of modern religious thinkers. At any rate, it is my view.

It is on this view that the question arises whether, under modern circumstances, there can be a Jewish philosophy at all. For if that view is correct, then religious thinking—at least Jewish religious thinking vis-à-vis revelation—is from beginning to end *committed* thinking, which stands in dialogical relation to the God of Israel. But, as has been said, philosophical thinking must be from beginning to end *detached* thinking. It may thus seem that there is now no basis for meeting, as there was under medieval assumptions, since revelation is accessible, if at all, only to a commitment which is *ipso facto* non-philosophical. At best there could be only an attempt to show the compatibility of modern reason with a modern acceptance of revelation; and even such an attempt, unlike its medieval precursors, would be more concerned with keeping the two apart than with binding them together.

It is in this precarious situation that the following essay seeks, nevertheless, to contribute to a revival of Jewish philosophy. Although insisting both on the detachment of philosophic thought and on commitment as the condition of the accessibility of revelation, I nevertheless assume that revelation is not *wholly* inaccessible to philosophic reason. Under what conditions can this be possible?

As has already been said, this requires, in the first place, that the philosopher, *qua* philosopher, should suspend judgment as to the actuality of revelation. The essay which follows confronts the revealed morality of Judaism with certain modern philosophical standards of morality. It does not commit itself to the actuality of a revealed morality.

But how, without such a commitment, can there be a philosophical understanding of the *nature* of a revealed morality? The essay undertakes such an understanding through what may be called a *sympathetic phenomenological re-enactment*. This remains bound to the limits of philosophical detachment, while at the same time seeking a sympathetic understanding of truths accepted only on the basis of a commitment. Such an understanding will obviously have certain limits. One cannot, for example, remain a detached philosopher and yet ask—let alone find an answer to—the authentic Jewish question, "What does the God of Israel demand of *me?*" At the same time, it would seem that to deny in principle the possibility that detached thinking might understand some of the meaning of committed faith is impossible, for it is to be led to absurd consequences, such as that unless one shares the faith of a religious literature it must be wholly unintelligible; or that a leap from detachment to commitment, if and when it occurs, must be wholly blind. It would also be to imply that a Jewish philosophy is impossible in the present age.

The argument for the possibility of such a philosophy, as presented in this preface, is obviously fragmentary. It is hoped that the reader may find less fragmentary the example of Jewish philosophizing given in the following pages.

I

Can a law be at once moral and the will of God? Can one accept it as at the same time a moral duty and divinely revealed? Or is, perhaps, a revealed morality, radically considered, nothing less than a contradiction in terms?

At one time, such questions would have seemed preposterous to uncritical religious believers, and even critically minded philosophers would have seen no need to ask them. Today, they have become part of the fabric even of popular religious thought. This is due, more than to anything else, to the influence of one single philosopher. Present-day academic moral philosophy may not pay much attention to Kant; most popular moral or religious tracts may not so much as mention his name. But on the topic of revealed morality, moral and religious thought at both levels is still much influenced—consciously or unconsciously—by Kant's moral philosophy.

A Jewish philosopher concerned with that topic does not therefore engage in a mere antiquarian academic exercise if he seeks a confrontation of Kant and Judaism; that is if, investigating this topic, he takes Judaism as his example of a revealed morality, and Kant as his main guide in moral philosophy. This is the undertaking of the present essay which, under double guidance, asks whether the moral characteristics of a religious law or commandment must clash with the way in which it is revealed. We say: "must clash." For that a clash is *possible* must be taken for granted, and one need not be either modern or a philosopher to know it. Rabbinic teachers, for example, knew well enough that human behavior falls short of true morality if it is motivated solely by fear of heavenly punishment or the hope of divine reward.[1]

II

Philosophy has always questioned revelation in general and revealed morality in particular. But no philosopher prior to Kant found it necessary to question all revealed morality as being less than truly moral simply by virtue of being revealed. The question whether all revealed morality might be a contradiction in terms is a question which was not asked.

This may be shown by a brief review of the most radical objection to revealed morality made by pre-Kantian philosophy on grounds of morality alone. Theologians often claim that revelation is the sole source of our knowledge of moral law. Philosophy has almost always been forced to reject this claim. For to be obligated to any law, a man must be able to know that law; and to qualify as moral, a law must be universally obligatory. But, on the admission of theologians themselves, revealed moral law is accessible only to those who possess the revealed Scriptures.

It will be noted that this objection by no means amounts to a rejection of revealed morality. It is merely a threat of rejection, unless a certain demand is met. The demand is for an independent, universally human access to moral law, in addition to revelation. *Fikᵧ ᵧᵃ⌣.*

Can Judaism meet this philosophical demand? One's first resort would be to the general Noachidic revelation which, unlike the revelation at Mount Sinai, is given to all men. But this can satisfy the philosopher only if he can exact a further concession. The Noachidic "revelation"—if one chooses to retain this term—must be accessible without a Scripture: for the Noachides have no Scripture. It must be, that is, a universal human capacity; in short, just what the philosopher has called reason all along.

Traditional Judaism may have misgivings about this concession. If pressed, however, it will nevertheless concede. For it must then, itself, distinguish between *moral* revealed laws which, "had they not been written by God, would have had to be written by men," and *non-moral* revealed laws, "to which Satan and the Gentiles object."[2] But if, except for divine action, men would have *had* to write moral law, they must be *able* to write it. And if the Gentiles—who object to non-moral revealed law—do *not* object to moral revealed law they must, in fact, have written or be able to write at least some of it.

This clarifies sufficiently for the present purpose the relation between Jewish revealed morality and philosophical rational morality, as set forth prior to Kant. However loudly and lengthily the two moralities may quarrel about the *content* of moral law, they have no necessary quarrel concerning its *foundations*. The philosopher has no moral reason for objecting in principle to a morality resting on revelation. And the Jewish theologian has no religious reason for objecting in principle to a morality resting on reason. What is more, this mutual tolerance concerning the foundations of morality produces opportunities for settling conflicts concerning its content as well. This is attested to by a long line of Jewish rationalists who believed that, since the same God was the creator of human reason and the giver of the Sinaitic revelation, the discoveries of reason and the teachings of Judaism could be in no genuine conflict.

III

This peaceful coexistence was upset by a thesis advanced by Immanuel Kant, first prominently stated in his *Fundamental Principles of the Metaphysics of Morals* (1785). Kant himself recognized that his thesis was both crucial and revolutionary; he held that previous moral philosophy did not contain it, and that, because of this failure, it had failed as a whole. Kant also recognized the revolutionary implications of his thesis for revealed morality. Indeed, this is a theme to which he kept returning, as if unable to leave it alone.

In a passage exemplary for our purpose Kant writes:

> [If the will is moral] it is not merely subject to law, but subject in such a way that it must also be regarded as imposing the law on itself, and subject to it for that reason only. . . . All past efforts to identify the principle of morality have failed without exception. For while it was seen that man is bound by his duty to laws, it was not seen that he is subject only to his own, albeit at the same time universal legislation, and obligated to act only according to his own, albeit universally legislating will. So long as one thought of man as merely subject to a law, whatever its content, without this

law originating in his own will, one had to think of him as impelled
to action by something other than himself. The law had to carry
with it some interest which induced or impelled him to action.
But in this way all labour to discover the supreme ground of duty
was lost beyond recovery. For one could thus never arrive at duty,
but merely at the necessity of acting for some interest.[3]

But this, Kant concludes, is at best only an impure morality. An
externally compelling or cajoling law must necessarily be heteronomous or impure so far as moral motivation is concerned. To
be pure, a moral law must be autonomous, or self-imposed.

We must be sure to grasp the essence of the Kantian thesis.
It is by no means the mere assertion—as we have seen, far from
new—that in order to be morally obligatory, a law must have a
universality enabling all men to know it. Kant would have thought
this condition satisfied by those ancient moralists who identified
the moral law with the law of the universe, or by their present-
day heirs who identify it with the laws of mental health. The
essence of the Kantian thesis is that neither of these laws, however universal, can by itself *obligate* a man to obedience; they can
do no more than promise happiness or mental health as the reward
of obedience, and threaten unhappiness or neurosis as the punishment of defiance. This is because both laws confront man only
from without. They are not imposed on man by man himself. A
law which cannot unconditionally obligate may be prudent, wise,
or beneficial. It cannot be moral.

According to Kant, then, there may be much that can induce
us or force us to obey. But no law in heaven or on earth can obligate us to obey unless we *accept ourselves* as obligated to obey.
And unless we can accept ourselves as obligated we cannot *be*
obligated. Once clearly identified, the Kantian thesis seems very
nearly irresistible.

It poses, however, an unprecedented challenge to every revealed morality, regardless of content, and simply by virtue of
its being revealed. *If in order to be moral a law must be self-
imposed, not imposed from without, then how can a law given or*

imposed by God have genuine moral qualities? Pre-Kantian moral philosophy, as was seen, could accept revealed morality conditionally. Kant's moral philosophy threatens it radically. It does so because revelation is either a gift to man from without—the gift of a God *other* than man—or else it is not revelation at all.

IV

According to one widely popular interpretation of Kant's thesis, the will, in imposing moral law on itself, *creates* that law. Moral law is the collective creation of the human spirit; and only because it is such a creation is it moral at all. In rising to the life of morality, man actively transforms his own being in the light of ideals which are themselves a creative human product. All true morality is creative simply by virtue of being truly moral. And all passive submission, no matter to whom or what, is less than truly moral simply *because* it is passive submission.

Philosophers who accept this version of the Kantian thesis must reject in principle all revealed morality, radically, unequivocally, and immediately. To them, such a morality must be at worst a mere passive submission to the whims of an alien Deity. Even at best, it is just a creative morality which fails to recognize itself for what it is, for it mistakes its own creation for a passively received gift. And by virtue of this mistake it still falls short in some measure of the ideal morality.

But it is a matter of great importance that this version of the Kantian thesis is decidedly not Kant's own.[4] Kant does not assert that the human spirit creates moral law; he emphatically denies it. And his denial dramatizes his conviction—often stated by Kant himself but frequently overlooked by his interpreters—that in order to impose moral law on himself, man need be neither its individual nor collective creator. He need be capable only of *appropriating* a law, which in fact he has *not* created, *as though* he had created it. The attacks of "creative morality" philosophies on revealed morality, whatever their merits, we may thus ignore.

Unlike these, Kant's own doctrine does not rule out revealed morality from the start. For if the moral will need only appropriate, and not create, moral law, why might it not be *prima facie* possible for it to appropriate a law given by God? This, however, seems possible only *prima facie;* while not ruling out revealed morality from the start, Kant's doctrine deeply threatens it in the end. Indeed, this threat may be described as far more dangerous than that of "creative morality" philosophies. These latter—which reject revealed morality on the basis of criteria external to it— invite a like treatment from the defenders of revealed morality. This is not true of Kant, who takes revealed morality in its own right with a considerable degree of seriousness before he questions it radically.

Kant does not rule out revealed morality from the start; his moral will does not create moral law. Yet he threatens that morality in the end: for his moral will must act as though it were the creator of moral law. This Kantian assertion confronts the believer in a revealed morality with a grave dilemma: *Either he concedes that the will can and must impose the God-given law upon itself; but then its God-givenness becomes irrelevant in the process of self-imposition and appropriation; or else he insists that the God-givenness of the law does not and cannot at any point become irrelevant; but then the will cannot impose the law on itself—it can only submit to it for such non-moral reasons as trust in divine promises or fear of divine threats.*[5]

Kant himself perceives this dilemma with the utmost clarity; only for him it is not a dilemma. In his view, the religious man must choose between what Kant terms, respectively, "theological morality" and "moral theology." But to choose moral theology is to gain everything and to lose nothing.

The religious man chooses theological morality when he accepts laws as moral because they are the will of God. In so doing he not only submits to an alien law, but he submits to it because it is alien. Hence he cannot impose that law upon himself; and he can obey it—if he does obey it—because of its external sanctions only.[6] "Theological morality" is, and must be, heteronomous morality.

The religious man can rise above this only if he embraces "moral theology." He must not accept laws as moral because they are the will of God, but he must ascribe laws to God because they are intrinsically moral, and known to be so, quite apart from the will of God. It is because the will is capable of recognizing their intrinsic morality that it can impose laws upon itself, thus achieving moral autonomy. But this achievement is bought at a price. In imposing moral laws on itself, the will need not and, indeed, cannot pay heed to their God-givenness. The same act which appropriates the God-given moral law reduces its God-givenness to irrelevance.

One might therefore well ask why Kant's religious man, when achieving moral autonomy, should still *be* a religious man. Why should he end up with "moral theology" rather than with morality pure and simple? What necessity is there for ascribing the moral law to divine authorship, and what is the function of this ascription? This is a question of some complexity. But so long as we move in a purely moral context—asking ourselves what our duty is and why we should do it—the question does not arise at all. In that context, the question of the authorship of the moral law may be, or possibly even must be, left open. Kant writes:

> The veiled goddess before whom we bend our knees is the moral law within us . . . To be sure, we hear her voice and clearly understand her commandments, but are, in hearing them, in doubt as to who is speaking: whether man, in the self-sufficient power of his own reason, or Another, whose nature is unknown, and who speaks to man through the medium of his reason. Perhaps we would do better to refrain even from inquiring. For such a question is merely speculative, and our duty remains the same, whatever the source from which it issues.[7]

V

Such, then, is the challenge of Kant to revealed morality. The student who in its light considers the revealed morality of Judaism makes two extraordinary discoveries. One is that this morality cannot be classified as either autonomous or heteronomous in the Kantian sense. The other is that, in the nearly two hundred years since the Kantian doctrine first appeared to challenge them, Jewish religious thinkers have noticed this fact but rarely, and, when they have noticed it, only dimly.

Apologetic tendencies have marred at least all the standard Jewish responses to the Kantian challenge. Thus, orthodox thinkers can certainly never have forgotten that, according to a central traditional Jewish doctrine, the commandments are not truly performed until they are performed for their own sake. Yet when faced with the Kantian challenge they have tended to behave as though they had indeed forgotten that Jewish doctrine. Rightly concerned to rescue the divine Law-giver from irrelevance, they have been prone to argue that, but for the divine sanctions behind the commandments, the latter woud remain universally and necessarily unperformed. They should have insisted that the revealed morality of Judaism is not heteronomous. What they did insist all too often was that all human morality must be so. But thereby they not only put forward a false doctrine but pleaded Judaism guilty to a mistaken charge.

Liberal responses to Kant have suffered even more gravely from apologetic bias. While orthodox thinkers argued that the morality of Judaism is revealed but heteronomous, their liberal colleagues have often acted as though it were autonomous but not revealed. They would have prophets and rabbis speak with the Kantian voice of self-legislating reason.

This can be done in one of two ways; but both are foredoomed to failure. One can say that prophets and rabbis taught an autonomous morality, as it were, unconsciously: for they still gave conscious fealty to a revealing God. But then their morality stood, after all, still in need of liberal purification which finally eliminated the revealing God. Or one can picture prophets and rabbis teaching an autonomous morality for what it is—but this picture is a scandalous distortion of historical fact.

Because of the haste with which they resorted to apologetics, both these standard reactions to Kant failed to bring to light the authentic revealed morality of Judaism, which takes it out of the realm of both autonomous and heteronomous morality. One group of apologists saw that the revealed morality of Judaism is not autonomous, because it stands in an essential relation to a commanding God. The other saw that it is not heteronomous because, bidding man to perform commandments both for their own sake and for the sake of God, it rises above all blandishments and threats. But neither group was able to perceive the essential togetherness of these two elements. And yet the source and life of the revealed morality of Judaism lies precisely in that togetherness; a divine commanding Presence which never dissipates itself into irrelevance, and a human response which freely appropriates what it receives. The Jewish thinker does not respond adequately to the Kantian challenge until he brings this togetherness to philosophical self-consciousness, in order to ask a question which Kant literally forces upon him: *How can man appropriate a God-given law or commandment, accepting and performing it as though it were his own, while yet remaining, in the very act of appropriation, essentially and receptively related to its divine Giver? How can man morally obey a law which yet is, and never ceases to be, essentially revealed?* According to Kant, this is clearly impossible. Puzzlement and wonder arise for the Jewish philosopher because —if he is to believe the testimony of both Jewish life and Jewish thought—what Kant thought impossible is real.

VI

We must take care above all lest what is essential in this re-markable togetherness slip from notice. This would happen if one were to attend now to the divine commanding Presence in its otherness, and then to the human response in its power of free appropriation, but not to the two together. This togetherness is essential. In displaying it, we shall find that it exists in Judaism from its beginnings and throughout its history. Only in periods of spiritual decay can the one element seem capable of existence without the other. And this *is* the decay. With the exception of such periods, there is no age in the spiritual history of Judaism so "primitive" as to manifest—in the style of "theological morality" —only a divine commanding Presence but "not yet" an act of human appropriation. Nor is there an age "advanced" enough to manifest—in the style of "moral theology"—only a free human appropriation but "no longer" a commanding God who can be present in all His otherness.

At no moment in the spiritual history of Judaism is the other-ness of the divine commanding Presence so starkly disclosed as in that pristine one in which the Divine, first reaching out to the human, calls him to His service. For in that moment there are as yet no specified commandments but only a still unspecified divine commanding Presence. Abraham is commanded to go to another country without being told of the country, nor of the purpose which his migration is to serve. Prophets are called as messengers, without as yet being given a specific message. Israel as a whole is challenged, knowing as yet no more of the challenge than that it is divine. In the pristine moment, the divine commanding Presence does not communicate a finite content which the human recipient might appraise and appropriate in the light of familiar standards. On the contrary, it calls into question all familiar content, and, indeed, all standards. Whatever may be true of subsequent history, there can be, at any rate, no mistaking this initial voice for one already familiar, such as conscience, reason, or "spiritual creativity."[8]

It may therefore seem that, whatever the nature of the human response to this pristine challenge, it cannot, at any rate, be free appropriation. There can certainly be no appropriation of specific commandments in the light of commensurate human standards; for there are as yet no such commandments. And how could there be an appropriation of the unspecified divine commanding Presence itself, when in the pristine moment it discloses itself as wholly other than human? It may thus seem that, if there is human freedom at all in the pristine moment, it can at most be only heteronomous freedom; the kind, that is, which is conditioned by fear or hope.

And yet a freedom of this sort could not survive the touch of the divine Presence. Such freedom might survive, perhaps, in moments of divine distance which, giving rise only to finite fear or hope, could leave room, as it were, for a freedom conditioned by them. But a fear or hope produced by the touch of divine Presence would of necessity be an absolute Fear or Hope; and as such it would of necessity overwhelm the freedom conditioned by them. If in relation to God man is capable of heteronomous freedom only, then the event of divine Presence would reduce him, while that event lasts, to a will-less tool of a blind fate.

Such a reduction is indeed the primordial experience of some religions. But it is not the primordial experience of Judaism. For here the Divine manifests Itself as *commanding*, and in order to do so it requires real human freedom. And since the Divine is *Presence* as well as commanding, the required human freedom cannot be merely conditional; it must be unconditional and absolute. Finally, this unconditional and absolute freedom must be more even than the freedom to accept or reject, for their own sake and on their own merit, specific commandments: there are as yet no such commandments. The freedom required in the pristine moment of the divine commanding Presence, then, is nothing less than *the freedom to accept or reject the divine commanding Presence as a whole, and for its own sake—that is, for no other reason than that it* is *that Presence.* It is such freedom that the prophet displays when he responds, "Here I am, send me"; or the people as a whole, when they respond, "we shall do and hearken."[9]

This pristine human freedom of choice is not autonomous. Without the Other, man might have the self-sufficient power for all kinds of choice, but the power of choice to accept or reject the divine commanding Presence he would not have. How could he accept God, unless God had become present to him, for him to accept? How could he reject Him, unless He had become present to him, for him to reject? The divine commanding Presence, then, may be said to *give* man choosing power. It may even be said to *force* the actual choice upon him. For in being present, It *singles out;* and in singling out It rules out every escape from the choice into some spurious third alternative.

And yet this pristine choice most decidedly *is* a choice. The divine commanding Presence may force the choice on singled-out man. It does not force him to choose God, and the choice itself (as was seen) is not heteronomous; for it accepts or rejects the divine commanding Presence for no other reason than that it *is* that Presence. But this entails the momentous consequence that, *if and when a man chooses to accept the divine commanding Presence, he does nothing less than accept the divine Will as his own.*

But how is this humanly possible? We have already asked this question, in a general form. But it may now be given a sharper form which states in full clarity what is at stake: *How can man, in the very moment which starkly discloses the gap between him and God, presume to bridge that gap, by accepting God's will simply because it is God's, thus making it his own? How can man presume to act out of love for the sake of God?* It is perhaps no wonder that a philosopher, when first coming upon this decisive question, should shrink from it in thought. Even prophets shrank from it, when first confronted with it in life.[10]

VII

It may therefore seem prudent for a philosopher to suspend if not to avoid that question, by turning from the pristine moment which initiates the revealed morality of Judaism, to the developed life of that morality itself. Here revelation has become a system of specified laws and commandments; and at least insofar as those are moral in nature they possess in Judaism undoubted permanence and undoubted intrinsic value.[11] A Jeremiah may believe that whereas in one situation God demands resistance to the enemy, in another He demands submission.[12] But one cannot conceive of him as saying that concerning justice or love and injustice or hatred. Just how moral law can assume permanence and intrinsic value within the framework of a revealed morality is indeed a deep and weighty question, which requires treatment in its own right.[13] The fact of its doing so, in Judaism at any rate, can be in no serious doubt.

This may suggest to the philosopher that, once permanent law of intrinsic value has made its appearance in Judaism, the divine commanding Presence of the pristine moment has vanished into an irrelevant past. What could be the function of His Presence? If it contradicted moral standards already in human possession, its voice would surely have to be rejected, as a voice of temptation. And if it confirmed these standards, it would only tell what is already known. In short, once revelation has become specified as a system of laws, new and revealing immediacy is either false or superfluous.[14]

If this were the full truth of the matter, then revealed moral law in Judaism would allow of only two human responses: One obeys it for its own sake, by recognizing and appropriating its intrinsic value. Then, however, one obeys it for its own sake *only*, and the divine Giver of the law becomes irrelevant in the process of appropriation, and so does the revealed quality of the law itself. Or one obeys it *because* it is revealed. But then one

could not obey it either for God's sake or for its own; not the former because the Divine, having lost commanding presence—
immediacy—after the rise of law, would have reduced itself to the
mere external sanction behind the law; and not the latter, because
the law would then need such sanctions. In short, one would be
driven back to the Kantian alternative between a "moral theology" which is essentially unrevealed, and a "theological morality" which is less than fully moral.

   But must the divine Presence pass into irrelevance once revealed moral law has appeared? To ask this question is to recognize that the Kantian alternative contains a hidden premise. This
premise, to be sure, is hard to reject, but Judaism implicitly rejects it. According to the testimony of Jewish life and teaching,
the divine commanding Presence does *not* pass into irrelevance
once moral law has assumed permanence and intrinsic value. The
Torah is given whenever men are ready to receive it,[15] and the act
of receiving Torah culminates in the confrontation with its Giver.
The prophet, to be sure, has a specific message; yet the words
"thus saith the Lord" are not an empty preamble but an essential
part of the message itself. Kant holds that, mediating between
man and God, moral law rules out or renders irrelevant an immediate divine commanding Presence. Judaism affirms that, despite the mediating function of the revealed moral law, the Divine
is still present in commanding immediacy. The Kantian premise is
that moral law is a *bar* between man and its divine Giver. The
premise of Judaism is that it is a *bridge*.

   How can the law be a bridge? Only by making a most startling
demand. For Kant, all morality, including religious morality, demands a two-term relationship between man and his human
neighbor. The revealed morality of Judaism demands a three-term
relationship, nothing less than a relationship involving man, his
human neighbor, and God Himself. If it demanded a human relationship only, then the God in Whose name it was demanded
would indeed reduce Himself to mere external sanction behind the

demand. The startling claim of the revealed morality of Judaism is, however, that God Himself enters into the relationship. He confronts man with the demand to turn to his human neighbor, and in doing so, turn back to God Himself. Micah's celebrated summary of the commandments does more than list three commandments which exist side by side. It states an internally related whole. For there is no humble walking before God unless it manifests itself in justice and mercy to the human neighbor. And there can be only fragmentary justice and mercy unless they culminate in humility before God. Here lies the heart and core of Jewish morality.[16]

What human response is adequate to this divine demand? The response remains fragmentary until the commandments are performed, on the one hand, for *their* sake, and on the other for *God's* sake. And each of these must point to the other.

Moral commandments, to be moral, must be performed for *their* sake. For unless so performed they do not realize a three-term relationship which takes the human neighbor in his own right seriously; they function merely within an attempted two-term relation between man and God. We say "attempted." For such a relationship is rejected by God Himself. It is God Himself Who bids man to take his neighbor in his own right seriously. To obey God, man accepts both his neighbor, and the commandment concerning him, as possessing intrinsic value. He performs the commandment for its own sake.

And yet the commandment remains fragmentary if performed for its own sake *alone.* For if such performance discloses the human neighbor, and ourselves, too, as beings of intrinsic value, it is ultimately *because the divine commanding Presence so discloses them.* This is why, even if beginning with the acceptance of the disclosure only, a man is finally led to confront the divine Discloser; why performance of the commandment for *its* sake points to its performance for *God's* sake. Both are certainly part of Jewish teaching. And they exist not contingently side by side, but in an internal and necessary relation. God is not barred from direct human access by the intrinsic value of man, or by the intrinsic value of the commandment which relates to man. On the contrary, *He discloses Himself through all intrinsic value, as its ultimate Source.* And the man who accepts this disclosure acts for the sake of God. In the hour of his martyrdom, Rabbi Akiba knew that the love of God is not one commandment side by side to others. It is the life of all.[17]

Thus, the territory in which we have sought philosophic refuge from the decisive but bewildering question raised by the pristine moment of divine commanding Presence, while no doubt safer, is by no means absolutely safe, if by "safety" is meant the comfortable distance, and hence the irrelevance, of the Divine. We first saw that in the pristine moment of divine commanding Presence there is already the possibility of free human appropriation, and we have now seen that, once human freedom can appropriate specific laws and commandments endowed with permanence and intrinsic value, the divine commanding Presence will still confront it. Divine commanding Presence and appropriating human freedom still point to each other. And the philosophical question raised by their togetherness can no longer be suspended or avoided. In the light of the foregoing, we may reformulate that question, to read as follows: *how can man presume to participate in a three-term relationship which involves not only his human neighbor but also God Himself? How can he—as he must, in order to participate in such a relationship—act out of love for the sake of God, when God is God while man is only man?* In Kantian language, what is the condition of the possibility of such action?

VIII

It is a testimony to Kant's genius as a religious thinker that he should not have wholly ignored this question. He even supplied it with an answer. But Kant's answer is not and cannot be the Jewish answer. Instead, we come to a final parting of ways.

Kant writes:

> The virtuous man fears God without being afraid of Him. This is because he is not worried lest he himself might wish to resist Him or His commandments. God is awe-inspiring to him because such resistance, while unthinkable in his own case, is not in itself impossible.[18]

For Kant's virtuous man, it is "unthinkable" that he might not will the will of God. For a prophet when first singled out, it is unthinkable how he *could* will it. To fear God at all, Kant's virtuous man must imagine himself as willing what he is in fact incapable of willing. The rabbis need no such strategy in order to stand in fear of God. Their impossible possibility is not the fear but rather the love of God.[19] For Kant, the oneness of the human with the divine will is automatic once virtue is achieved. For prophets and rabbis, such oneness is very far from automatic even for the virtuous man, and, in a sense, for him least of all. For prophets and rabbis, there is a radical gulf between God, Who is God, and man, who is only human. How then is a oneness of wills possible at all?

It is possible if God Himself has made it possible. Man can appropriate divine commandments if they are handed over for human appropriation. He can live by the Torah in the love and for the sake of God, if the Torah itself is a gift of divine love, making such a life a human possibility. He can participate in a three-term relationship which involves God Himself if God, Who in His power does not need man, in His love nevertheless chooses to need him.

The belief in the reality of such a divine love is as pervasive in Judaism as is the belief in revealed law itself. For here divine commandment and divine love are not only coeval, they are inseparable. The Torah manifests love in the very act of manifesting commandment; for in commanding *humans* rather than angels, it accepts these humans in their humanity.[20] Hence in accepting the Torah, man can at the same time accept himself as accepted by God in his humanity. This is why to attempt to perform the commandments, and to do so both for their sake and for the sake of God, is not to attempt the humanly impossible. At least in principle, the commandments *can* be performed in joy.[21]

This belief in divine love manifest in the divine commandment is present in Judaism from its pristine beginnings and throughout its history. From its beginnings: having first shrunk from the divine commanding Presence, the prophet ends up accepting it because he has experienced the divine love which makes acceptance possible.[22] Throughout its history: our daily prayer renders thanks for the divine love in which God has given the commandments.

If this faith permeates Jewish life so universally and so obviously, one may well ask why Jewish thought, when confronted with the Kantian challenge, should have failed to bring it clearly to philosophical self-consciousness. Had it done so, it would not have accepted so meekly the terms of the Kantian dilemma, between a morality which, because genuinely moral, cannot be essentially revealed, and a morality which, because essentially revealed, must be less than truly moral. It would have repudiated this dilemma, recognizing—and clearly stating—that, if divine love is manifest in the revealed commandments, the dilemma does not arise.

Perhaps it is not far-fetched to identify as the cause of failure, in the case of non-Jewish philosophers like Kant, an ancient prejudice against Judaism bolstered by ignorance of Judaism; and, in the case of Jewish philosophers, uncritically assimilated reliance on non-Jewish modes of philosophical thought.

An ancient prejudice contrasts Jewish law with Christian love; and this is only slightly modified by the concession that love "evolves" in later stages of Judaism as well. Against this prejudice, it is by no means enough to insist that divine love is as ancient in Judaism as is divine commandment. For such love might still be confined, in Pelagian style, to the remission of sins which strict justice would condemn; and this would still leave law itself prior to love, and in itself loveless. In Judaism the primordial manifestation of divine love is not subsequent to but *in* the commandments; primordial human joy is not in a future subsequent to the life of the commandments but in that life itself.

Now it is precisely this teaching which Paul either could not comprehend or could not accept. Paul did not merely assert that the commandments cannot be performed wholly, which to the rabbis was not new. He asserted that they cannot be performed at all. This was because, while accepting one aspect of Jewish teaching he did not accept the other. He saw man commanded to act for God's sake, by a God incommensurate with all things human. But he did not see, or was personally unable to experience, the divine love which, handing the commandments over for human appropriation, makes their performance a human possibility. Hence he thought man was obligated to do the humanly impossible.

Kant's moral philosophy may be regarded, among many other things, as a protest against this Pauline conclusion. It rightly insisted that man can be morally obligated to do only what he is able to do, and hence that, if an unbridged gap exists between the human and the Divine, divine commandments cannot be moral commandments. It also properly refused to divorce the Divine from the moral. But this compelled it to deny the gap between the Divine and the human. And the result was that the divine will became a moral redundancy.[23] In all this, Kant's anti-Pauline protest shares one assumption with Paul's own position; the denial of divine love manifest in the God-given commandment. From the standpoint of the revealed morality of Judaism, Kant may therefore be viewed as the nemesis of a tradition which begins with Paul.

IX

Throughout our essay, the term "Judaism" has meant classical Judaism which finds literary expression in the Hebrew Bible and in rabbinic literature. Re-enacting this Judaism in thought, we have rejected the Kantian dilemma between a morality which, if autonomous, is not essentially revealed, and, if essentially revealed, must necessarily be heteronomous.

But can the Jewish philosopher of today do more than give a phenomenological re-enactment of the classical faith? Can he accept it himself? It is all too obvious that faith in a divine love manifest in revealed commandments, always under much pressure in life, is subject to pressures of the gravest kind not only in modern life but in the realm of modern thought as well.

This is a question for separate inquiry, the results of which one cannot anticipate. One can only be certain that the Jewish philosopher who conducts it must not, at any rate, surrender quickly to modern pressures. For if there is anything that makes him a *Jewish* philosopher, it is precisely the duty to confront, and take seriously, his own Jewish tradition. He would fail in his duty if he were ever to forget that his ancestors could often live by the belief that "when the Torah came into the world, freedom came into the world."[24]

15

On the Eclipse of God

In one of his writings, Martin Heidegger quotes with approval, as applying to the present, these words of the early 19th-century German poet Hölderlin: "Alas, our generation walks in night, dwells as in Hades, without the Divine." When Hölderlin wrote those words, there cannot have been many people who agreed with him, for it was an age which thought of itself as about to reach the very summit of religious enlightenment. In our own age, by contrast—an age which is acquainted with catastrophe and stands in fear of even greater catastrophes to come—hardly anyone can think of himself as walking in anything but night. And while it is not immediately clear whether this means that we must dwell "without the Divine"—indeed, that is the question to which these reflections are addressed—it is at any rate perfectly clear that we are undergoing an unprecedented crisis of religious faith.

According to a widespread view, it is the very catastrophes of the 20th century which have brought the crisis about. The ancient belief that the Divine is with us—that God lives and cares—cannot, it is said, be sustained in the face of these catastrophes, for to sustain it requires smugness and blindness to tragedy. Yet the fact is that this view reflects a complete lack of understanding of the nature of religious faith in general and Biblical faith in particular. Biblical faith—and I mean both Jewish and Christian—is never destroyed by tragedy but only tested by it; and in the test it both

Reprinted from *Commentary* (June 1964), pp. 55-60.

clarifies its own meaning and conquers tragedy. Here, precisely, lies the secret of its strength.

Consider a few representative examples. The prophet Jeremiah lives to see the destruction of the Temple, of Jerusalem, of the whole national existence of Judah. He does not deny the tragedy or seek to explain it away. But neither does it occur to him that God's existence has now been refuted, or that He can no longer be conceived as just, or as loving His people, Israel. To Jeremiah the destruction of the Temple *is* a manifestation of divine justice. And it does not mark the end of divine love: "There is hope for the future."

The case of Job is still more extreme because Job is struck by tragedies which are explicitly said to be beyond the bounds of any conceivable divine justice. Yet Job never denies the existence of God; nor does he follow his wife's suggestion that he curse God and die. His faith is reduced to utter unintelligibility, yet he persists in it.

Let me give a final example which, at least in one respect, is still more extreme—the example of the Psalmist. Even in the midst of unintelligible tragedy, Job never wholly loses his sense of the presence of God. The Psalmist *in extremis*, however, does, when He complains that God has "hidden His face." God is not—at least not now—present. Unlike Job, the Psalmist does not ask that God's ways be made intelligible to him. He does not ask that the valley of the shadows or the netherworld be made to vanish; he asks only that God be present while he walks through them, as God was present to him before. Yet even in this most extreme of all crisis situations—God having "hidden His face"—the Psalmist never loses his faith. He never says that God does not, after all, exist; nor that, though existing, He has finally ceased to care. (In practice the two assertions would amount to the same thing.) What he does say is that, unaccountably, God has hidden His face; that He has hidden it for only a while; and that He will turn His face back to man again.

Put radically, this means that there is no experience, either without or within, that can possibly destroy religious faith. Good fortune without reveals the hand of God; bad fortune, if it is not a matter of just punishment, teaches that God's ways are unintelligible, not that there *are* no ways of God. A full heart within indicates the Divine Presence; an empty heart bespeaks not the non-existence or unconcern of God, but merely His temporary absence. *Religious faith can be, and is, empirically verifiable; but nothing empirical can possibly refute it.*[1]

Philosophers of science rightly assert that such an attitude toward the empirical is in principle illegitimate in the sciences. It is, however, hardly surprising that it should be of the essence of religious faith. Science is forever hypothetical. But what could one make of a religious faith which was forever hypothetical, wavering between belief in good times and unbelief in bad? Since, as we have seen, the characteristic of genuine faith is not only to survive in tragic times but to survive in them most triumphant, it is no accident that adherents of Biblical faith should always have regarded times of external or internal darkness not as evidence against God, but rather—to use Martin Buber's expression—as evidence of an "eclipse of God." To follow Buber's metaphor, an eclipse of the sun is something that occurs, not to or in the sun, but between the sun and the eye; moreover, this occurrence is temporary. Hence the catastrophes of our time, however great, cannot by themselves account for the contemporary crisis of religious belief; or rather, they can be regarded as having produced this crisis only on the assumption that religious belief was already undermined. What, then, undermined it?

MOST people would say: modern science. The story begins wih Copernicus, who shows that the earth is but one of many stars; it is carried forward by Darwin, who shows that man is but a higher animal; and it culminates with Freud, who shows that the one indubitably distinctive human characteristic—rationality—

is neither very significant nor even very distinctive. Once at the center of the universe, man has been moved to the periphery. Once the crown of creation, man has become a fleck of dust.

Another and related aspect is perhaps still more important. The pre-modern universe was shot through with value: there was a hierarchy of purposes into which man with his human purposes could fit and feel at home. By contrast, the universe of modern science is a universe of fact without purpose; and because man cannot live without purpose, there arises a dichotomy between "fact" and "value." Values are now human *only:* man finds that he and his values have no counterpart in the world of sheer fact around him—he is radically alone. When Aristotle gazed at the stars, he could regard them as manifesting purposes somehow akin to human purposes. When the Stranger of Albert Camus's novel gazes at the stars, he must regard them as neutral. Thus it seems that man is not only a marginal being within the universe of modern science, but also that his purposes and values, inextricably bound up with any conceivable religion, lack the kind of "objective" warrant which could be given them by some Archimedean point outside himself. How, then, can he still look upon himself as being under the special care of a cosmic God?

But this whole argument, however plausible on the surface, is utterly invalid. Since Biblical belief is empirically irrefutable, scientific evidence can no more affect it than the evidence of historical tragedy or the evidence of an empty heart. The Biblical God, to be sure, has always revealed Himself. But He has always concealed Himself as well. At most, therefore, modern science should have had no greater effect on Biblical belief than to show that its God was even more inscrutable than had hitherto been thought, and His revelations even more ambiguous and intermittent.

Perhaps, however, it would be rash to dismiss the threat of modern science to Biblical faith on such general grounds alone. Conceivably there is a special affinity between that faith and the

Weltanschauung of the pre-modern world, and conceivably the very different *Weltanschauung* that goes with modern science is radically in conflict with Biblical faith. Science may be unable to refute faith, yet it may be that one cannot really live by both.

But is it true that pre-modern science and Biblical faith are temperamentally compatible, while modern science and Biblical faith are mutually hostile? A. N. Whitehead argues, and argues plausibly, that the opposite is the case. According to Whitehead, pre-modern and modern science differ not only in their conclusions about nature but also in their approach to nature. Pre-modern science did not experiment with—"torture"—nature: who would wish to torture something divine, or shot through with divinity? It was because they regarded nature as divine that the Greeks thought only of contemplating it and not of putting it to human use. Thus, though they developed so much else, they never systematically developed experimentation. To the Protestant mind, schooled in the Bible, nature is not divine, but the *work* of God; and God created it for human use. It was this belief—still according to Whitehead—that made modern experimental science possible. Hence one might well conclude that in some ways modern science is closer in spirit to Biblical faith than its pre-modern predecessor. Is there not rivalry between a science which finds gods in nature and a faith whose God is beyond nature? And is not a science for which nature is at any rate un-divine free from conflict with a faith which, however different in all other aspects, agrees at least on this one point?

Nevertheless, it might still remain true that this un-divine nature of modern science threatens, if it does not rule out, any religious recourse to a Divinity beyond nature. If man is a mere fleck of dust in a blind universe, can he plausibly resort to such a God— a God, furthermore, essentially concerned with *him?* But closer inspection reveals that this is, and has been since the rise of modern science, only half the story. As the *object* of scientific investigation, man may be infinitely small. As the *subject* undertaking the investigation, however, he is infinitely large, if only because he knows that he is infinitely small. Man, growing ever smaller in stature as modern science progressed, at the same time grew ever larger as well; for whereas all else in the universe was only part of a whole, it was man who *knew* the whole and his own position within it. And so far as we can tell even today, man is unique in this respect. What makes him unique, moreover, is not a mere capacity for abstract theory which is relevant to a few thinkers alone; it is the power this capacity gives him to transform nature, as well as to transform the whole human condition. Because of technology man can be more fully controlled than ever before; he becomes the object of physical and social engineering. But the engineer is himself human.

I hope it is clear that my purpose is not to exalt human greatness in an attempt—like those of earlier times—to struggle by means of faith in man toward faith in God. Rather what I want to stress is man's dialectical condition: that he is at once small and large, part of the universe and yet not reducible to a mere part— in short, and for better or worse, a terror, wonder, and mystery to himself. Now in this regard, modern man is not really so far from the Psalmist who writes: "What is man that Thou art mindful of him, and the son of man that Thou shouldst think of him? Yet hast Thou made him but little lower than the angels, and crowned him with honor and glory." It is, to be sure, a decisive difference that the Psalmist feels at once small and large *before God.* His feeling and ours, however, have much in common.

If, then, the historical catastrophes of our time cannot explain the crisis of contemporary religious belief, neither can modern science and all its works. Indeed, one might go so far as to say that the whole battle between science and religion rests on nothing but gigantic misunderstandings on both sides. It was because faith had *already* been undermined by the time this battle was joined in the 19th century, that religion had to resort either to a fundamentalism hostile to all science, or else to a modernism seeking props for its own weakness in a science which would not and could not provide them.

OUR question concerning the cause of the modern crisis of faith thus remains unanswered. In seeking the answer, we do well to keep a firm grasp on the essence of Biblical faith, which is the *believer's certainty of standing in relation to an unprovable and irrefutable God*. What could have undermined such a certainty? The process was extremely complex, but let us for the sake of better understanding try to describe it as though it took place in three clearly distinct stages.

First came what may be called the discovery of the circle of authority and faith. A pre-modern man, asked about the grounds of his religious certainty, would presumably have pointed to an authority—a prophet, a sacred scripture, a church, even the voice of his own heart. This, however, involves a circle. If Moses beheld the Presence of God in the burning bush, it was because he was already open to that Presence; a modern agnostic, beholding the same bush, would perceive only a chemical phenomenon. No conceivable datum—neither a natural fact, nor an inner experience, nor an existing scripture—can serve as an authority authenticating a religious truth except for those already prepared to accept that truth on faith. Faith may base itself on authority; but the authority *is* an authority only where faith can be presupposed.

The discovery of this circle is not by itself fatal to faith, as can be seen from the fact that pre-modern thinkers were by no means wholly unaware of it. (Saint Thomas Aquinas knew, for example, that he could not argue with a nonbeliever on the basis of the revealed Scriptures, since the issue between them was precisely whether the Scriptures *were* revealed.) Nevertheless, the discovery, by focusing attention on faith instead of on authority, leads the modern critic to a second and more decisive step. To the believer, faith is the *immediate relation* between himself and God.

To the critic, faith is merely the *feeling* of standing in such a relation, plus an *inference* from that feeling to an actual God.

The step just described may seem a matter of mere philosophical subtlety; yet everything centers around it. For once this second step is taken, the third—and it is the *coup de grâce*—quickly follows: the elimination, with the help of Ockham's razor, of the inferred God. Ockham asserted the rational necessity of eliminating unnecessary assumptions, as one shaves off an unwanted beard. And it is all too clear that God, as an assumption made to account for the feeling of His Presence, is indeed both unwanted and unnecessary.

In the first place, a God inferred to explain religious feelings would at most be a probable inference, capable of refutation and never really certain. And in the second place, anyone in agreement with Kant (and with a good many other philosophers as well) would regard such an inference—moving from a natural effect to a supernatural cause—as in principle illegitimate.

Thus modern criticism, operating through three stages, explains faith as an inference from religious feeling, and eliminates the inference as a redundancy. To complete the destruction of faith, it remains only to explain how the inference should ever have been mistaken for an immediate relationship. *That* is achieved by defining God as in fact an unconscious projection, and faith as in fact a solitary disport with religious feelings (however these, in turn, are to be explained).

The reason we can consider this whole process—which may be termed subjectivist reductionism—as *the* cause of the modern religious crisis, is that it is not a mere intellectual argument carried on by abstract thinkers. Subjectivist reductionism has become a modern—perhaps *the* modern—way of life. Which came first— the argument or the way of life—we need not here inquire.

MUCH that passes for an independent assault on religion is actually a version, or an application, of the three-stage argument just presented. Consider, first, Biblical criticism, which, it is sometimes supposed, constitutes a refutation of the claim that the Scriptures are the revealed word of God. But in fact Biblical criticism either presupposes what it imagines itself to be proving, or else it leaves the issue open. For if the critic declares that what the Bible itself regards as the reflection of human dialogues with God is nothing more than an expression of the evolution of religious feelings and ideas, it is he who has brought such categories to the Bible, not the Bible which has yielded them to him. His criticism, in other words, already assumes a position of subjectivist reductionism.

Consider, next, humanism. Feuerbach, possibly the greatest of modern humanists, speaks for all: "What man is not, but wills to be or wishes to be, just that and only that, nothing else, is God." But to the religious believer, God is not what *he* wills to be; He is the other-than-human with Whom the believer stands in relation. How, then, does the humanist refute the believer? Only by a form of subjectivist reductionism. And what is true of Feuerbach is true of Marx and Freud as well. To unmask *some* gods as pseudo-gods, they can rely on specific empirical evidence in specific spheres. But to unmask all gods as pseudo-gods is in the end to rest one's case not on specific empirical evidence but on an *a priori* philosophical argument; and the argument is a form of subjectivist reductionism.

So pervasive is subjectivist reductionism in the modern world that it has enlisted friends of religion as well as foes in its ranks— although it must be said that this friendship is of the most dubious kind. Its nature may be illustrated by two examples, the one widespread and popular, the other more or less confined to academics. Pragmatism—and a good deal of popular psychology as well—is apt to assert that while religious beliefs are mere wish- or need-projections, they are useful, or even necessary, for comfortable survival in an uncomfortable world. The question thus arises as to how they can be preserved, and the answer would appear to be: by keeping their illusory character concealed. For who can live by a belief which he knows to be illusory? Yet such conceal- ment is not only practically impossible in the modern world; the particular friends of religion presently under consideration do not even seem to desire it. Hence in many circles religion has become a collective make-believe: something which is good for most, ac- cepted as true by others, rejected as false by oneself. Religion of this sort is not a bulwark against religious crisis; it is one of its gravest manifestations.

Much the same can be said of the other, more academic form of friendship for religion displayed by some of the linguistic phi- losophers who have now taken over from the logical positivists. Logical positivism was a clear foe of religious faith. It declared religious language to be emotive only, referring to no objective reality. Thus "God" really meant "three cheers for the world"; and a revivalist preacher, urging his congregation to give three cheers for God, was really saying "Let's give three cheers for three cheers for the world." Here was subjectivist reductionism accompanied by forthright hostility. The heirs of logical positiv- ism, the linguistic philosophers, on the whole feel no such hos- tility. Science tells us about the world, they say, while religion re- flects attitudes toward the world—and why should we not have attitudes? Indeed, how can we live without them? But if religion is acknowledged to be an attitude *only,* and the God toward whom religion is an attitude is excluded, then subjectivist reduc- tionism has won the day. Defending the attitude *as* attitude does not protect religious faith: it helps bring about its doom.

Has subjectivist reductionism, then, won the day? It has not. For the Biblical faith has been restated in our time, both by Jews and Christians, with a purity perhaps unmatched in cen- turies; and this restatement has fully risen to the challenge posed by subjectivist reductionism.

Here are two quotations, one taken from Bertrand Russell's *My*

Philosophical Development, the other from Buber's *Eclipse of God*. Russell writes:

> If A loves B the relation . . . consists in certain states of mind of A. Even an atheist must admit that a man can love God. It follows that love of God is a state of the man who feels it, and not properly a relational fact.

Contrast this with Buber:

> Great images of God fashioned by mankind are born, not of imagination, but of real encounters with Divine power and glory.

Russell here admirably states the subjectivist-reductionist view. Although he expressly speaks only of the love of God, what he says would apply equally well to faith. Just as an atheist can "admit that a man can love God," he can admit faith in another man. Faith would be a subjective state and God would become an inference made by the believer which the atheist would declare invalid.

Buber's statement, once contrasted with Russell's, is seen in its full significance and polemical power. Man does not have private feelings from which he infers the Divine. *If related to God at all, he is primordially open to Him; and his subjective feelings and the images of God he fashions are mere by-products of this primordial openness.* No doubt man can be imprisoned by images and feelings, and no doubt he can seek to escape from the prison of these images and feelings by inferring from them to a God beyond them. But such imprisonment is pseudo-religion, and the attempt to escape from it is futile. Or rather, the true escape is not to infer God from images and feelings, but to turn away from these to God Himself.

On Buber's thesis, an atheist can certainly "admit that a man can love God." But it is questionable whether an atheist can do something far more important—understand what the love of God *means*. For how can he distinguish between the pseudo-love which, being feeling *only*, is a disguised love of self, and the real

love which obtains between God and man? And what holds of
the distinction between love and pseudo-love also holds of the
distinction betweeen "great" images of God and trivial or superficial ones. Perhaps the atheist does not wholly lack the power to
make these distinctions; but then, not everyone protesting atheism is a simple and unequivocal atheist.

Here we have, then, two assertions. How are we to judge between them? I will approach this decisive question through a
perennial problem, though it can carry us only to the threshold of
an answer. Philosophers often ask how one can know other
minds. I can immediately know my own feelings; and I can immediately observe other people's behavior. But how can I know
the feelings of others? Well, I can infer them from their behavior.
But this inference would seem to presuppose that their behavior
is like mine—that, for example, they behave when they feel pain
as I do when I feel pain. This assumption may be perfectly plausible. But it *is* an assumption. Hence I can never know, and certainly never know *immediately*, that I am not radically alone.

I am persuaded that, while this line of reasoning has some value
in bringing to light certain specific philosophical issues, it is altogether misguided. A self is primordially open to other selves; and
unless it were thus open it would never become a self at all. A
child *becomes* an "I" in a relation of openness to a "Thou"; indeed, he knows the meaning of "Thou" before he knows the
meaning of "I." There is, to be sure, a problem involved in knowing other selves. But the problem is not whether they exist; it is
who they are. And it arises, not because the self is to begin with
in a subjectivist prison from which it must subsequently try to
escape; it arises because, born free of prisons of this kind, the self
is subsequently cast into them by the breakdown of communication. And when the breakdown is complete there is mental disease.

THIS much, at least, would seem arguable or even demonstrable: genuine love between humans does not consist of

subjectivist solitudes externally related; it is *one* relation, although always impaired in its unity, often threatened by temporary eclipse and sometimes by total destruction. A demonstration of this proposition, however, would—as has already been said—take us only to the threshold of the question we have been struggling with. For it might well be the case that, whereas genuine love between humans consists of an immediate relation, the love of God consists of feeling *only*. Indeed, this is bound to be true if the faith which knows this God is itself nothing more than subjective feeling. What, in the light of the foregoing, are we to make of this possibility?

The first thing to say is that if it is true, there can be no genuine love of God at all, since there can be no openness to the other which even love between humans requires. The second thing is that pseudo-love of God is the legitimate object of destructive criticism, and that from a perspective like Buber's, one cheerfully supports the criticism. And the third and most important thing to say is that genuine love of God—if there be such love—escapes the grasp of the subjectivist critic. For genuine love of God, which is openness to the Divine, can be known only in actual openness, and this is precisely what the critic cannot or will not have. Hence he is left only with the images and feelings which are its by-product. How then can he judge them *as* by-products? How, indeed, can he safely distinguish between the pseudo-faith and pseudo-love which are merely feelings projected onto a pseudo-god, and the genuine faith and love which constitute a relation to God? It would seem, therefore, that the critic's reduction even of pseudo-faith must always remain ambiguous, and can never be final.

This does not prevent him, however, from *deciding* that religious images and feelings are *never* "born of real encounters," that they are *always* mere "imagination." Only in making this decision, he does not give a *demonstration*. Buber's response to the challenge of subjectivist reductionism has disclosed that it

does not refute Biblical faith, but rather that it opposes one faith
to another. Biblical faith stakes all on man's primordial openness
to the Divine—an openness, to be sure, which is interrupted by
eclipses of God. The reductionist "faith" stakes all on the thesis
that man is primordially shut off from God, and that all supposed
openness is mere self-delusion. But in the perspective of Buber's
modern reaffirmation of the Biblical faith, reductionism itself appears as a self-delusion: it mistakes withdrawal from God for the
natural and inevitable human condition.

　　　　IN SUCH manner does faith refute the refutation proposed by subjectivist reductionism. But this is not to say that
faith can prove its own case against subjectivist reductionism. It
cannot refute but only reject it; and it can testify against it. For
the argument cuts both ways. The reductionist cannot use observable data—religious images and feelings—to demonstrate the subjectivity of faith. But neither can the believer use these same data
to demonstrate the objectivity of faith. For not only is it the case
that the reductionist critic cannot or will not enter into the actual
relation of openness to God; it is also the case that for the believer
himself the "knowledge" obtained is shot through with the gravest of risks. After all, does not disguised self-love, being disguised, mistake itself for love of God? Are not god-projections,
being unconscious, mistaken for real gods by those who are prey
to them?

Some part of this risk has always been understood by believers
in the Biblical tradition, who realized that false prophets, no less
than true, can be sincere. The full extent of the risk, however, has
become obvious only to the modern believer. His ancestor rarely
doubted that man was in principle open to the Divine; hence the
risk of which he was aware extended for the most part only to
deciding when and how such openness was truly manifest. The
modern believer, by contrast, has glimpsed the possibility that *all*
openness to the Divine may be pseudo-openness only—that man

may be radically alone. He does not stand in immediate openness to the Divine. He seeks, in Kierkegaard's expression, an immediacy after reflection. The Psalmist *in extremis* experienced an eclipse of God. The extremity of faith in the modern age is uncertainty as to whether what is experienced *is* an eclipse of God, or the final exposure of an illusion.

Hence if the modern believer works and waits for an end to this eclipse, he must carry in his working and waiting a uniquely modern burden. The Psalmist *in extremis* could rest in the irrefutability of faith. The modern believer *in extremis* must endure the full impact of its being undemonstrable as well; he must suffer the knowledge that to the world around him the concealed God is a non-existent God, and that he himself can do no more than testify to the contrary.

Under these circumstances, it is natural that there should be those who wish to be told whether the present crisis of religious faith will lead to a renewal. But anyone who asks for a prediction does not understand what has been said. Pronouncements upon the future that is at stake here could not take the form of scientific or historical prediction, but only of indulgence in prophecy. And a rabbinic sage wisely observed that when Biblical times came to an end, prophecy was taken away from prophets and given over to fools and children.[2]

16

Judaism and the Meaning of Life

I

Religions—which differ in much else—differ in substance according to their experience and understanding of the meeting between the Divine and the human: whether, when, and how it occurs, and what happens in and through it. In Judaism, the fundamental and all-penetrating occurrence is a primordial mystery, and a miracle of miracles: the Divine, though dwelling on high and infinitely above man, yet bends down low so as to accept and confirm man in his finite humanity; and man, though met by Divine Infinity, yet may and must respond to this meeting in and through his finitude.

Some scholars attribute to the God of early Jewish faith mythological finitude. But this reflects blindness to the religious realities of Judaism—a blindness arising out of modern prejudice. In the very beginnings of Jewish faith, God is experienced and conceived as the all-demanding God; and it is only a question of time until the one-important God becomes the one-existing God.

Reprinted by permission of The Ryerson Press from *The Meaning of Life in Five Great Religions*, ed. R. C. Chalmers and John A. Irving (Toronto, 1965), pp. 56-78. Published in the USA by The Westminster Press, 1966.

Hence even His earliest followers smash the idols: Judaism is anti-mythological from the start.

Just as the God even of "primitive" Judaism is infinite, so the man even of "advanced" Judaism remains finite. Man, though created in the Divine image, is still a creature; he is neither a fragment of Divinity nor potentially Divine. Such notions—the product of modern humanism—remain unassimilable to the Jewish faith.

As a consequence of the miracle of miracles which lies at the core of Judaism, Jewish life and thought are marked by a fundamental tension. This tension might have been evaded in either of two ways. It might have been held—as ancient Epicureanism and modern Deism, for example, do in fact hold—that the Divine and the human are after all incapable of meeting. But this view is consistently rejected in Jewish tradition, which considers Epicureanism tantamount to atheism. Or, on the other side, it might have been held that the meeting is a mystical conflux, in which the finite dissolves into the Infinite and man suffers the loss of his very humanity. But this view, too, although a profound religious possibility and a serious challenge, is rejected in Jewish tradition. Such thinkers as Maimonides, Isaac Luria, and the Baal Shem-Tov all stop short—on occasion, to be sure, only barely—of embracing mysticism. And those who do not—such as Spinoza—pass beyond the bounds of Judaism. The Infinity of the Divine, the finitude of the human, and the meeting between them: these all remain, then, wherever Judaism preserves its substance; and the mystery and tension of this meeting permeate all else.

In the eyes of Judaism, whatever meaning life acquires derives from this encounter: the Divine accepts and confirms the human in the moment of meeting. But the meaning conferred upon human life by the Divine-human encounter cannot be understood in terms of some finite human purpose, supposedly more ultimate than the meeting itself. For what could be more ultimate than the

Presence of God? The Presence of God, then, as Martin Buber
puts it, is an *"inexpressible* confirmation of meaning. . . . The question of the meaning of life is no longer there. But were it there, it
would not have to be answered."[1]

II

In Judaism, however, this "inexpressible confirmation of meaning" *does*, after all, assume expression; and this is because the
Divine-human meeting assumes structure and content.

First, it is a universal human experience that times of Divine
Presence do not last forever. But this experience does not everywhere have the same significance or even reality. Conceivably
mythological religions—for which the world is "full of gods"
(Thales)—may find divinity even in the most worldly preoccupation with the most finite ends: this is not possible if the Divine is
an Infinity and radically other than all things finite. Mystical religions, for their part, may dismiss all such worldly preoccupations
as mere appearance, and confine reality to the moment in which
the human dissolves into the Divine: this is not possible if the
moment of Divine-human encounter itself confirms man in his
human finitude. In Judaism, man is real at every moment of his
finite existence—including those moments when he is divorced
from the Divine. The God of Judaism, while "near" at times, is—
for whatever reason—"far" at other times. But times of Divine
farness must also have meaning; for the far God remains an existing God, and nearness remains an ever-live possibility. These
times of Divine farness, however, derive their meaning from times
of Divine nearness. The dialectic between Divine nearness and
Divine farness is all-pervasive in Jewish experience; and it points
to an eschatological future in which it is overcome.[2]

Secondly, the Divine-human meeting assumes structure and
content in Judaism through the way man is accepted and con-

firmed as a consequence of this meeting. In Judaism God accepts and confirms man by *commanding* him in his humanity; and the response called for is *obedience* to God—an obedience to be expressed in finite human form. Here lies the ground for the Jewish rejection of the mystic surrender. Man *must* remain human because in commanding him *as* human, God accepts him in his humanity and makes him responsible in His very presence. In Judaism, Divine Grace is not superadded and subservient to Divine Commandment. Divine Grace already is, primordially, *in* the commandment; and were it not so, the commandment would be radically incapable of human performance. It is in the Divine Law itself that the Psalmist finds his delight, not only in a Divine action subsequent to observance of the Law; and if the Law saves him from perishing in his affliction, it is because Divine Love has handed it over to humans—not to angels—thereby making it in principle capable of human fulfillment.[3]

Because the Divine acceptance of the human is a commanding acceptance, the inexpressible meaning of the Divine-human encounter assumes four interrelated expressions of which two are immediately contained within the commandment itself. First, there is a dimension of meaning in the very fact of being commanded as a human by the Divine: to be thus commanded is to be accepted as humanly responsible. And before long the undifferentiated commanding Presence will give utterance to many specific commandments, which particularize Divine acceptance and human responsibility according to the exigencies of a finite human existence on earth.

Secondly, if to be commanded by God is to be both obligated and enabled to obey, then meaning must be capable of human realization, and this meaning must be real even in the sight of Divinity. The fear induced in the finite human by the Infinite Divine Presence may seem to destroy any such presumption. Yet the acceptance of the human by the commanding Love makes possible, and indeed mandatory, human self-acceptance.

A third aspect of meaning comes into view because the Divine commandment initiates a relation of *mutuality* between God and man. The God of Judaism is no Deistic First Cause which, having caused the world, goes into perpetual retirement. Neither is He a Law-giver who, having given laws, leaves man to respond in human solitariness. Along with the commandment, handed over for human action, goes the promise of *Divine* action. And because Divine action makes itself contingent upon human action, a relationship of mutuality is established. God gives to man a *covenant*—that is, a contract; He binds Himself by its terms and becomes a partner.

The meaning of the Divine-human encounter, however, has yet a fourth expression; and if this had not gradually emerged, the Jewish faith could hardly have survived through the centuries. Because a pristine Divine Love accepted the human, a relation of mutuality between an Infinite Divinity and a finite humanity—something that would seem to be impossible—nevertheless became possible. Yet that relation remains destructible at finite hands; indeed, were it *simply* mutual, it would be destroyed by man almost the moment it was established. Even in earlier forms of Jewish faith God is long-suffering enough to put up with persistent human failures; and at length it becomes clear that the covenant can survive only if God's patience is absolute. The covenant, to be sure, *remains* mutual; and Divine action remains part of this mutuality, as a response to human needs. But Divine action also breaks through this limitation and maintains the covenant in *unilateral* love. The human race after Noah, and Israel at least since the time of Jeremiah, still can—and do—rebel against their respective covenants with God. But they can no longer destroy them. Sin still causes God to punish Israel; but no conceivable sin on Israel's part can cause Him to forsake her. Divine Love has made the covenant indestructible.

In Judaism, covenantal existence becomes a continuous, uninterrupted way of life. A Divine-human relation unstructured by commandment would alternate between times of inexpressible meaning and times of sheer waiting for such meaning. A relationship so structured by commandment, yet failing to encompass both Divine nearness and farness, could not extend its scope over the whole of human life. For if it were confined to times of Divine nearness, covenantal existence would be shattered into as many fragments as there are moments of Divine nearness, with empty spaces between them. If, on the other hand, it were confined to Divine farness, it would degenerate, on the Divine side, into an external law sanctioned by an absent God and, on the human side, into legalistic exercises practiced in His absence. But as understood and lived in Judaism, covenantal existence persists in times of Divine farness. The commandment is still present, as is the Divine promise, however obscured for the moment. The human power to perform the commandment, while impaired, is not destroyed; and he who cannot perform the commandment for the sake of God, as he is supposed to do, is bidden to perform it anyway—for performance which is not for His sake will lead to performance which *is* for His sake. Times of Divine nearness, then, do not light up themselves alone. Their meaning extends over all of life.

III

So much for the general characteristics of the Divine-human relationship according to Judaism. What humans partake of this relationship? Individuals or communities? And some individuals and communities only, or potentially the whole of the human race? It will become evident that in Judaism these are not mutually exclusive alternatives, and indeed, that those modern conceptions which would make them so—"individualism" versus "collectivism," and "particularism" versus "universalism"—are alien to the dynamic of the Jewish faith.

Consider, first, "universalism" and "particularism." Because the God of the Divine-human encounter is Infinite, each meeting discloses Him—potentially at least—as the One of every meeting. Because the man of this encounter is finite, and accepted in his finitude, each meeting singles him out—potentially at least—as a unique individual or a unique group. Mythological deities may remain "particularistic"—i.e., confined to limits of time and space: the Jewish God who smashes the idols breaks through such limits. The mystical conflux may dissolve the here-and-now into a "universalistic" eternity; the Jewish encounter with God accentuates the here-and-now in which it occurs. If He did not from the start transcend the here-and-now of the encounter, the Jewish God would fragment himself (in Buber's phrase) into "moment-gods" according to the moments of meeting; and if He did not in every encounter single out *this* individual, *this* people, in the here-and-now, He would accept not existing humans but only unreal abstractions. The Biblical God is indeed the God of all the nations; but there is no word for the abstraction "mankind" in the Hebrew scriptures.

To be singled out by the Divine is a crucial and persisting Jewish experience. The first commandment given to the first Jew—that Abraham leave his country—is addressed to him only; it does not call for a universal migration of peoples. The commandment to become a holy people unto God constitutes Israel as a unique people; it does not enunciate a universal principle. The Talmud teaches that God has made each man unique and speaks to him in his uniqueness, and this teaching is powerfully reaffirmed in modern Hasidism. Even today, Jewish existence cannot be understood without reference to such singling out. To be sure, some modern Jewish thinkers (Mordecai Kaplan, for example) have identified the "essence" of Judaism with universal moral and religious principles shared by all higher religions, but though they take great pains to connect this "universal" essence with the "particular" existence of the Jewish people, their efforts always end in failure.

Just as the human remains singled out even in the most "advanced" Jewish experience, so God transcends, even in the most "primitive" Jewish experience, the here-and-now in which such acts of singling-out occur. The significance of the commandment addressed to Abraham is realized only in future generations. The covenant between God and Israel has from the outset a scope which transcends Israel; in time it will encompass the whole of the human race.

"Universalism" and "particularism," then, are not only both present throughout Jewish religious experience; they are also internally united, and their union is manifest in *history*. History is not history unless each of the events that makes it up is unique; and it remains fragmented into many histories unless these unique events nevertheless constitute one "universal" whole. In Judaism, the events of history become one through the *direction* it assumes as a result of Divine incursions into it. The Jewish God is from the start a God of history; eventually He will become the Lord of *all* history.

A crucial dimension of meaning in Judaism is therefore historical. The Hebrew prophets do not only proclaim a universally applicable Divine Will; it is their inescapable agony to be men of their own day. Jeremiah demands passive submission to the enemy, well aware that armed resistance has been the Divine Will at other times. And when he is confronted by another would-be prophet offering the opposite counsel, he suffers—and the people suffer—because no resort to general principles can settle the issue between them. This issue may indeed be settled by the future. But by then it will be too late for an action which is needed now: so radically singled-out and singling-out can a prophetic message be, so wholly historical can a commandment be. And yet, though a man of his time, the prophet is not for his time alone. His moment is an epoch-making moment significant for all of history.

In addition to becoming historical in this way, the Divine commandment also establishes the historical meaning of human action. A Providence which in pursuit of its historical purpose reduced man to a will-less automaton would not be a Providence which governed history, but rather a blind Fate which destroyed it. The prophets do not predict an inescapable future. Their predictions—such as they are—are contingent upon human action. Human action, therefore, assumes a decisive historical meaning; and this action is no less epoch-making than the prophetic message which demands it. For it leaves an indelible mark on all future history.

This would, however, be impossible if history were composed of human action only, albeit responding to Divine command. Human action is finite: how can it give direction to history, or leave indelible marks upon it? The answer is that it can do so only if it is not left to itself, only if it works in persistent mutuality with a Divine action which responds to it. Thus, in Judaism, the relation of mutuality between the Divine and the human becomes manifest in history. Such early Jewish documents as the Book of Judges can see an exact correlation between Israel's obedience and national victories, and between Israel's defiance and national defeats: the victories are given by God and the defeats are sent by Him. And naïve though this view may seem, *some* degree of belief in such a correlation remains an element of all subsequent forms of the Jewish faith. For a history dependent for meaning on human action alone would lead to despair, while Divine incursions into history that were devoid of all reference to human action would deprive human action of meaning.

Later stages of Jewish faith, however, modify the naïve view of history reflected in the Book of Judges in three main respects. We have already noted how in Judaism Divine action, mutually related to the human and contingent upon it, is gradually seen to have a unilateral aspect as well. Such unilateral Divine action comes to be part of the Jewish understanding of history, and traces of it are already in the Book of Judges itself: behind the Divine punishment which is a reaction to man's sinfulness is a Love which seeks to produce repentance. This Love, to be sure, was not conceived as wholly unilateral so long as it was considered possible that sufficiently grave sins on Israel's part might cause God to abandon or destroy His covenant with her. But at least from Jeremiah on, Jewish faith rules this possibility out.

IN RABBINIC literature, the inextricable connection between Divine-human mutuality and Divine unilateralness becomes the object of explicit theological reflection. God is Judge, and God is Father; and unless He were both the world could not exist. God is Judge: love without judgment would destroy the distinction between the righteous and the wicked, and hence all human responsibility. God is Father: judgment without love would place on human responsibility a greater burden than it could bear.

The Book of Judges harmonizes with ease a Divine power encompassing all history with a human freedom to rebel against it. For its interest is confined to Israel, and it sees Divine power as responding to Israel's deeds. But later Biblical writings reflect the awareness that a Providence limited by human deeds would lose its providential character. Biblical thought is not philosophical thought, and therefore it does not confront the problem posed by the conflict between Divine omnipotence and human freedom.[4] Neither, however, does it fall into the dilemma of having to choose between the two. Nebukhadnezzar is the instrument of a Divine Providence which uses him to punish Israel. Yet he remains a free and responsible agent, and hence is punished for his sins.

The rabbis of the Talmud recognize the paradox involved here, but being no more philosophical than the Bible itself, they agree with the Bible in rejecting the dilemma. Human action limits Divine power, which is why men "strengthen" it when they obey the Divine will and "weaken" it when they disobey. But human action limits Divine power only "as it were": finite man cannot literally either weaken or strengthen the Infinite God. And yet human thought must remain content with such paradoxical symbolic statements. It cannot rise to a literal truth which is free of paradox; it can only hold to the double truth that "everything is foreseen, yet freedom of choice is given."

The implication is that history is wholly in Divine hands even while man has a share in making it; that, whereas righteousness makes man a partner in the realization of the Divine plan, sin, for all its reality and power, is unable to disrupt or destroy it.

There is still a third respect in which the fully developed Jewish understanding of history departs from the naïve view of the Book of Judges. In opposition to this view, Jeremiah complains that the way of the wicked prospers, and the Book of Job is wholly devoted to refuting the belief—persisting elsewhere, and in secular form even in modern times—that prosperity and good fortune are a proof of virtue, adversity and disaster a proof of vice. Such complaints might have been belittled either by the admonition to worry about virtue only and not its reward, or by the restriction of meaning in history to a spiritual dimension, exclusive of all worldly fortune, good or ill. But while Jewish thought does occasionally give voice to such an admonition, it rejects any suggestion that history is not, after all, in Divine hands; and as for the restriction of significant history to the domain of pure spirit, Judaism always and wholly repudiates it. The complaint of Jeremiah and Job, then, cannot be evaded; and here, the Jewish quest for meaning in history runs into certain limitations.

We have already come upon the outlines of two such limitations. First, if Divine omnipotence co-exists with human freedom; if Divine power is manifest in what yet remains the criminal act of a Nebukhadnezzar (or, for that matter, the righteous act of an Abraham or Moses): then meaning in history, even if and when disclosed, is disclosed only within the confines of finite understanding. And this falls radically short of the understanding of God. Secondly, meaning is not everywhere disclosed in history. Nebukhadnezzar is seen as serving a Divine purpose; but not every tyrant is a Nebukhadnezzar. And while a prophet proclaims the will of God to one generation, most generations are lacking in prophets.

In such times, however, men are not left alone with their own wisdom when engaged in historical action; nor are they forced to deny meaning to history where none is disclosed. For even when God is far, His commandment is still near; it is not merely on his own counsel that man falls back in fathoming the task of the present hour. And the events of the present, although *disclosing* no meaning, nevertheless *possess* meaning. For history remains in God's hands even when all is dark.

THIS distinction between meaning and disclosed meaning in history is crucial in Judaism and has been among the most vital factors in its survival. Without it the Jews might have identified meaning in history with what history discloses, and celebrated naked success: but how could they have done so and yet resisted Babylonians and Romans in the name of their faith? Or they might have abandoned history as a sphere of religious meaning: but how could they have done so and yet carried forward a religious existence inextricably bound up with history? Finally, they might have distinguished between a sacred history in the keeping of God and a secular history outside the Divine concern: but how could they have done so and remained true to fundamental Jewish realities? The pristine Divine-human meeting in Judaism accepts man in his totality; and the Divine commandment specifies itself socially, politically, and economically, as well as individually and spiritually. A meaning at once manifest in history and yet indifferent to poverty, war, and tyranny is unthinkable to the Jewish mind.

But the Jewish search for meaning in history is bounded by yet a third limitation, and this only gradually emerges. Not only is the *disclosure* of meaning in history fragmentary; the meaning *itself* is fragmentary. Past and present point not only to a finite future but to one which is absolute and all-consummating as well.

Not until an eschatological dimension, a messianic belief, comes into view is the Jewish understanding of meaning in history complete.

A Jeremiah sure of history, and ignorant only of a portion of its contents, would not contend with God but merely seek Divine enlightenment; a Job sure of history would begin where in fact he ends: with the incommensurability of the Divine dispensation with all things human. Both Jeremiah and Job, however, are forced to contend with God by the very nature of the primordial Jewish experience. Divine Love has singled out man so as to make him humanly responsible; is it not bound, then, to the consequences of its own action—to a Divine Justice not *wholly* incommensurate with responsible human action? Jews were thus forced to go beyond acceptance of an undisclosed meaning in history. They had to question meaning in history itself, in the light of historical realities. This questioning, to be sure, did not result in wholesale skepticism, or a despair of meaning in history. But it did result in the belief that meaning has remained incomplete in past history, and must remain so in any future that does not differ qualitatively from the past.

The question to be asked of Judaism, then, is not so much why the Messianic belief appeared on the scene as why it appeared so late. Is the prosperity of the wicked or the suffering of the righteous so rare a phenomenon, or one so difficult to perceive?

A partial answer may be that for early Biblical man the meaning of life, when that meaning remains incomplete, can find completion in the lives of others. If Abraham dies satisfied, it is because of a Divine promise extending to his descendants. If the Book of Judges perceives complete justice in history, it is at least to some extent because justice is due to the people only, not to the individual members of it. Early Biblical man takes no offense at a God who punishes the children for the sins of the fathers: and here lies one reason why for him a finite future can consummate the meaning of past and present.

But the God of Jeremiah and especially of Ezekiel will not tolerate the visitation of the sins of the fathers upon the children: for the God of Israel is God of each person as well. Once this becomes the explicit Jewish faith—after long being implicit—the contention of Jeremiah and Job becomes inescapable. Individuals *do* suffer unjustly, and their suffering cannot acquire meaning through historical events after they have died. Meaning in history, then, is fragmentary; and a merely historical future, no different in nature from the past, cannot complete it. Thus an eschatological future comes into view.

IV

We have already rejected the disjunction of "universalism" and "particularism" as alien to the dynamic and structure of the Jewish faith. We must now do the same with the disjunction of "collectivism" and "individualism." Jewish faith ends by repudiating any reduction of the individual to his communal or historical role, but this repudiation is implicit from the beginning. For the acceptance of man in the pristine Divine-human meeting would be incomplete if it did not encompass the individual in his own right as well as the community. There is Jewish authenticity in the rabbinic legend which makes the Sinaitic revelation address each individual Israelite.

Aspects of such "individualism" are present even where the emphasis is "collectivistic." In binding the community, the Mosaic code nevertheless recognizes the individual within the community, which is why its scope can also extend beyond the community, to strangers and slaves. This motif becomes still more radical in post-Biblical thought. In the view of the rabbis, the Divine spirit rests on all individuals according to their actions, whether they be Gentiles or Israelites, men or women, slaves or handmaidens; and the righteous among the Gentiles are priests of God.

The consequence of such "individualism" is that historical

change can hold no total sway over the commandments. Orthodox belief, of course, considers the Mosaic Law to be exempt from historical change in any case, but all Jewish belief takes this view concerning those laws which state what is morally due to individuals: the wrongness of theft or murder does not depend on historical circumstances. The distinction between the historical and trans-historical commandments becomes fully explicit—and inescapable even for Orthodox belief—in the prophets. Jeremiah proclaims submission to the enemy as the task of the hour when armed resistance has been the task of another hour. But it is unimaginable that he should adopt a similar position regarding what is owed to widows and orphans.

"Individualism" is as much present in Divine promise and its fulfillment as it is in the commandment. It is the individual who in the Psalms comes upon Divine salvation—both that which rewards human faithfulness and that which is the sheer gift of a gratuitous Love. Nor does this reflect an "individualistic" piety unrelated to, let alone at odds with, the "collectivistic." Not a few Psalms were written in and for public worship, and they retain an essential place in public Jewish worship today. Indeed, the Jewish liturgy is so structured as to unite its communal and individual aspects into an organic whole. The God addressed as God of Abraham, Isaac, and Jacob by the whole community is also addressed as *his* God by each individual member. And the Jewish calendar which includes Passover, celebrating the origin of the community of Israel, also includes the Day of Atonement, on which the individual stands before God in radical solitariness—in the midst of the congregation.

But just as history comes at length to point to an eschatological dimension, so does the life of the individual. Early Biblical man may immediately rejoice in a commandment wholly fulfilled or in a salvation suddenly made manifest. In due course Jewish faith comes to accept that the saving moment does not vanquish evil permanently, nor absolutely even while the moment lasts; and that no man is free of sin. To be sure, there is forgiveness wherever there is repentance, and a man ought to repent a day before his death. Yet repentance itself remains fragmentary, and even the most righteous of men—such as Abraham and Moses—do not die sinless. The Pharisaic insistence on life after death is in the Jewish spirit; and there is poetic if not literal truth in the rabbinic view that this belief is present in the Bible itself.

V

Since prophetic times Jewish faith has looked to a Messianic future. The goals of this future are no longer limited—to a united people, a promised land, a central Sanctuary. They are, rather, all-encompassing: all nations flow to Jerusalem; the Kingdom of God is forever established; and it extends over the whole earth.

This is a hope for history. And it arises from a decisive historical experience: the land was given as promised to Abraham, and the central Sanctuary established, but the covenant still has at best only a precarious existence. Time and again Israel has returned to God only to forsake Him once more. And in the end the wearisome cycle is broken by catastrophe and exile.

It was doubtless the original Jewish belief that the Divine commandment is capable of total human performance, and that the Jewish commitment to the covenant, once made, might have been kept with total fidelity. Under the impact of historical experience, however, the prophets were led to qualify this belief, and Judaism acquired a new dimension through the qualification.

Israel has broken the covenant; so long as she can, she will always break it *sometimes*. Man will always sin so long as he is able: for sin, though not original, is nevertheless universal. The covenant, then, remains threatened, and from without as well as from within. For the nations not only tempt Israel to idolatry but also endanger her very survival. History, in short, seems to have lost the direction it once had; and it cannot re-acquire direction from a future which does not differ qualitatively from present and past.

In the teeth of these perceptions, the prophets nevertheless re-affirm the ancient faith in the direction of history. Revelation has initiated meaning in history: it points to a Redemption which will complete that meaning. The revealed commandment demands human performance; a Messianic Redemption will place the commandment in man's inward parts. Man has been able to obey the Divine Will ever since the Divine commandment accepted him in his humanity; in the Messianic future he will be neither willing nor able to disobey it. For all Nature will have been cured of its anti-Divine potential: the wolf will lie down with the lamb. And since Redemption will extend to all nations, all history will be embraced in total consummation: the Kingdom of God on earth will be complete.

For such a future, incommensurate as it is with human historical action, men must wait, radically uncertain of the time of its arrival. Throughout Jewish history, there seemed to be moments of human righteousness ripe for Redemption in the sight of Divine Justice, and long periods of human suffering ripe for it in the sight of Divine Compassion. But even popular legend came to picture the Messiah as bound in fetters—anxious to come and yet held back by a God who alone knows the secret of the right time. And the rabbis prohibited all attempts to calculate the end.

And yet men must work for the Messianic end even as they wait for it. A Messianic future simply incommensurate with all historical human action would retroactively destroy the historical meaning which it was intended to consummate; yet if Jewish faith has come to expect this future at all, it is precisely because meaning, however fragmentary, is nevertheless actual in pre-Messianic history. Hence men must, here and now, "prepare the world for the Kingdom of God"; and it is to this goal that Jewish obedience to the commandments is in due course directed. And so aware does

Jewish faith become of the weight of its Messianic obligation as to imagine that a single day of wholehearted obedience would cause the Messiah's immediate arrival.

But the incommensurability of human action with its Messianic goal remains. When, for one thing, is the individual or community capable of even a single day's total faithfulness? How, for another, would the righteousness of some cause all sinners (tyrannical rulers, for example) to repent? The Messianic future, then, is at once connected with human action in pre-Messianic history and yet incommensurate with it. The Messiah will arrive when the world has become good enough to make his coming possible; or evil enough to make it necessary. Men must act as though all depended on them; and wait and pray as though all depended on God.

Because the Messianic end is tied to present history, the prophetic expectation can even now imagine it; because it remains incommensurate with all pre-Messianic history, the prophetic imagination cannot make it literally intelligible. Thus, the Messianic peace is no unearthly mystery but one in which men beat their swords into plowshares. And the hunger stilled is not of the soul alone, but of the body as well. Yet such a peace and prosperity transcend all literal comprehension. What transfiguration will make the wolf lie down with the lamb—or men incapable of oppressing one another? Jewish thought moves between a "left-wing" view which sees the Messianic world as rid of tyrants but otherwise unchanged, and a "right-wing" view which sees an apocalyptic transfiguration. But the mainstream of Jewish thought flows between these extremes.

THE Messianic future, while the earliest, is not the only eschatological expectation in Judaism. Beside and beyond it emerges the hope for a "world-to-come"—a hope which, although post-Biblical in origin, was always implicit in the Jewish belief that God gives meaning to individual lives wholly and in their own right. Whereas the Messianic future redeems an incomplete history, the world-to-come redeems the incomplete individual lives which exist in history.

Classical Jewish thought never achieves clarity as to the relation between these two expectations, but all attempts to assimilate one to the other are consistently rejected. Despite the absence of the belief in life after death from the Hebrew Bible, Orthodox post-Biblical theology quite deliberately embraces it. For the Divine commandment has accepted the individual and therefore any Redemption would remain incomplete—as the Messianic end by itself does—if it did not give completion to the individual. But no more can the Messianic goal of a redeemed future be identified with an Eternity beyond all time. A primordial Divine commanding Love has endowed history with meaning, in that it calls for meaningful human action. The great Divine-human drama of history thus initiated cannot be retroactively destroyed by an end which makes this world merely a place in which to prepare for another, and in itself meaningless. Redemption must consummate both the history in which men work and wait, and the lives of the individuals who work and wait in it.

The two aspects of the eschatological expectation, then, must remain mutually irreducible, even despite the conscious recognition that Eternity must surely supersede all future history. This can be so because the world-to-come remains radically unintelligible. The rabbinic sources confine themselves to saying that it will redeem the whole man whom the Divine commandment has accepted from the beginning—not an immortal soul only, but a resurrected psychosomatic totality. They are well aware that this is past all understanding, and they view silence on the subject as a necessity imposed by the silence of the Bible itself. "Rabbi Yohanan said: 'Every prophet prophesied only for the days of the Messiah; but as for the world-to-come, no eye has seen what God has prepared for those who wait for Him.' "[5]

17

A Jew Looks at Christianity and Secularist Liberalism

I

Ever since the Age of Enlightenment, Jews have had a special sense of kinship with secularist liberalism. For whereas modern Christians have often acted, and sometimes still act, as if full human rights should remain reserved for Christians, secularist liberals have consistently been in the forefront of fighters for the extension of full human rights to all men—and hence to Jews. Is it to be wondered at that even religious Jews opposed to their secularism should be drawn to their liberalism? What self-respecting modern man can accept second-class citizenship?

At the same time, even secularist-minded Jews, provided they remain Jews, find it difficult to identify themselves wholly with secularist liberalism. Throughout the ages, the choice to remain Israel has been based on a commitment to the God of Israel; and even today a Jew cannot persist in his Jewishness without hanging on to some remnants at least of his religious past. The God of Israel, however, is rejected by the secularist liberal. Moreover, He is the God shared by Jew and Christian. In the modern West, therefore, the Jew has existed and still exists between secularist

Reprinted by permission of McClelland and Stewart Ltd. from *The Restless Church,* ed. William Kilbourn (Toronto, 1966), pp. 86-99. Published in the USA by J. B. Lippincott Company.

liberalism and Christianity. And the conflict which has existed and still exists *between* these two ways of belief and life has contributed to a secularist-religious conflict *within* Jewish existence.

For these reasons, the Church's initiation of a dialogue with a secularist liberal is of profound concern to a Jew; and if invited to have a share in it, he does well to speak from the midst of that situation into which the history of Christian-secularist conflicts has placed him. He must try to convert the insights born of his situation into a testimony—made to both Christian and secularist liberal—to Him whom he knows as the living God.

II

The modern Church, Pierre Berton charges,[1] stands condemned in the light of what is good in the modern world. But what is the good that he accepts and uses as overall criterion? In a Hegelian formulation, the good is what makes modern man capable of being at home in his world; whereas pre-modern men were forced to look beyond their world. In the pre-modern world, the infinite value of the human person was at best the belief of a few religious groups and confined, moreover, to a passive waiting for the fulfilment of other-worldly hopes. In the modern world, it is becoming a universal rational ideal, capable of this-worldly realization. Social evils such as poverty, tyranny, the oppression of nation by nation or race by race, as well as natural evils such as starvation and want—all these might not be eliminated by modern man any more than by pre-modern man. But for modern man their elimination has become a rationally necessary ideal. He will, in fact, reduce, if not eliminate, these evils as human self-confidence combines with human social conscience to use the instruments made available by modern science. Such, in brief, is the creed of secularist liberalism.

We may as well accept from the outset the general accuracy

of Pierre Berton's charge that the modern Church has sometimes opposed and at other times only belatedly supported liberal drives, and that it has rarely, if ever, spearheaded them. To quarrel with the details (and much quarrelling could be done, some in defence of the honour of Christian saints and martyrs) would only obscure a far more important question—*Why has the modern Church on the whole been lukewarm, indifferent or downright hostile to liberal drives when it might well have wholeheartedly embraced or even spearheaded them?* Or to put the same question in a still more radical and hence still more significant way: *why has the liberalism of the modern age been allowed to be shot through with a thorough-going secularist bias, when it might conceivably have been given a religious and Christian impetus?* This question is vital for the appraisal of the future of Christianity in the modern world. And it is of vital concern for the Jew as well. For it has a direct relation to the secularist-religious conflict within Jewish existence. Moreover, the secularism which has proved to be so profound a modern challenge to Christianity is no less a challenge to Judaism.

Why has modern Christianity stood over against liberalism, while Jewish existence has freely exposed itself to it, even at the price of internal conflict? For the fact of Jewish self-exposure is beyond doubt. Jews have contributed their Freuds and Einsteins far out of proportion to their numbers. They have vigorously supported liberal causes of every kind. Even when orthodox loyalty makes them hostile to one facet of the secularist-liberal creed, they are still committed to many others.

Only absurd racists would account for this Jewish behaviour in terms of some native Jewish genius for liberalism. The simple truth is that the Jew was originally made a modern liberal by his pariah status in pre-modern Christian society. If he remained a liberal when he was a pariah no more, it was because he could not forget what it was like to be a pariah—and that there still are pariahs.

When the Jew first emerged from behind Ghetto walls the liberal ideal seemed to promise everything and threaten nothing. It threatened nothing, for all it would destroy were Ghetto walls and mediaeval oppression. It promised everything, for, to a people which had been denied liberty and equality and fraternity throughout Christendom for many centuries, the realization of these ideals was indeed bound to seem everything, or nearly everything. If, to begin with, Jews trusted the liberal promise naively it was because, thrust suddenly from mediaeval darkness into the modern world, they were dazzled by its light. Even today, however, when the darkness in the modern world has often come close to extinguishing the light, Jewish loyalty to liberal ideals remains. For the memory of past Jewish disabilities (and they are by no means all past) remains alive; and so does Jewish sympathy, strengthened by this memory, with the fate of those as yet disabled.

How, in the light of his own liberal commitments, must a Jew look on that Christian hostility and lukewarmness toward liberalism of which *The Comfortable Pew* offers such depressing evidence? If self-critical enough not to attribute Jewish liberalism to some mythical innate Jewish virtue, he will be fair enough not to attribute Christian anti-liberalism to some equally mythical Christian vice. If the one is bound up with the pre-modern experience of impotence, is not the other bound up with a pre-modern experience of power and privileged status?

The evidence, one fears, is incontrovertible. On behalf of a human equality, transcending differences not only of race, nationality, and sex but of creed as well, modern liberalism has demanded a state and society essentially secular; and Christians such as Kierkegaard have supported that demand in the name of Christianity. Yet few Christian churches have ever been quick or happy to surrender pre-modern positions close to the seats of established power, or cease to behave as though the state must somehow remain Christian, with non-Christians reduced to second-class citizenship. In the Ontario of 1965, few churches still seem much concerned with the effect on non-Christian children of Christian religious education in the public schools. And in the Canada of 1965 it still takes a fight for atheist immigrants to be granted citizenship. Indeed, such are the temptations of numbers and power that until today the Christian establishment sometimes treats even some Christians as more equal than others, and—what is more—more equal than others in the sight of God. Or so one must judge in the case of churches which are only for the rich or for whites.[2]

Of such behaviour Jews have frequently been the especially singled-out victims. A Jew must therefore testify that throughout the long struggle for Jewish human rights the secularist liberal has usually fought alongside the Jew, while the established Christian forces were—on the whole, but with very notable exceptions—ranged against him. No doubt much stood and still stands between the Christian as Christian and the Jew as Jew. Even so, might not Christian churches, professing as they do one Father of mankind, have matched secularist liberals (who do not profess Him) in recognizing the Jew, if as nothing else, as a full member of mankind? Yet until today even Jewish minds filled with love for the Christian faith cannot but associate two meanings with the term "Christian": commitment to a God who is Love and "Jews not wanted." Is it any wonder that modern Jews have been drawn to secularism when it alone seemed to stand for liberalism? One of the major charges a religious Jew must make against modern Christendom is that it has tempted Jews to throw in their lot with secularism, thereby turning their back on Him who is the God of both Israel and the Church.

Nor is this all. A religious Jew would be profoundly relieved had he to testify only against non-Christian forces abusing Christianity for their own purposes. (Is a "Christian" country club interested in the Christianity of its members? Or only in the exclusion of Jews from membership?) Such, however, is not the case. It is his bitter but ineluctable duty to testify against what have been official Christian teachings for many centuries, and to report clearly that even today—twenty years after Auschwitz!—few Christians have radically re-examined or turned against these teachings. The horror of Auschwitz was assuredly not a Christian but an anti-Christian responsibility. Yet would this horror have happened except for centuries of Christian teaching concerning Jewish responsibility for the crucifixion? And can one report even now that Christian self-examination has radically confronted this question with all its vast implications? Here is the view of Roy Eckhardt, a Methodist clergyman, on one such re-examination:

> In vain does one search the draft of Vatican II for even the slightest sign of Christian contrition, for even a single word of recognition that the church of Jesus Christ has been a knowing and willing participant in the centuries-long demonry of anti-semitism. If by some trick of time this schema could have been promulgated in the thirteenth century, the ideology in it would have been redeemed a little. The powerful are sometimes brought to justice to the powerless. But in the present instance, while the voices are voices which foster understanding, the hands are hands which have clasped death: the death of Christendom, the "death of God" and the death of six million Jews. How admirable of us now to exonerate the Jewish people for all their reputed transgressions! Could there be a more damning judgment upon the church of our century than this one—that not until the day after Auschwitz did Christians see fit to fabricate a correction of the record?[3]

Nor are such criticisms of church pronouncements confined to Roman Catholicism. An Episcopalian scholar, Frederick C. Grant, assails a statement adopted by his own Protestant Episcopal House of Bishops in October 1964 (exonerating all except "some" Jews), among other reasons because, while speaking of the guilt of all men for the death of Christ, it makes no reference to any need for the church itself to repent for Christian maltreatment of Jews. "If I were a Jew," Grant writes, "I would tear up the resolution and stamp on it."[4] How many Christian theologians would even today state flatly: "A theology which consents to verbalize respecting 'Jewish responsibility for the crucifixion'—*and it does not matter which side it takes*—is not theology at all, or, if that word must be used, it is a devilish theology?" [italics ours].[5]

But to pursue that issue further would be to turn this Jewish contribution to a Christian-secularist dialogue into a contribution to a Christian-Jewish dialogue. Our main issue in this section has been Christian intolerance of the Jew, not as Jew, but as a representative of non-Christian humanity. And this section must end with a question concerning the future—a question of common Jewish-Christian concern. The present-day world is no longer white and Christian, but multi-racial and multi-religious. What will happen if secularist liberalism alone espouses clearly and without hedging the cause of man's common humanity? Unless the Church passionately embraces the liberal ideal, who will witness to this world—a world much too vast for the tiny and scattered community of Israel alone, rent as it is by its own religious-secularist conflict—who will bear witness of Him who is the living God of both Jew and Christian?

III

But what if the past Christian fear of liberal drives has been a justified fear? What if the liberal ideal threatened, not merely Christian or pseudo-Christian vested interests, but rather the very substance of the Christian faith? As science advances, must faith necessarily recede, and as modern man becomes ever more at home in this world, must God become ever more remote from it? Must a liberalism which increases human freedom in the world be a secularism which makes him self-sufficient in it—and God superfluous? We here pass beyond what has thus far separated Jews from Christians to what unites them. For the challenge posed by secularism is posed to both.

The questions we ask are not new questions. Throughout the nineteenth century secularism assumed a militant anti-religious posture, and religion, whether militant itself in the form of fundamentalism or appeasement-minded in the form of modernism, was on the defensive. Far from being new, our questions may well seem by now wholly outmoded. For in twentieth-century North America, militancy and warfare have given way to mutual tolerance and dialogue. Yet in a true dialogue one must closely inspect what is offered by the partner. And to judge by what *The Comfortable Pew* offers to Christianity, the old warfare may well be preferable to the new tolerance.

Can a Christian believer accept Berton's "reverent agnosticism"? What would he then have that non-believers lack? Surely there is no Christian monopoly on the belief that "truth is better than a lie, honesty better than a deceit, love and mercy better than hate and mistrust." True, non-Christians would not accept these "general principles" on the authority of the "founder" of Christianity. But this, far from making the Christian superior to the secularist liberal, might actually make him inferior. For the secularist liberal might claim, as Kant long ago did, that he can dispense with all external authorities, because the general principles of morality dwell in his heart. Clearly, a "reverent agnosticism" prepared to say to *all* questions "because of the limitations of my mind and the nature of the subject, I cannot know the final answer" is poles apart from a faith which moves mountains. And this alone would surely be enough to make Berton's peace-offer religiously unacceptable.

Matters are made worse because Berton himself does not, after all, leave *all* questions open. The questions not open are those to which secularist liberalism has the answer. And the final upshot is that Berton's "new-look-Christianity" would reduce itself to a willing tool in the pursuit of the goals of secularist liberalism. But can there be peace at such a price? Can any Christian reduce his faith to a mere cure for human weakness, and his God to a mere instrument of human purposes however worth while?

Is this the best shape in which Christianity can emerge from radical self-exposure to the modern world? Rather than accept the word of a secularist, one must surely first look at actual Christian self-exposures. And one must state bluntly that *The Comfortable Pew* has not looked closely, thereby giving a scandalously one-sided picture of Christian realities. The book dwells rightly on the conservatism of Christian establishments. It says little of way-out Christian radicals, anti-Nazi Christian resistance fighters, or the critical thought which has existed in the Church for well over a century. To charge that such stirrings have had much too limited an effect on established Christian institutions or the general Christian consciousness would have been one thing. Virtually to ignore them is quite another.

It must be admitted that most nineteenth-century Christian self-exposures to liberal and critical ideas were half-hearted, apologetic, and lacking in complete integrity; and for this reason alone, perhaps, foredoomed to ineffectiveness. Thus while nineteenth-century fundamentalists would attack the theory of evolution, their modernist contemporaries would accept it—and promptly find a religious meaning in it! Or (to give another example) Protestant biblical scholars would subject the Old Testament to a purportedly objective criticism, yet make its inferiority to the New Testament a foregone conclusion—a practice deserving the remark that "the higher criticism is the higher anti-semitism."

But present-day self-exposure to the challenge of liberalism and criticism in significant quarters of the Church cannot be said to suffer from such shortcomings. Here "demythologizing" is the word of the hour, and it is apparently carried on without set limits. Secular man with his concerns is the man of the hour; it is by his standards that Christian faith is to measure its relevance. And among the theological heroes are Marx and Nietzsche. Nor are these stirrings only theoretical or academic; witness the sit-ins in Mississippi and Alabama, and the sales of *Honest to God* or, for that matter, of *The Comfortable Pew*. Never in history has Christian self-exposure to the secular world and all its works been so radical, honest, and fearless of consequence.

Indeed, if self-exposure to the modern world were all that mattered, one would have to be wholly satisfied with the quality if not the quantity of these stirrings. But if the *Christian* quality of this self-exposure matters as well, one must have a sense of uneasiness. This Christian self-exposure is much needed and much delayed, hence impatient and turbulent. Could it be that it does not always know what it is doing? Is there no danger that the present "religionless Christians" will reject, along with the pseudo-gods whom Marx and Nietzsche destroyed, the true God whom these heroes of theirs defied? Demythologizing is a necessity, and a God "up there" is an outdated metaphor. But may a Christian say the same of a God "out there"—pictured spatially outside man because other-than-human?[6] It is more than four decades since Karl Barth and Martin Buber first pointed out the vast difference between a radically open Christian or Jewish encounter with the world, and surrender to the world, a surrender made wholesale because presupposing the world's standards. One sometimes feels today that their lesson must be stated and thought through all over again.

Coming from a Jew, this warning may seem to have a strange source. To the Christian it must often seem that Jewish interest in Christianity is confined to the growth of liberal attitudes in it; and that if these attitudes foster a secularism that undermines the Christian faith Jews are not much worried. Yet, we have advisedly said earlier that Jews have existed between secularist liberalism and Christianity since the rise of the modern age; and we must now add that events in this century have done much to produce conscious Jewish awareness of this condition.

Religious Jews, at any rate, might have felt some uneasiness with secularist liberalism in the very period, immediately following the French revolution, which was instrumental in proclaiming their emancipation. The revolution, in a famous phrase, would "grant to the Jew as man everything, and to the Jew as Jew nothing." But who was here doing the granting and denying? Sovereign man. And what sacrifice did he demand of the Jew? Part of what had been his relation to God. For two good reasons, however, little uneasiness was felt at the time. First, man, though sovereign, was not absolute sovereign; the domain of private conscience remained untouched, and the Jew, bidden to become a man abroad, was permitted to remain a Jew at home. Secondly, the man who was sovereign was Universal Man—the core of the secularist liberal creed even today; and who could not give some considerable loyalty to Universal Man?[7]

But there soon began in continental Europe two ominous and interrelated developments. Universal Man became a particular man—the man of modern nationalism. And this man had religious, or rather pseudo-religious, pretensions. His voice (especially, but not exclusively, in Germany) became ever more strident, and the realm reserved for private conscience ever more precarious. In the end, Nazism made the national state total, destroyed the realm of private conscience, demanded absolute conformity, and murdered Jews.

Such has been the contemporary Jew's experience with a secularism become deified, all-encompassing, demonic and mad. A Jew can hardly bear to transform this experience into testimony. For it is a tragedy unequalled in all of Israel's tear-stained history; and, having been singled out as no other group of men, he must fear that few non-Jews will understand his testimony. Yet out of the midst of tragedy, must he not warn today's Christian against surrender, however well-intentioned, to *any* secularism, however far removed from Nazism? Would not such Christian surrender be an invitation to secularism to appropriate the vacated religious sphere, thus becoming what Jews and Christians have always known as idolatry?

It would of course be absurd to hold all secularism responsible for Nazi madness—as absurd as to try to inspire a "return to religion" by issuing dire warnings of the danger of its recurrence. Secularist liberals are foes of Nazism. And Nazi "paganism" is not cause for Christian self-congratulation but much rather for such agonized self-appraisals as *The Deputy*.

Even so, the Nazi experience (and not it alone) forces Jewish and Christian believers to raise one fundamental question. The world which demands their involvement is complex. Only rarely, as with racial justice, is the stand required straightforward. On most issues they cannot easily be sure of what is morally required, or protect themselves against giving unwitting support to all sorts of dubious forces. One special question above all must be asked: *What is the firm ground of faith on which they may stand as they try to meet the demands of the world?* What may they *bring* to the world, lest self-exposure end up with total surrender?

There is no easy answer. Still, Christian behaviour under the Nazi trial furnishes one invaluable lesson. Throughout the nineteenth century, modernist Christian thought had been in search of easy adjustments. What if criticism did reduce the word of God to that of man! Was not the human word the product of creative culture, hence itself divine? Thus a process of Christian surrender began, the more thorough when the deified human word was nationalist or fascist. Much German Protestantism had been "German-Christian" long before the advent of Nazism. And when the word of Hitler became the word of God it offered little or no resistance.

Contrast Hitler's German-Christian church with the German Confessional church. Its subsequent leaders—notably Karl Barth —had been forced to question modernist compromises during the first war, when clergymen of every warring nation had claimed the Christian God on behalf of their national causes. This was worship, not of a God immanent in culture, but of a deified culture against God. And it demanded—after demythologizing had done all its necessary work—the reaffirmation of the *distinction* between the word of God and the word of man. It demanded that man, rather than idolize his human concerns, stand before Him who is the Judge of states and cultures—and of churches and liberal ideals. When the Nazi trial occurred, it found few Christians prepared. But the few prepared were prepared well. They were not tempted to deify the voice of either their nation or its leader. Indeed, they knew that, precisely because the voice of this leader made claims to divinity, it was the voice of the Antichrist.

Such has been the ground on which some contemporary Christians have stood, in the very midst of a multitude eager to mount swastikas on the spires of Christian churches. But is the ground a firm ground? Can the modern believer—Jew or Christian—*bring* the word of God *to* the modern world, even as he exposes himself to it freely and without reservation?

IV

Here it is at long last time to bear direct witness to Him who has been the God of Israel for more than three millenia, and the God of the Christian church since its inception. *He is the One who is infinite, yet relates Himself to finite man; who in His power does not need man, yet in His love chooses to need him; who in His self-sufficiency does not require the world yet wishes to require it—and bids man do His will in it.*

Such a God does not require demythologizing. He already *is* demythologized, and has been so ever since He first revealed Himself in an infinity destructive of all finite idols. (Only the images man forms of Him require demythologizing, but even these are already *recognized* as being mere images.) Nor does a man whom such a God has singled out have to be turned to the world; he already *is* turned to the world, by a God who bids him work in it. Such a man, moreover, does not need to learn of human freedom; he is already given such knowledge by an infinite God who has accepted him in his finite humanity and made man ruler over the earth. Nor, finally, must such a man still rise above a parochialism which would accept the humanity of one group of men but deny that of others. He is already raised above it, by a God who reveals Himself as the God of all men, even as He is present to one group of men.

Such, in brief, is the testimony. And it must be made first to the secularist liberal, so as to embrace his liberalism and repudiate his secularism. The infinite value of the human person, always part of both Jewish and Christian faith, must now by faith be accepted as a rational ideal, if by "rational" and "ideal" is meant a goal demanding secular realization—by and on behalf of all men. And in accepting this demand, modern Jew and Christian must descend into this secular world, from what has often been, and sometimes still is, a remote Heaven. Yet in this very descent they must refuse to grant that God is absent from this world, or that, reduced to a finite presence in a finite world, He is Himself finite.

In this refusal, they must confront the secularist liberal with a direct challenge. Like Jew and Christian, he would assert the infinite value of the human person. But how can finite man possess such a value when he is cut off from the infinite God? And how can the secularist liberal defend it against anti-liberal secularists who threaten it? On one side secularism would reduce all human value to mere finiteness, thus making all human persons mere means to supposedly higher ends. And on another it would raise to pseudo-infinity some finite values—true values such as talent or accomplishment or false values such as colour of skin—thus making some men the slaves of others. Can the secularist liberal resist such anti-liberal, secularist pressures? And if he can and does, could it be because of a genuine, albeit hidden, commitment to Him who is God of Israel and the Church? Might it conceivably be the case that, if the modern secularist liberal ever did become a secularist, it was in the end only because of the inveterate anti-liberalism of the established religious forces?

At this point, what may begin as a Jewish or Christian testimony against the secularist liberal must inexorably turn into, and culminate in, Jewish and Christian self-criticism. How could either believer ever have been indifferent, lukewarm, or hostile to the liberal ideal—and this in the name of their faith!—when that ideal is the most authentic modern secular expression of their faith? How could they ever have feared the free scientific exploration of the world when, long freed of idolatrous worship of the world, they should have been the freest of all scientific explorers? Why afraid of technology, when they were the first to believe that the earth is handed over to human rule? Above all else, how could any Jew or Christian who ever believed in one Father of all men have failed to rally to the modern struggle on behalf of man's common humanity, or have sabotaged secularists who led this struggle?

The answer to all these questions is surely not faith, but lack of faith; not confidence in a God present in the modern, no less than in the pre-modern, world, but rather the fear that this God, present no longer, must become in the modern world a pious but lifeless memory. Mixed with the fear of His absence, is there a fear of His presence? The fear that God might be present to judge Church and Synagogue in their unrepentant failure to be open to both Word and world—open to the word which is "like a fire . . . a hammer that breaketh the rock in pieces" (Jer. 23:29), open to the world into which they are commissioned to "bring good tidings to the poor . . . to bind up the brokenhearted, to proclaim liberty to the captives and the opening of the prisons to them that are bound"? (Isa. 61:1, quoted Luke 4:18-19). One cannot doubt that this unbelief and fear is a cause—if not *the* cause—of the tragic modern split between those who espouse the cause of men but reject the God who first espoused it, and those who, seeking to espouse God's cause, are in flight from the modern world and thus from real men.

Is the hour too late for the healing of this split? Not if the ancient promise is true, the promise which was given through the mouth of Joshua: "Have not I commanded thee? Be strong and of a good courage; be not afraid, neither be thou dismayed; for the Lord thy God is with thee whithersoever thou goest." (Josh. 1:9.)

18

On the Self-Exposure of Faith to the Modern-Secular World:

Philosophical Reflections in the Light of Jewish Experience

I A Contemporary Reversal of Traditional Fronts

Ever since the Age of Enlightenment there has been a tension between the traditional religions of the West—Judaism and Christianity—and the secular world then beginning to emerge: its science, technology, economics, politics, and, in general, its attitude toward life. And since the modern-secular world would not go away and could not be wished away, its effect on orthodox belief was one of crisis—whether orthodox belief declared itself under total siege, ventured the odd sortie, or even undertook a wholesale assault on the alien territory and in so doing became itself transformed. By now, this crisis has existed for so long that it has become a permanent condition of religious belief in the modern world; and most of the recent talk about a brand-new religious crisis in our own age merely reflects the permeation of the old crisis into nearly all parts of modern society. Among the factors

Reprinted by permission of the editor from *Daedalus* (Winter 1967), pp. 193-219.

responsible for this recent development are the fast pace of modern technology, the rapid growth of the secular city, and two world wars fought in one generation.

A new crisis, or at any rate a new dimension of the old crisis, has nevertheless made its appearance in the present generation. This is indicated by a remarkable current reversal of traditional fronts among those professionally competent to consider the estate of religion. Believers now exalt secular "relevance" and "celebrate" secular culture at the precise time when some former protagonists of secular culture look beyond it or even despair of it.[1] Sociologists occupationally geared to the here-and-now take the long view of secularism and the religious crisis,[2] while theologians (whom one would expect to take the long view) see the most startling, not to say apocalyptic, upheavals in the mid-twentieth century.[3] Christians, traditionally far more suspicious than Jews of the secular world and all its works, now seek total self-exposure to it, whereas Jews, long dwellers in the secular city and in love with secularist-liberal ideas ever since these had been instrumental in securing their emancipation, now warn Christians lest too uncritical a self-exposure to the secular world issue in total surrender.[4] Most startling of all, at the precise time when some agnostics have become cautiously open to traditional religious claims, they are told by some Christian theologians that, in the mid-twentieth century, "God is dead."[5] When has such a battle cry ever issued not from the lips of a self-declared "anti-Christ" such as Nietzsche, but from those espousing, and insisting on continuing to espouse, the Christian gospel?

This essay seeks to bring philosophical reflection to bear upon the present reversal of traditional fronts; yet, written in the perspective of Judaism and Jewish experience, it is essentially within rather than above the battle. In a case such as the present, partisanship is inevitable; a phenomenon such as "the present crisis of religion" eludes, in the end, any wholly objective appraisal. A statistician can measure church or synagogue attendance; he cannot measure the depth of a religious commitment. A psychologist can uncover the neurotic etiology of spurious religion, but that of all religion only on the prior dogmatic assumption that it is all spurious. A sociologist can correlate religious behavior with social forms, but can see it limited by the "laws" of these forms only after having denied the freedom of both God and man. Philosophy, like the social sciences, has limits in this area that cannot be transcended. Philosophers seek universal conceptual clarification, including that of religious concepts. They may possibly even venture beyond the logical and linguistic forms of religious belief into its substance, and seek to decide what can and cannot be believed. They cannot, in any case, *qua* philosophers, descend from the realm of the universal into that of the particular in order to decide what tenable beliefs are, in a given situation, live options. Such a decision can be made not by the philosopher who rises above the situation but only by the man who lives in it. And this is a particular man whose experience is partial and fragmented.

Ever since the Jew became modern, he has existed, as it were, between Christianity and secularist liberalism. If a believer, he has shared with Christianity the Biblical God; and if not, at least a regard for a religious tradition to which he owes his survival. With secularist liberalism he has shared the ideals that have produced democracy and his own emancipation; so far as these are concerned, even orthodox Jews are secularist liberals. The conflict that came to exist *between* these two forms of modern belief and life has contributed to a religious-secularist conflict *within* Jewish existence. The one conflict still exists, and so does the other. In any contemporary reversal of traditional fronts, the Jew is obviously not an impartial bystander but rather a participant; his stance, whatever its nature, is informed by his Jewish situation.[6]

This first experience has been joined, if not overshadowed and dwarfed, by another in this generation. The one experience the Jew has lived with and assimilated for nearly two centuries; the other is, as yet, wholly unassimilable. The events that are associated with the dread name of Auschwitz still pass human comprehension. But they have shaken Jewish existence to the core, even when they are uncomprehended. They call everything into question: for the believing Jew, for the unbelieving Jew, for the Jew who is neither believer nor unbeliever but merely asks unanswered or unanswerable questions. Only one thing is as yet clear. The Jew may not authentically think about religion, or its modern crisis, or the goods and ills of the modern-secular world as though Auschwitz had not happened.

11 On Dietrich Bonhoeffer's Christian Confrontation of a "World-Come-of-Age"

The present reversal of traditional fronts in Protestantism may be said to originate with Dietrich Bonhoeffer's *Letters and Papers from Prison*,[7] written in a Nazi jail and concentration camp in 1943-44 prior to his execution. This is an oversimplification historically, but not poetically. These documents were written in a country which, once the heart of Western Christendom, was then in the grip of demonic, anti-Christian powers; and by a member of a church which, alone among German churches, clearly opposed these powers, in the name not of modern humanism but rather of the ancient gospel, brought by neo-orthodox theology to new life. The man who wrote these documents did not only die a martyr; he suffered this death because he had given his Christian witness a political expression by participating in a plot on Hitler's life. No more dramatic example can be found in this century of what has since come to be the basic issue at stake in the current reversal of traditional fronts: *the radical religious—in this case, Christian—self-exposure to the modern-secular world and all its works.* The example is all the more compelling because it occurred in a country in which Christianity, since Luther, has been prone to cut off the "inner" world reserved for Christian conscience from the "outer" world, handed over to Machiavellian princes and autocrats.

No less dramatic than the occasion and the author of the *Letters and Papers from Prison* are those of its passages—terse, radical, though, as will be seen, in the end profoundly problematical—which were destined to be the most influential. The confrontation between Christianity and the modern-secular world demanded in these passages is indeed radical. The modern-secular world is taken as it takes itself, and as such confronted; and what it is confronted with is not weak, diluted apologetics, but rather the pristine Christian gospel.

For the present purpose, Bonhoeffer's crucial passages may be summed up in four basic affirmations. First, the modern-secular world has "come of age." Its science, politics, morality, even its philosophy and religion stand in no need of God as a "working hypothesis," in terms of which they must be explained.

Secondly, the "autonomy" of the modern-secular world rules out any honest Christian recourse to "the so-called ultimate questions—death, guilt—on which only 'God' can furnish an answer." Thus is rejected any Christian use of "the existentialist philosopher and the psychotherapist" who "make it their object first of all to drive man to inward despair, and then it is all theirs." For "whom [do such efforts] . . . touch? A small number of intellectuals, of degenerates. . . . The ordinary man who spends his everyday life at work, and with his family . . . is not affected. . . ." Modern-secular man exists "*etsi Deus non daretur.*"

Yet, thirdly, while even the Christian ought to live in this godless world, he lives in it "before God." God is no longer needed as a crutch. Everywhere he is confronted by faith and love.

Fourthly and finally, to confront God in faith is to find him in the midst of life, not merely at such of its margins as guilt and death. And to speak of him to secular man is not to "speak ill of . . . his worldliness" but to "confront him with God at his strongest" rather than at his weakest point. Far from letting "this world be written off prematurely," the Biblical God—in the New as well as in the Old Testament—focuses his primary concern not on other-worldly salvation, but on this-worldly life.[8]

Their radicalism lends these affirmations a tremendous liberating power. Swept aside is all apologetic nineteenth-century half-heartedness—toward the scientist, the secularist reformer, the agnostic moralist, each of whom used to be told that he stood in need of religion, no matter how much his thought and his life gave the lie to this story; it was to be replaced by a radically honest self-exposure. Swept aside, too, is the halfhearted Christian testimony that used to define itself in alien terms—the terms of a world for which it could still perform some useful function, or the terms of philosophies still left with a gap of some kind. This was to be replaced by a testimony to a God who, ever-present to man, can confront modern-secular man as surely as his less secular ancestors. Radical, modern-secular honesty is united with radical Biblical authenticity.

A Jew's Jewish affirmations may differ from Bonhoeffer's Christian ones. Yet the Jew is bound to be moved by them and, indeed, become deeply involved. For one thing, the profane-sacred, temporal-eternal dichotomy has always been alien to Judaism and Jewish existence; and Bonhoeffer opposes it because of Hebraic inspiration. For another (as has been said), modern Jewish existence has been exposed to special strains because of the modern conflict between secularist liberalism and Christianity. But, when more closely considered, Bonhoeffer's affirmations are, in the end, profoundly problematical; and, as will be seen, what is problematical about them is augmented in the thought of his disciples.

Two questions are left hanging in mid-air. First, who is the God to be *confronted*, and how is he related to the "God-hypothesis" to be *discarded*, the hypothesis through which things were once *explained*? Although this may seem an abstract theoretical question, it is, nevertheless, inescapable. What if Bonhoeffer's modern-secular man were to reject—indeed, were in all honesty *obliged* to reject—the God with whom Christian testimony confronts him as a mere myth of bygone ages, now in need of demythologization? As will be seen, this question haunts Bonhoeffer's theological disciples.

The second question is even on the surface not abstract and theoretical only. Who is Bonhoeffer's "man-come-of-age," happy in his secularity and free of guilt? Is he an ideal man as pictured by Spinoza, Kant, or Hegel? But that man is himself only an ideal. Or is he an actually existing man? Doubtless he is this latter, for he alone is an "ordinary man who spends his everyday life at work, and with his family." It is a tragic irony, however, that Bonhoeffer should have cleared this man of guilt at the precise time when he became implicated, all around him, in a guilt without historical precedent: not only when his "work" was to drive gas-chamber trucks or to fight Hitler's war, but also when it was merely to clean the streets—and hold his peace. Bonhoeffer aimed at two great goals: a gospel found in the midst of life and joy rather than merely in death and guilt; and the protection of the secular man against religion-inspired slander. A nearly incredible lack of realism made him fail to rise to what would have been not slander but judgment—of "ordinary" Christians and secularists alike.

Clear-sighted witness, apostle of Christian self-exposure to the secular world and himself martyr to his cause, Bonhoeffer nevertheless failed wholly to grasp—almost no one to this day has succeeded in wholly grasping—the monstrous evil in the actual world about him. This painful truth, in retrospect inescapable, cannot escape his Jewish reader. In a concentration camp filled with Jews subjected to every imaginable form of torture, Bonhoeffer writes that Protestants must learn about suffering from Catholics.[9] No mention is made in the *Letters and Papers* of Jewish martyrdom.[10]

III On the Self-Exposure of Faith to the Secular City

The ambiguities implicit in Bonhoeffer's affirmations become explicit among those of his British, American, and Canadian disciples who currently demand radical Christian self-exposure to the modern-secular world and all its works. This current Christian demand is producing a Jewish reaction that, while sporadic, is possibly highly significant. Time was when even orthodox Jewish believers would ask of Christians a more wholehearted acceptance of those secular-liberal ideals that have separated state and church, established the equality of all citizens, and emancipated Jews. Now that some leading Christian thinkers urge precisely that, they are warned against abandonment of the Biblical God by Jews not all of whom are self-declared believers.[11] One could not altogether blame Christian thinkers if they felt that, so far as Jews are concerned, they can never do right.

This present Jewish stance is due not to greater Jewish religious firmness but to recent Jewish experience. At a time when Christian thinkers are becoming aware of the gap between the modern Christian church and the modern-secular world, Jewish thinkers are becoming aware of the bond between Judaism and Christianity, even when their commitment to Judaism is problematical.

Only in recent decades have Jews had occasion to realize fully the bonds they have with Christianity as well as with secularist liberalism. In the heyday of nineteenth-century optimism, the Western Jew was apt to throw in his destiny wholly with secularist liberalism "abroad" even if he remained an orthodox Jew "at home,"[12] and to have no very positive relation to the forces of Christianity except insofar as these, too, threw their weight behind liberal ideals. But what if secularist liberalism were to become wholly omnipotent? Would it remain liberal? Could it be counted on to respect the Jew's right to his Jewishness, of which it had little appreciation, and to his Judaism, of which it had less? Might it, in fact, even be perverted into a demonic pseudo-religion and deny the Jew's very humanity?

Some of these questions have *in abstracto* been present ever since, after the French Revolution, the Jew was requested to surrender his public Jewishness "abroad" (if not his private Jewish faith "at home") as the price of his emancipation. In the mid-twentieth century, these questions have assumed a reality of which no wild imagination could have dreamed in the nineteenth. Soviet secularism seems bent on a policy designed to dissipate both Jewish culture "abroad" and Jewish faith "at home." And the Nazi secularist pseudo-religion of blood and soil has succeeded in the physical destruction of one third of the world's Jewish population. These two events must, under no circumstances, be viewed as in the same class, and can be so viewed only by indiscriminate cold-war warriors. They have, nevertheless, had the common effect of making many Jews view secularism with newly critical eyes. The modern Jew has been obliged to look to secularist liberalism for the recognition of his humanity in the past. The momentous and fearsome events of the present have made him wonder whether, if to anyone, it is not to the Christian that he must look for the recognition of his singled-out Jewish condition.[13] Indeed, may contemporary events not indicate that secularist liberalism itself stands in secret need of Biblical inspiration for its liberalism? If bereft of this inspiration, or subjugating and thus perverting it, may secularism not become illiberal and totalitarian, or even a demonic pseudo-religion?

Such fears are obviously not felt by those Jews who grasp the opportunities offered by the secular city for surrendering their Jewishness in the faith that such a surrender will make them "simply human." But despite statistics concerning assimilation and inter-marriage, their response to the secular city does not represent what must be called mid-twentieth-century American Jewish normative behavior. To the astonishment of many, the normative American Jewish response to the events of this century has been a reaffirmation, if not of Judaism, at least of Jewish group-survival. (In the light of the dynamic of present Jewish life, it is the Jewish intellectuals whose intellectualism has led them to surrender their Jewishness who are out of step, not the community which they have abandoned.) The causes of this re-affirmation are complex: among others, a flight from the anony-mous society of megalopolis to the community—such as it is—of suburbia; loyalty to the martyred European millions which, once aroused by plain need, refuses to vanish; a new seriousness about Judaism among formerly perfunctory believers; and even a new openness to Jewish religious resources among formerly confirmed secularists. All these responses, from a minimal commitment to Jewishness to a maximal commitment to Judaism, imply some de-gree of criticism of the modern-secular world where before there was little or none.

In the light of this experience, how will a Jewish reader react to such a work as *The Secular City*?[14] On first reading he may well seem to be perceiving messianic signs. Has he come upon a genuinely Christian-Biblical effort to make peace with those liberal-secular ideas with which the Christian forces have been at odds too long—an alienation of which the Jew has been a special victim? There is such an effort, and it aims at peace not with a mere abstract idea of secular freedom but with its actual carriers in the secular city: social mobility and big-city anonymity, cultural pluralism and pragmatic scepticism, and an open marketplace governing religious beliefs as much as all else. Their acceptance, moreover, is by a faith far more Hebraic than Hellenic in inspira-tion: a faith which will not freeze a past world into permanence, nor divide reality into an all-important heaven and a worthless earth. *The Secular City* seeks a worldly God who speaks *into* the here-and-now; not a conservative God confined to the past, but a God of the present who is geared to the future. Jewish faith has, since Biblical times, sought a worldly God of the present and the future; and it is largely by dint of circumstances not of their making that modern Jews have been split into those seeking the old God, but able to find him only in seclusion from the modern-secular world, and into those embracing the modern-secular world, but unable to find the old God in it. Are unprecedented opportunities now in the making for a tripartite secularist-Christian-Jewish dialogue in which what is at stake is the word of the old Biblical God for the modern-secular world?

This may indeed be cautiously affirmed, no less because of events in Alabama and Mississippi than because of events in theological seminaries. A Jew's duty is to bring Jewish experience to bear on his participation in the tripartite dialogue. Part of so doing, however, is to express caution to Christians lest an indiscriminate self-exposure of faith to the modern-secular world end in surrender.

The Secular City justifies caution. No single item of the work will strike a Jewish reader more forcefully than its failure—twenty years after—to come to grips with Nazism. The work warns in a general way against the dangers of the modern-secular world; yet such is the degree of its infatuation that it has no room for Nazism in that world. Nazism is a mere "throwback to a lost tribalism." What an insult to any tribe ever in existence. And what a staggering failure to grasp that Nazism, far from being a mere falling-out-of-step innocuous to all who are *in* step, is, alas, a distinctly modern phenomenon. How, except for modern anonymity and modern technological quantification, could Nazism have engaged in its grisly mathematics of mass-murder? So blithely is *The Secular City* in love with the virtues of modern secularity that it is able to commit this enormous tautology: "When a political leader makes religious or totalitarian claims, when a Hitler or Stalin tries once again to assert himself as the pure expression of the *Zeitgeist* or the dialectic, free [*sic*] men recognize this as an affront to their deepest convictions about politics."[15] As if the question raised by Nazism were not precisely why Germans preferred slavery to freedom, and even "thought they were free"[16] when in fact they were slaves. Moreover, for long and crucial years, even "free" Western leaders—both Christian and secularist—appeased Hitler not only as the lesser evil to war but also as the savior of Western civilization from Communism.

The Secular City comes to grief over Nazism not because of moral blindness but rather because, like Bonhoeffer, it fights on one front and ignores the simultaneous need to fight on another. It fights for the recognition of the challenge of the liberal secular-city dweller to the religious believer, in particular to the rural believer. It fights, too, against all religious efforts to reduce the former to a guilt or despair for which there is neither need nor cause. It ignores the real *grounds* for despair and guilt—among secularists and believers alike. Is there no guilt in an America well-fed in the midst of world-wide starvation and with enough arms to destroy the human race? And no despair in the secular city even if guilt can be shut out? Not if those novelists are to be believed who discover meaninglessness in busy suburbia as well as in the slums. American "pragmatic man" may waste "little time thinking about 'ultimate' or 'religious' questions," and be able to live "with highly provisional solutions."[17] But only the idolization of pragmatism can shut out those ultimate moral dilemmas of the present time in the light of which all the provisional solutions must be groped for; or fail to notice that it is precisely when his actual needs are filled that pragmatic man falls either to restlessly inventing ever-new unneeded needs or to asking the desperate and utterly unpragmatic question: "What is the use of use?"[18]

The secularist must find his own way out of the dilemmas of the secular city. The believer—Jewish and Christian—must surely seek the word of the ancient Biblical God as it applies to the modern-secular world. Such a search, if it remains for the Biblical God, will not result in a surrender to secularism, if only because

the Biblical God *judges* the world—the modern-secular world as
much as any other—even as he accepts it in love.

The Secular City, to be sure, does not surrender. It culminates
in the attempt to speak "in a secular fashion" of God, socio-
logically, politically, and even theologically. It is, however, virtually left without speech. So deeply is the work impressed with
the novelty of modern-secular man as to see virtually no continuity between him and the whole preceding human species.
Hence, it cannot hear a divine voice from the past in the present
and is faced with a future that is wholly open.[19]

Less reliance on sociology and more metaphysical discipline
might have prevented such a hollow outcome. Following an old
and shopworn doctrine harking back to Auguste Comte, *The Secular City* views metaphysics as primitive guesswork about the
universe the necessity of which disappears with the rise of science.
In fact and at its best, metaphysics is radical thinking about the
totality of human experience. As such, it helps see in perspective
all changes, including those in the human social condition and
those that the believer may affirm about the Divine. The famous
passage (Exodus 3:14) that *The Secular City* translates as "I will
do what I will do"[20] assuredly contains no ontological information
about the divine nature. But neither does it command an openness to the future so total as to fragment the One God of Israel
into as many "moment-gods"[21] as there are historical moments.
The Hebraic believer confronts the future with a present knowledge coming from the past; the word from the past is judging
justice and accepting love. He who revealed himself to Moses as
"I shall be who I shall be" may disclose himself in the future by
yet unknown names. He will be the same already-known "I."

I V On the "Death" of God

But what if a truly uncompromising self-exposure of faith to
the modern-secular world *ipso facto is* surrender to secularism?

We have noted Bonhoeffer's failure to clarify the relation between the "God-hypothesis" that is to be discarded, and the Biblical God who is to be confronted. Its nemeses are the current so-called "God-is-dead" theologies.

The expression covers a variety of different and possibly incompatible assertions. The first is purely metaphorical: not God is dead in our time but merely human belief in him. This latter is dead not so much because men no longer, in fact, believe, but rather because the legitimacy of belief would have vanished even if belief were still widely alive.[22] Modern science has demythologized the world of fact, thus disposing of the need for a God-hypothesis; and modern philosophy—it is linguistic empiricism, mostly Oxford-inspired—has reduced the meaning of the word *God*, as employed by the believer, to a mere expression of emotion. The believer imagines that the assertion "God exists," although not necessarily demonstrable, nevertheless refers to an objective truth. Philosophy disposes of this illusion. The believer's statement is not "about the world," but merely about his own attitude toward the world.

The philosopher may or may not find this attitude legitimate; on his part, he is clearly incapable of himself adopting it. How, having acquired knowledge, can he return to innocence? How, having unmasked the word *God* as a mere projection upon the world, can he ever again adopt an attitude dependent on the belief that a truth beyond his mere attitude is disclosed in it? Belief in God, then, is dead among the scientifically and philosophically enlightened; and it would never have been alive among previous generations had they been blessed with our present enlightenment. As for God himself, he is not dead. He was never alive.

There is nothing either new or startling about these assertions ——except that they should be made in a theological work, *The Secular Meaning of the Gospel*.[23] Here they are the more startling because what is aimed at is not a return to pre-neo-orthodox liberalism but rather a position that has incorporated neo-orthodox Christian insight. What is here wanted is not the Sermon on the Mount and the ethical preacher Jesus, but the Christ on the Cross and the Easter. How can this goal be attained when the Father and the resurrection have both fallen prey to a demythologizing philosophy?

The goal cannot be attained. The Christ, Son of the Father, becomes the "man free toward others"; and the Easter becomes his "contagious" effect, in the first instance upon his immediate disciples, and at length upon the Christian church.[24] One need not raise obvious historical objections to this reduction, nor ask embarrassing questions as to how the "contagious" effect of the Christ compares with that produced by other charismatic figures, not all of them admirable. It suffices to point to an internal contradiction upon which *The Secular Meaning of the Gospel* suffers inescapable shipwreck. The secular gospel is "freedom-toward-others," *total* in the Christian only when it is *secular*, when it is freed of faith in the Father. This freedom, then, supersedes that of the Christ himself, who was *not* secular but believed in the Father. And yet it is faith in the Christ that makes the secular Christian free. *The Secular Meaning of the Gospel* is secular, to be sure; but it cannot be gospel. It is a surrender to secularism.

More important than this surrender is why it should have been thought necessary, at least on the grounds that are here offered. It is, to begin with, highly questionable whether even in the minds of Biblical authors God ever was a hypothesis needed for the explanation of fact. A myth such as creation does not, after all, *explain* anything. Nor is God in the Bible ever accepted hypothetically only, as a mere assumption in need of confirmation and capable of refutation. The prayed-for rain may confirm him; it confirms not his existence, but merely his mercy, even as lack of rain evidences not divine non-existence, but merely divine refusal. Linguistic empiricists resort with tiresome repetitiousness to Elijah at Mt. Carmel.[25] But their reflections are thoughtless as well as tiresome. Is it really imaginable that an Elijah—of all prophets—would have become one of the priests of Baal if fire had consumed not his sacrifice but theirs? That the Jew's faith, at any rate, is no hypothesis is shown by its very survival; if empirically refutable, it should stand refuted a thousand times. And must a Jew really remind a Christian of Paul's view of faith as the evidence of things not seen? Or that the "fool who says in his heart that there is no God" (Ps. 14:1; 53:1) is a fool not because he lacks eyes and ears, but because the lacks the eyes and ears of faith?

Does philosophy reduce faith to a mere expression of emotion, or, in any case, to a mere attitude toward the world without access to objective truth? Only when it begs the main question from the start. Empiricism accepts as objective "data" only what is accessible to a detached—unbelieving—observer; thus the objective realm is confined to "the world," which in turn is empirical data and the hypotheses needed to explain them. On these grounds, faith certainly reduces itself to a mere attitude toward the world. But empiricism does not understand faith as faith understands itself. In its own self-understanding, faith is a committed confrontation of the world, not a detached observation; and in this confrontation of the world, it is receptive of a God who speaks in and through the world. Faith, to be sure, is a "subjective attitude"; but because it is a *believing* attitude, it takes itself as receptive of an objective truth accessible only in the believing attitude and inaccessible otherwise. Linguistic empiricism poses as a refutation of faith; in fact, it merely takes its stand outside the circle of faith, in a circle of its own in which the word of God is not heard and only "data" are given. As for *The Secular Meaning of the Gospel*, it does not follow an inexorable imperative of intellectual honesty when it leaves the circle of faith. It merely confesses its atheism.

The Secular Meaning of the Gospel reduces affirmations made from within the circle of faith to affirmations made from without. "God-statements" dissipate themselves into "man-statements": "God loves me" means no more than "I feel secure."[26] This reduction evidently follows for one who has moved outside the circle of faith and judges faith by the standards of agnostic empiricism.

The reduction is totally fallacious, however, within the circle of faith itself. The believer who stands before God does *not* "feel secure." He is, on the contrary, exposed to the most radical of all insecurities. When the revelation of divine love breaks into this insecurity, it comes as the absolute surprise that the Divine who in his glory does not need him should yet choose to need him, and that he, the believer, should in all his unlovableness nevertheless be loved. That this revelation is inaccessible to the detached observer is not strange but expected; his reduction of "God-statements" to "man-statements" has cut him off from God.

The surrender of *The Secular Meaning of the Gospel* to secularism, then, is sadly unnecessary. There is, in any case, no need for it on the grounds of either empirical science or linguistic philosophy.[27] A Jewish reader will have a special sense of sadness; for the surrender here carried out cuts off ties that have existed between Jew and Christian through the centuries. Few New Testament passages are more alien to Jewish faith than the following: "For it is the God who said 'let light shine out of darkness' who has shone into the hearts to give the light of the knowledge of God in the face of Christ" (II Cor. 4:6). Yet even here Jew and Christian, at odds over "the face of Christ," still share the God who speaks. This bond is destroyed when *The Secular Meaning of the Gospel* reinterprets the passage so as to eliminate God.[28]

In its self-exposure to the modern-secular world, can Christian faith come upon deeper challenges than those faced by *The Secular Meaning of the Gospel*? Is it faced not only with the long-obvious threat of externally opposing forces, but also with a threat from within? Or, to stay with the previously used image, is Christian faith challenged not only to *abandon* its own circle for the secularist circle external to it, but also to *transfigure* itself radically, so as to become absorbed by the secularist circle without remainder? With this question we come upon a far more profound Christian self-exposure to the modern-secular world, and at the same time one far more dangerous. *The Secular Meaning of the Gospel* merely abandons the Biblical God for an atheistic humanism. *The Gospel of Christian Atheism*[29] literally affirms and indeed wills the death of the Biblical God; and its affirming and willing produces the spectre of idolatry.

The Gospel of Christian Atheism revels in sweeping generalizations and unsubstantiated assertions,[30] as well as in a dialectic which, while at times the Hegelian movement of spirit which transfigures what it negates, is at other times merely incoherence made into a theological virtue. But rather than pounce on such vices, one must attend to its central virtue, a radicalism than which one bolder and more extreme it would be difficult to imagine. Here the central theological issue left hanging in mid-air since Bonhoeffer is confronted head-on and dealt with in a manner that leaves no room for ambiguity or compromise. *The Gospel of Christian Atheism* is a work which itself must be confronted head-on, if only to be uncompromisingly rejected.

For all its lack of intellectual discipline, the work states its central thesis with admirable clarity. The spirit of the modern-secular world is most clearly expressed in modern speculative philosophy; this is neither simply indifferent to Christianity nor simply hostile to it. Modern speculative philosophy—and the whole modern-secular world—are the dialectical result of Christianity, as well as its dialectical negation. Its result: only the Christian God incarnate in the world has made possible "profane" modern worldliness. Its negation: only as modern worldliness negates the transcendent otherness of the Biblical God, so as to appropriate it into total immanence, does it, *qua* worldliness, become complete. This movement is already, in principle, complete in modern philosophy—above all, in Hegel and Nietzsche; for here the "death" of the transcendent God is effected by means of an immanent self-elevation of thought toward divinity. If the movement is as yet incomplete in the modern-secular world as a whole—if at the present time there is a chaos in which the old Christian values have already vanished while new, post-Christian values have not yet emerged, it is in large measure because Christian theology has opposed modern autonomous-godless thought in the name of the transcendent God, when to transfigure itself into just that mode of thought, and hence to accept the death of the transcendent God, is in truth its inescapable destiny. Christian theology must therefore accept and even "will" the death of God—anyhow occurring in the midst of Christendom "in our time, in our history, in our existence,"[31] and in effect write a third testament. The Old Testament knew only the alien, transcendent, externally commanding Father. He became the Son, incarnate and immanent, in the New Testament. It will be left for the third testament to come dialectically to deny the Son's resurrection to transcendence, and along with it the Father who makes this resurrection possible. This step will lay "faith . . . open to the most terrible darkness"; yet in precisely that darkness will it "be receptive of the most redemptive light." And the redemption-to-come will be the "full and actual presence of the Christ who is a totally incarnate love."[32]

Such, in brief, is *The Gospel of Christian Atheism.* In this essay, it calls for both a philosophical and a Jewish response. This response must begin with noting the work's totally inadequate grasp of Hegel, more obviously even than Nietzsche its philosophical patron saint. Hegel *does* transfigure Christian faith into autonomous philosophical thought. He does *not* in the process produce the death either of God or of the Christian faith. Hegel's philosophy rests on two crucial presuppositions: on the one hand, the faith which receives the descent of God into Christ; on the other, the ascent of modern secularity to freedom and autonomy. Its task is to reconcile these two presuppositions in the form of philosophical thought, and yet so to reconcile them as not to destroy them. Thought transfigures secular and religious life into a union of *thought;* but it also *re-instates* them in that creative difference in which they exist *in life.*[33] If taken at his full word rather than selectively made use of, Hegel lends no support to *The Gospel of Christian Atheism.* On the contrary, he anticipates the move taken in that work and rejects it.

But there is, of course, ample precedent for the kind of selective reading of Hegel that takes a left-wing turn and denies transcendence. It is instructive to consider the fate of nineteenth-century left-wing Hegelians. Their denial of Hegelian transcendence led them to seek an absoluteness immanent in actual humanity; yet in the process of this search virtually every left-wing Hegelian accused his predecessor of dissipating concrete man into an unreal abstraction. This process may be said to have culminated in Marx and Nietzsche, both left-wing Hegelians in a wider sense. Scorning the spurious "freedom" of Feuerbach's "abstract" humanity, as well as the "mere idealism" of "utopian" socialists, both men sought an *actual* humanity *absolutely* free, in the one case in the future classless society; in the other, in the future "Overman." But with what success? In retrospect, Marx's dialectical socialism is far more utopian than "utopian" socialism. As for Nietzsche's Overman, he is a mere myth, and one far more unreal—and dangerous—than all those transcendent deities that he was meant to replace.

Nietzsche assuredly is not a proto-fascist. He is, however, a reckless and apocalyptic mythmaker, divorced from reality as all apocalyptic mythmakers are. Americans have only lately discovered Nietzsche. Now that some American theologians idolize him, they stand in need of a warning from someone who never has had to discover him behind false stereotypes. Karl Löwith, lifelong German student of Nietzsche and author of a classic study of him as far back as in 1935, writes in 1956:

> He is still close to us, yet already quite remote. . . . [In his case] the question of . . . the historic responsibility of all public thought, speech and writing is inescapable. For in the case of Nietzsche it is undeniable that he wished from the beginning to be effective through his writing and be as philosopher a "physician of culture." Thus in the end he sketched a world-historical program designed for "great politics." . . . And he coined maxims with an unheard-of harshness and recklessness of which in his personal life he never was capable, maxims which entered into public consciousness and then were practised for twelve years. Among these

were the maxim of the dangerous life, of contempt for sympathy
. . . , of a decisive nihilism of action, according to which that which
already falls is yet to be pushed down.[34]

What responsible secular philosopher of the age of Auschwitz and
Hiroshima would utter the Nietzsche-style demand to "abandon
all those moral laws which the Christian Church has sanctioned"?[35] It seems strange that theologians should embrace
Nietzschean apocalypticism when secular philosophers—Sartre
and Camus come to mind—have abandoned all reckless human
aspirations to an immanent divinity, leaving man with a responsible but finite freedom.

But perhaps this is not strange. Theologians, after all, cannot
let go of infinity and divinity, even if the search for these is at the
cost of a reckless antinomian disregard for morality. Is this disregard necessary? And is the search successful? It is tempting to
contrast the goal of *The Gospel of Christian Atheism* (which is to
lay hold of concrete present worldliness) with its actual result
(which is the apocalyptic dissipation of everything concrete and
present into what Hegel would have called a "night in which all
cows are black"). One is all the more tempted to dwell on this
result because apocalyptic nihilism is not uncommon among present post-Christian writers, who respond to our present despairs
with the indiscriminate surrender of all those things in the present
which must under no circumstances be surrendered, but, on the
contrary, loved and nurtured.[36] But we must turn at once to what
in the context of this essay is the crucial theological issue: between
any possible form of Jewish faith and this Christian (or post-
Christian) theology—possibly the most radically anti-Judaic theology ever nurtured in the bosom of the Christian church.

Why must *The Gospel of Christian Atheism* accept and even
"will" the death of God? Not because modern belief in God is no
longer genuine; the work would attack it as reactionary even when
it was genuine. Nor because God is ruled out by modern science

and empiricist philosophy; the work cares little about science and less about empirical evidence. The death of God must be willed because "God . . . is the transcendent enemy of the fulness and the passion of man's life in the world, and only through God's death can humanity be liberated from that repression which is the real ruler of history."[37] In short, it is the Lord of Israel whose otherness—and hence lordship and divinity—is the enemy; and only as Christianity rids itself of this Jewish element can it consummate the salvation aimed at ever since the time of its origin, but until now unconsummated because of its failure to emancipate itself from Judaism.[38]

Such views must produce from a Jew one fundamental question. Who is this hostile God, foe of human freedom and source of every repression? He is not and never has been the authentic God of Israel: not in the Hebrew Bible, not in the rabbinic writings, not in the history of Jewish religious thought until this day. He is not the God of the psalmist when he "delights" in the divine commandments (Ps. 119:47); not the God of the rabbinic sage who declares that "when the Torah came into the world freedom came into the world" (*Midrash Genesis Rabba, Wayyera* LIII 7); not the God of the ordinary Jewish worshiper who daily proclaims that it is in his love that God gave commandments to Israel. The enemy-God is a caricature. The authentic God of Israel is he who in his transcendent otherness does not need man and yet chooses to need him; who in his love makes man free and responsible, and thus as commanding demands a free response. He is, in short, a God of grace. But must a Jew tell a Christian about grace?

From time to time this would appear to be necessary. In the perspective of Judaism, Nietzsche's titanic war on the Biblical God is not a modern necessity, inevitably waged in behalf of human freedom. It is the nemesis manifested in this parson's son of an age-old Christian—or is it pseudo-Christian?—blindness to a grace that is manifest in the commandments, to a grace that does not diminish or vanquish human freedom but rather augments and, indeed, establishes it. This same nemesis is manifest in *The Gospel of Christian Atheism.*[39]

V On the "Eclipse" of God

Philosophers have always been demythologizers.[40] More to the present point, the Bible demythologizes when it reduces nature to the un-divine product of a divine Creator that is intended for human use. (It has been plausibly argued that modern science and technology are Biblical in inspiration when, rather than contemplate nature with a religious awe, they subject it to experimental "torture" and technological control.) But while the Bible demythologizes the creation, it does not demythologize a divine word that may enter into it, in order to be present for man in and through it. It is the possibility of just this presence that the modern-secular world calls radically into question; and when the question is given an unequivocally negative answer, modern secularity has turned into secularism.

The essence of secularism may be formulated as an answer to one of the questions left hanging by Bonhoeffer. Suppose a secularist experienced, with or without the witness of a Bonhoeffer, the presence of the "confronting" God: Would he believe in him? If he were an unrepentant secularist, he would "explain" the confronting God as the mere unconscious projection of his subjective "experience." This explanation, moreover, would encompass in principle all similar experiences throughout human history. Secularist man may or may not deny "the existence of God." He is, in any case, cut off from his presence. According to his lights, man—every man—is radically and inescapably alone.

Faith does not radically expose itself to the modern-secular world if it avoids the challenge of secularism. Yet self-exposure to secularism involves a risk without precedent in the history of faith. When faced with false prophets, an ancient prophet recognized the possibility and the risk that he himself might be false. When faced with secularism, modern faith recognizes the vastly more shattering possibility that all human witnessing to a divine presence ever made might have been based on a radical illusion: the possibility that man is, as secularism holds him to be, radically alone.

The modern believer dare not ignore this possibility, lest his self-exposure to the modern-secular world fail precisely when it is most serious. Yet dare he embrace the possibility as actuality? This would be to surrender to secularism. The modern believer walks on the "narrow ridge" of total risk.

On this ridge the great modern theologians have been walking for nearly half a century. To give one example, whatever questions may be asked about the "positivism" of Karl Barth's neo-orthodoxy,[41] it does not ignore secularism but arises from self-exposure to it.[42] To give another, Martin Buber's *I and Thou* [43] is not a mere homily that expresses its author's experience of a "divine Thou" and ignores the secularist objection that such experiences are in principle illusory. It confronts the secularist objection and repudiates it. *I and Thou* does not refute a Feuerbachian secularism that makes all I-Thou relations human. Faith can neither refute secularism nor itself be proved. The work does bring about, however, a significant confrontation; from this, it emerges that Biblical openness to a divine presence and the unyielding solitariness of secularism are both equally unprovable and irrefutable. They are, in this sense, rival faiths.

Secularist unbelief dissipates the present divine Other into a projection of human feeling. Belief on its part takes human feeling as the mere by-product of an actual encounter with Divinity: Only if man is "withdrawn" from the encounter is he left with mere feeling. Secularism asserts that belief deifies the projection of feeling. Faith retorts that secularism deifies its withdrawal from God; it holds that to repent of his secularism a man must not in his withdrawn state cast about for "religious experiences," but rather "turn" away from his self-absorption and toward the God who speaks.

This self-exposure is in principle adequate;[44] it bears witness to the "confronting" God while, self-exposed to a secularism that would "explain" away belief in this God, walking on the narrrow ridge of risk. It falls short, however, in at least one crucial particular. Committed to the thesis that God speaks constantly,[45] *I and Thou* stakes all responsibility for "hearing" on a human "turning." But the weight of such a responsibility was too great even in Biblical times. In the modern-secular world it is intolerable.

But perhaps the greatest achievement of Buber's career is the steadfastness with which it moves from an original resort to romantic illusions toward an ever-greater realism. About thirty years after *I and Thou*, Buber writes:

> Let us ask whether it may not literally be true that God formerly spoke to us and is now silent, and whether this is not to be understood as the Hebrew Bible understands it, namely, that the living God is not only a self-revealing but also a self-concealing God. Let us realize what it means to live in the age of such a concealment, such a divine silence. . . . It would be worthier not to explain it to oneself in sensational and incompetent sayings, such as that of the death of God, but to endure it as it is and at the same time move existentially toward a new happening, toward that event in which the word between heaven and earth will again be heard.[46]

This statement is made in direct response to Sartre's atheism, but in indirect response to all modern secularism and, in anticipation, to all the "God-is-dead" theologies. Faith stands here self-exposed to all the evidence that secularist unbelief might cite against it in the contemporary world; yet it remains faith because it continues to listen to God even if, there being no hearing, there may be an "eclipse of God." An eclipse does not destroy the sun; moreover, it is temporary. A faith which accepts a divine eclipse listens even in a time of silence, in the trust that the divine word will again be heard.[47]

Can such a faith endure in the present age? This is an as-yet unanswered question. The contradictions in which this endurance must prove itself today are nearly nowhere confronted. In this age, there is celebration of the freedoms of the secular city, coupled with dread of its emptiness. Democratic tolerance coexists with unprecedented violence and with the spectre of universal disaster. Modern man is torn between an at-homeness in a secular world exalting human autonomy, and flights from both into an apocalyptic nihilism. The listening endurance of faith will have to exist steadfast *in* this world, exposed at once to its marvels and terrors.

The Jew is singled out for special contradictions. In America he enjoys a freedom and security unparalleled in his history; yet he is but twenty years separated from the greatest and as yet uncomprehended Jewish catastrophe. His trust and joy in the modern-secular world cannot but coexist with radical distrust and profound sorrow. The authentic Jewish religious witness in this age must both face up to Auschwitz and yet refuse a despair of this world which, wholly contrary to Judaism, would hand still another victory to the forces of radical evil. Insofar as he is committed to Jewish survival, the Jew has already taken a stand against these forces. But survival-for-survival's-sake is an inadequate stand. The Jew can go beyond it only if he can reopen the quest of Jeremiah and Job, who for all their agony refused to despair either of God or the world.

VI Despair, Silence, Waiting, Interrogation

Is there an authentic Jewish enduring of the contradictions of present Jewish existence? Is it giving rise to a quest, to a listening, indeed, to an interrogating of God which, born of faith, may itself bespeak a Presence while as yet no voice is heard? Perhaps one must not look to philosophers or even theologians. Perhaps one must look to a novelist whose heaven-storming shatters conven-

tions and literary forms.[48] Elie Wiesel's *Night* is no mere specula-
tion upon imagined darkness. It is an eye-witness account of the
most terrible actual darkness, by a man who experienced it when
he was a fourteen-year-old boy. In this document—the document
of our time of the impact of radical evil on Jewish faith—we read:

> One day when we came back from work, we saw three gallows
> rearing up in the assembly place, three black crows. Roll Call. SS
> all round us, machine guns trained: the traditional ceremony.
> Three victims in chains—and one of them, the little servant, the
> sad-eyed angel.
> The SS seemed more preoccupied, more disturbed than usual. To
> hang a young boy in front of thousands of spectators was no light
> matter. The head of the camp read the verdict. All eyes were on
> the child. He was lividly pale, almost calm, biting his lips. The
> gallows threw its shadow over him. . . .
> The three victims mounted together onto the chairs.
> The three necks were placed at the same moment within the
> nooses.
> "Long live liberty!" cried the two adults.
> But the child was silent.
> "Where is God? Where is He?" someone behind me asked.
> At a sign from the head of the camp, the three chairs tipped
> over. . . .
> I heard a voice within me answer. . . . :
> "Where is He? Here He is—He is hanging on this gallows. . . ."[49]

The hero of *The Accident* has listened to Sarah, former "SS
whore" who has been forced into every degradation conceivable
by a satanic imagination.

> I shouldn't have listened. I should have fled. . . . Whoever listens
> to Sarah and doesn't change, whoever enters Sarah's world and
> doesn't invent new gods and new religions, deserves death and
> destruction. Sarah alone had the right to decide what is good and
> what is evil, the right to differentiate what is true from what
> usurps the appearance of truth.[50]

The Town Beyond the Wall ends with a legend. Man once was
granted by God his request for a temporary exchange of places.

The request granted, he immediately assumed omnipotence and refused to return to his place. In the years or centuries or eternities following:

> The past for one, the present for the other, were too heavy to be borne. As the liberation of one was bound to the liberation of the other, they renewed the ancient dialogue whose echoes come to us in the night, charged with hatred, with remorse, and most of all, with infinite yearning.[51]

In *The Gates of the Forest*, Gregor remains in an inconclusive argument with the Hasidic rabbi.

> Gregor was angry. "After what has happened to us, how can you believe in God?"
>
> With an understanding smile on his lips the Rebbe answered, "How can you *not* believe in God after what has happened?"[52]

Yet Gregor reaches an affirmation, or the fragment of an affirmation, or the fragment of a fragment.

> "Whether or not the Messiah comes doesn't matter; we'll manage without him. It is because it is too late that we are commanded to hope. . . . The Messiah isn't one man, Clara, he's all men. As long as there are men there will be a Messiah. One day you'll sing, and he will sing in you. . . ."
>
> At the appropriate moments Gregor recited the *Kaddish*, that solemn affirmation, filled with grandeur and serenity, by which man returns God his crown and sceptre. He recited it slowly, concentrating on every sentence, every word, every syllable of praise. His voice trembled, timid, like that of the orphan suddenly made aware of the relationship between death and eternity, between eternity and the word.[53]

19

A Response to Five Questions

(In its August 1966 issue, *Commentary* sponsored a Symposium on *The State of Jewish Belief*. The following reproduces *Commentary's* questions and my response. The Symposium is published as *The Condition of Jewish Belief* [New York: Macmillan, 1966].)

The Questions

1. In what sense do you believe the Torah to be divine revelation? Are all 613 commandments equally binding on the believing Jew? If not, how is he to decide which to observe? What status would you accord to ritual commandments lacking in ethical or doctrinal content (e.g., the prohibition against clothing made of linen and wool)?

2. In what sense do you believe that the Jews are the chosen people of God? How do you answer the charge that this doctrine is the model from which various theories of national and racial superiority have been derived?

3. Is Judaism the one true religion, or is it one of several true religions? Does Judaism still have something distinctive—as it once had monotheism—to contribute to the world? In the ethical sphere, the sphere of ben adam la-chavero, *what distin-*

Reprinted by permission of the editors from *Commentary* (August 1966), pp. 87-89.

guishes the believing Jew from the believing Christian, Moslem, or Buddhist—or, for that matter, from the unbelieving Jew and the secular humanist?

4. *Does Judaism as a religion entail any particular political viewpoint? Can a man be a good Jew and yet, say, support racial segregation? Can a man be a good Jew and be a Communist? A Fascist?*

5. *Does the so-called "God is dead" question which has been agitating Christian theologians have any relevance to Judaism? What aspects of modern thought do you think pose the most serious challenge to Jewish belief?*

Commentary's questions must be answered clearly, straightforwardly, and without evasion. But answers will inevitably seem evasive when no evasion is intended; complex and ambiguous when what is aimed at is clarity and simplicity; above all, they will seem far harsher and more dogmatic than their author actually is. Judaism is a spiritual life—dynamic, open, and whole. Answers to a questionnaire cannot capture that life but only open a door.

(1) The Torah reflects *actual events* of divine revelation, or incursions into human history, not a mistaken human belief in such incursions. But it is a *human* reflection of these events of incursion; the reception is shot through with appropriation and interpretation. Even a human listening to a human voice is inevitably an interpreting; this is *a fortiori* inevitable when the human "listening" is in faith and the "voice" heard is divine.

This rejects, on the one hand, the view that God dictated to Moses, a mere secretary. (Even orthodox tradition does not reduce human reception to such extreme passivity. Why, in that case, would there be any need for a Moses to receive the Torah? And why, in that case, would the rabbis elicit what is implicit in the Torah, instead of, in the style of fundamentalism, passively accepting its letter?) It rejects, on the other hand, any liberal dissipation of the event of divine incursion into "creative" human "insight," mistaken for revelation by those who achieved it. (This rejected view inevitably exalts the modern liberal above the ancient authors of the Torah, if only because, unlike them, he recognizes creative human insight for what it is. On any such view, the modern liberal cannot *listen* to God through the Torah. Nor can he truly listen to its ancient human authors. His own standards are *a priori* superior, and the Torah merely provides selective confirmation of his modern insights.)

The view I have sketched implies that not all 613 commandments are equally binding. Shot through with *human* appropriation and interpretation, both the Torah and the subsequent tradition which is oral Torah inescapably reflect the ages of their composition. But it also follows that it is both naive and un-Jewish to distill, as still binding, "eternal" commandments from a complex composed of both eternal and "time-bound" ones, the latter simply to be discarded. (This is done by old-fashioned liberalism, with its rigid distinction between the "principles" of prophetic ethics and mere external "ceremonial" laws, a distinction which derives its standards from external sources—Plato, Kant, Jefferson, and the like—and considers the standards by which it judges to be superior to what is judged by them; this is an inversion of the Jewish view in which a God speaking through the Torah does the judging.) A modern Jew can escape his own time-bound appropriating no more than could his fathers; but his interpretation is Jewishly legitimate only if it confronts, and listens to, the revelation reflected in the Torah, which continues to be accessible only through the ancient reflection which *is* the Torah. Our modern appropriating is both possible and necessary because Sinai is not an ancient event only: the Torah is given whenever Israel receives it. But the act of present appropriation is mediated through the original Sinai. It is this listening appropriation which creates historcial continuity.

"Ritual commandments" ostensibly "lacking in ethical and doctrinal content" in fact display a religious meaning by their very presence in the Torah—that the ancient Jewish response to the divine challenge is a *total* response which encompasses all of life. If a modern Jew rejects a particular ancient response as invalid for him, he must do so not because his response to the divine challenge has been reduced to a mere compartment of life, but because the divine challenge demands of his life a different total response. Thus, new commandments are given even as ancient ones lose their reality.

(2) In revelation, the Divine meets the human: It does not remain in inaccessible transcendence. While meeting the finite human, It yet remains in divine infinity: the finite is not idolatrously deified. And It enters *into* the human situation: It does not force the human into a mystic surrender of its finitude. The Divine commands, and commands humans in their humanity.

But it cannot do so except by *singling out* particular humans in their particularity. A philosopher may rise above his particular situation to the perception of a timeless truth. Every prophet must remain *in* his situation, in which the divine word singles him out. And the same is true of the whole people Israel. A Jew may wish to abandon his belief in the chosen people (I would prefer: his covenant with God), and seek to transform, in the style of philosophy, his Judaism into a set of timeless universal truths to which he has risen. To do so, however, is to fragment the one reality of the covenant into two realities only accidentally connected: a Judaism reduced to purely universal principles, and a Jewish people reduced to a merely accidental particularity. To some this fragmentation is a modern necessity. To the believer in a singling-out revelation, it is a religious impossibility. To the be-

liever, a Jewish self-understanding of Jewishness as a merely acci-
dentai manifestation of humanity-in-general, only accidentally
having a special obligation to the "universal principles" of Judaism, is not a rise to a higher level of humanity. It is a betrayal of
the post given to the Jew.

That the chosen-people concept has nothing in common with
racism is shown by the traditional doctrine concerning converts,
who become sons of Abraham. That it is diametrically opposed to
racism—as well as to the religious tribalism which may be viewed
as its ancient counterpart—follows from the being-singled-out
which *is* the chosenness. Tribal deities, as finite as the tribes
themselves, are bound to their respective tribes. Only an infinite
and therefore universal God can single out the particular. Tribal
deities behave by the standard of "my people, right or wrong,"
and modern racism makes the race itself divine. The God of Israel
judges Israel's iniquities because He is no tribal deity but the God
of all men: He who has singled out Israel, not for the sake of Israel
only, but for the world.

In the light of the foregoing, the charge referred to in this question may be understood as reflecting a special form of religious
anti-Semitism, which, having rejected a singling-out God, regards
an Israel still singled out, and accepting itself as singled out, as
an offense to its religious (or anti-religious) sensibilities. Such an
anti-Semitism finds its extreme form in a racism which, rejecting
the Judge, makes the master race judge of all things. Milder forms
are shown by those Jewish assimilationists, or "liberals" of all
kinds, who are scandalized by Jewish particularity, and those
Christians (or pseudo-Christians) who contrast Christian "universalism" with "narrow" Jewish "particularism." Such a Christian view reflects a refusal to recognize that Christianity shares
with Judaism the scandal of a singling-out God, and that the
Jewish no less than the Christian God singles out the particular
for purposes transcending the particular, i.e., nothing less than
the world.

(3) If revelation is a reality, it follows that religious truth does not find primordial expression in propositions. Propositions merely reflect the relationship between a universal, singling-out God and the men singled out by Him. It is not therefore impossible that there can be more than one true religion; for the one God of all men may relate Himself differently to different men or groups of men. (The biblical God does not relate Himself even to Abraham quite in the same way as He does to Abraham's descendants; and He who has led Israel out of Egypt has also led the Philistines out of Caphtor and the Cushites out of Cush.) Not all religions, however, can be true; idolatry, ancient and modern, is false. And some religions are only incompletely true. This is the believing Jew's best judgment, for example, concerning a highminded agnostic humanism. He may view the agnostic as doing the will of God even though he recognizes no God; he may even view the agnostic as superior to less highminded believers. This, however, is not tantamount to acknowledging the truth of agnosticism but only to acknowledging that there are fragments of truth within it.

Are there, then, any completely true religious alternatives to Judaism? It is no evasion to give only a partial answer to this question. The Bible, while in principle recognizing Gentile prophets, makes no real attempt to understand and judge their significance; for to do so would fall outside the scope of prophets sent to Israel. How non-Jews, and non-Jewish religions, may be singled out by Him whom the Jew knows as the God of Israel can be discovered by the Jew, if at all, only in dialogue with the testimony of these non-Jews and non-Jewish religions. Indeed, this discovery is what, from a Jewish standpoint, "dialogue" *means*. Hence it is not evasive to refuse to comment on such religions as Buddhism with which there has as yet been no Jewish dialogue, and to comment only inconclusively on Christianity and Islam with which dialogue has hardly begun in earnest.

Abstractly, a true religion is one in which individual men or groups of men know themselves to be related, and responsible, to Him whom the Jew knows as the God of Israel. This much a Jew cannot deny of either Christianity or Islam. But by itself this is only an abstraction. Thus, those in earnest about Jewish-Christian dialogue cannot avoid the fact of conflicting—rather than merely different—testimony. To give a crucial example: by his faith, his actions, and indeed his whole existence, the Jew testifies to a world still unredeemed and yet destined to be redeemed. In this he testifies against the Christian faith in a redemption already actual, a faith splitting history in two through the event which has made redemption actual. Can the Christian take seriously history since the time of his Christ? Can he face those aspects of it—war, poverty, hate or, for that matter, the suffering of Israel—which to the Jew make history unredeemed and yet in need of being redeemed? For the sake of the God of both Israel and the church, the Jew cannot suppress such questions; or, if he must, it were better that dialogue be suspended, and replaced by an agreement to abide by a pre-messianic disagreement.

The foregoing implies a clear difference between the believing Jew and the unbeliever in the ethical sphere. Everything else being equal, what to the one is a two-term relation between him and his neighbor commanded by conscience, is to the other a three-term relation commanded by God.[1] God is no mere external sanction behind the ethical commandment; if He were, the unbeliever would rightly dismiss Him as morally unnecessary and perhaps even impossible. His commanding presence *enters into* the relation, disclosing to the believer that the person with whom he is in relation is a creature created in the divine image. Jewish as well as non-Jewish unbelievers remain with a two-term relationship; but in the mind of a Jewish believer, the nonbelieving Jew fulfills a fragment of the divine covenant with Israel even while failing to recognize it.

Christian as well as Jewish believers stand in a three-term relation. The difference is that whereas Christian ethical life is lived in the context of a grace which has already redeemed the world, Jewish ethical life is pre-messianic, and finds grace primordially *in* the commandments, a grace which makes possible a human share in the preparation of the messianic kingdom. Only future dialogue can disclose whether this difference is as sharp as here stated. But even now a Jew knows that he can, however rarely, anticipate messianic redemption; and he sees many a Christian behaving as though the world were still unredeemed.

(4) To bind Judaism to any *one* political standpoint would be sheer parochialism. To make it hospitable to *all* political viewpoints would be to fall prey to a political quietism Jewishly tolerable only as a tactical device designed to avoid fruitless persecution. The God of Israel commands into a human situation which has an inescapable political dimension.

At least some political viewpoints are clearly ruled out. No good Jew can support on principle (as distinguished from mere tactics) racial discrimination; for he knows that his God created only one man in the beginning, lest anyone regard his ancestors as superior to those of others. Nor can he be a Communist when Communism is based on the principle of total human self-redemption, a principle which implies atheism and is used to justify human totalitarianism. Least of all can he be a Fascist, since Fascism combines atheistic political totalitarianism with racism.

But such is the burden of man's pre-messianic condition that whereas Judaism rules out some political viewpoints, it does not entail an absolute and unalterable commitment to any positive viewpoint. The ideas of universal freedom, equality, justice, and peace are authentic secular expressions of divine commandments pointing to an ultimate messianic dimension. But by themselves they are not concrete enough to amount to a political viewpoint; and what *is* concrete enough can rarely be directly or unambiguously identified as the will of God. The basic dilemma is that the Jew must decide what to do toward the messianic end while living in the here-and-now of a pre-messianic present. That such decisions are rarely either simple or unambiguous is as clear in this age as in any—when few Jews dedicated to the messianic idea of total peace can advocate immediate and total disarmament. It is all the more profoundly exhilarating that moments of grace occur in history in which all ambiguity vanishes. Such a moment is occurring in present-day America when the time is ripe for the total recognition of the humanity of the American Negro. Yet even here the ways in which this recognition is to be accomplished are not simple or unambiguous.

(5) The "God is dead" slogan covers a variety of different and even incompatible assertions: (a) that the "God-hypothesis" is no longer needed when science alone can explain the universe; (b) that *in point of fact* few contemporary men have a meaningful belief in God; (c) that whether or not they have such a belief, they *ought* not to have it, inasmuch as it reflects immaturity and modern man has "come of age."

(a) The first assertion restates the hoary positivistic view that religion is primitive science. But the biblical God is no hypothesis in need of empirical verification and capable of empirical refutation. Nor does He serve the pre-scientific function of explaining facts.[2]

(b) The second assertion is true but not new to inhabitants of the secular city—only to those freshly arrived from the farm. By itself, it at most means that the long association between Christianity and majority opinion is ended: that henceforth Christian faith must choose between minority status and surrender to secularism. For the believing Jew, this choice never existed.

(c) The third assertion is religiously serious. Does *radical* human freedom necessitate the death of God? In view of centuries of religiously-imposed unfreedom, this is no mean question. And yet, can a Jew believe that this of all ages—the age of Auschwitz, rarely mentioned by the Christian "God is dead" theologians and never, it seems, really faced—is the age of man "come of age"? Still more seriously, must God be dead in order that man may be free? Most astounding in all the present Christian turmoil is the lack of witness to a divine love which, rather than diminishing or destroying human freedom, on the contrary establishes and augments it. No doubt the present rebellion is the nemesis of past religious decadence. Yet, instead of rebelling against decadence, one may seek renewal. The Jew finds such renewal when his life bears witness that "when the Torah came into the world, freedom came into the world."[3]

(d) There is yet a fourth meaning to the "God is dead" slogan, most serious of all: that modern man is *incapable* of hearing the word of God *even if he listens*. Only to apply the slogan here is to prejudge what is in fact the central problem of religious faith in the modern world. According to Jewish tradition, God, often distant, "hides His face." Modern secularist man regards this distance as *necessary* distance, if not non-existence; and he *a priori* regards moments of divine presence—if *per impossibile* they should occur—as human self-delusion. Modern man seems incapable of accepting himself as related to a divinity beyond him.

But does this seeming incapacity signify that God is dead? Or that the great religious demand made of this age is a radical *t'shuvah*—a *turning* and listening to the God who can speak even though He is silent? And is not, in that case, the Jew of the generation of Auschwitz required to do what, since Abraham, Jeremiah, and Job, Jews have always done in times of darkness—contend with the silent God, and bear witness to Him by this very contention?

Notes

Notes enclosed in brackets represent additions to the original texts

1. These Twenty Years: A Reappraisal

1. See section 6.

2. I have deliberately kept this section free of all technical philosophical discussion. See my article, "Martin Buber's Concept of Revelation," *The Philosophy of Martin Buber*, ed. P.A. Schilpp and Maurice Friedman (La Salle, Ill.: Open Court, 1967), pp. 273-96.

3. See section 5.

4. See *Central Conference of American Rabbis Yearbook* (Philadelphia: M. Jacobs, 1953), pp. 399-455.

5. See essays no. 2-6.

6. See essays no. 4 and 6.

7. See my *Metaphysics and Historicity* (Milwaukee: Marquette University Press, 1961).

8. See essay no. 18, section III.

9. See essay no. 7.

10. See more fully essay no. 15. Other examples of confrontations between Judaism and philosophy are essays no. 14 and (in a less obvious way) no. 13.

11. See essay no. 14, Preface—a discussion which is in no way meant to be conclusive. The clearest example of "philosophizing, or something akin to it" within Judaism is essay no. 16, but see also nos. 7, 10, 12, 13.

12. See essays no. 4, 8, 19. For my later view of the issue dealt with in the Rosenzweig remark, see especially the notion of the interpretation of the nameless experience, essay no. 7, section II, and the notion of the divine commanding Presence, essay no. 14, section VI.

13. This last notion fully emerges only in essay no. 18, section VI.

14. See my *The Religious Dimension in Hegel's Thought* (Bloomington: Indiana University Press, 1968).

15. To the two mentioned external challenges, which are obviously

of the greatest weight ever since the rise of the modern-secular world, I here deliberately refrain from giving any kind of positive response. Such a response, if direct and pretending to be complete, could not avoid false apologetics. In my later essays, the two challenges are dealt with only obliquely and fragmentarily in nos. 7, 15, and 17.

16. On the connection between revelation and radical surprise, see "Man and His World in the Perspective of Judaism," *Judaism* (Spring 1967), pp. 166-75.

17. I may here be brief on the subject of Midrash, as preoccupation with Midrash is constant in all my essays. The notion of Midrash as dialectical and a whole is constant, but the notion of an open whole appears only in my more recent essays.

18. It is of course evident that the Midrashic framework may be broken by a step outside it, such as into modern secularism or into a rival religious framework. In the remainder of this essay I am solely concerned with the vulnerability which exists for those who faithfully remain within the Midrashic framework.

19. On the subject of this section, see further, "Jewish Values in the Post-Holocaust Future: A Symposium," *Judaism* (Summer 1967), pp. 266-99.

20. See essay no. 18, section VI.

21. Ibid.

22. See essay no. 18.

23. See essay no. 17.

24. My brief remarks on Dietrich Bonhoeffer (essay no. 18, Section II) have been criticized by Eberhard Bethge, possibly the most authoritative of Bonhoeffer interpreters. With regard to his first objection—Bonhoeffer's "modern-man-come-of-age" is not better but only more responsible than pre-modern man—I will only say that this would still seem to leave the Bonhoeffer of 1944 to some degree prey to that "lack of reality-relatedness" which Bethge himself ascribes to the Bonhoeffer of 1933. Surely no pre-modern believer using God as a crutch was more irresponsible than Germans using Hitler as a crutch; and if, as Bethge maintains, Bonhoeffer's term was meant to apply only to the minute minority of anti-Nazis taking responsibility for the situation, then it failed to come to grips with the unprecedented, and still uncomprehended, idolatry of the vast majority. (For the above, see "Bonhoeffer's Christology and His 'Religionless Christianity'," *Union Seminary Quarterly Review* (Fall 1967), pp. 65, 68, 69.)

More important in the present context is Bethge's second objection that Bonhoeffer showed only necessary caution, and not unconcern or unawareness, when in letters smuggled out of a Nazi prison he made no mention of Jewish suffering. I am happy and relieved to be thus instructed, for without doubt the fact that Bonhoeffer took personal risks to save Jewish lives bears Bethge out. ("Turning Points In Bonhoeffer's Life and Thought," *Union Seminary Quarterly Review* [Fall 1967], pp. 5-6.) What this shows, however, is a tremendous development between 1933 and 1944, and I was misled because I underestimated its extent. For the (in retrospect nearly incredible) fact is that in 1933 Bonhoeffer confined his opposition to Nazi Aryan legislation to its application to converted Jews and, indeed, did not hesitate to write:

> Now the measures of the state towards Judaism in addition stand in a quite special context for the church. The church of Christ has never lost sight of the thought that the "chosen people," who nailed the redeemer of the world to the cross, must bear the curse for its action through a long history of suffering . . . (*No Rusty Swords* [London: Collins, 1965], p. 226)

In commenting on this passage, J. Coert Rylaarsdam writes:

> We all think of Dietrich Bonhoeffer as a good Christian, even as a martyr, perhaps. With great courage he insisted on the crown rights of the Redeemer within his own church. Moreover, he insisted that Jews who had converted to Christianity were entitled to the same rights in the church as other Christians, a position by no means unanimously held in the church of Hitler's Germany. Nevertheless, standing in the Christian tradition of the curse, Bonhoeffer did not hesitate to appeal to it to rationalize Hitler's program for Jews faithful to their own faith. ("The Disavowal of the Curse: A New Beginning?" *Dialog* [Summer 1967], p. 192)

25. See essay no. 18, n.13.

26. See "Jewish Values in the Post-Holocaust Future: A Symposium," *Judaism* (Summer 1967), p. 296.

2. Self-Realization and the Search for God: A Critique of Modern Humanism and a Defence of Jewish Supernaturalism

1. Kaufmann Kohler, *Jewish Theology* (New York, 1918), p. 15.

2. Psychologists may argue that all men are sick. But if this is true to an extent rendering all human responsibility relative, then men can neither heal themselves or each other, and no one can lay down standards of health and sickness.

3. F.D.E. Schleiermacher, *Dogmatik,* §36; cf. also *Ueber die Re-ligion* (Leipzig, 1880), p. 75; *Psychologie* (Berlin, 1862), p. 461.

4. That Schleiermacher actually came close to such a position is shown by Reinhold Niebuhr, *The Nature and Destiny of Man,* vol. i (New York, 1945), pp. 86 ff.

5. We are here concerned only with the naive, uncritical acceptance of revelation and its critical dissolution into humanism. We are, of course, very far from holding that revelation must ultimately be inter-preted in terms of experience-of-revelation, and that humanism, rather than supernaturalism, has the last word. [Cf. essay no. 4.]

6. In these paragraphs, we do not, of course, attempt to give a com-plete picture of biblical and rabbinic views on the subject. Our task here is rather to select such aspects as will clarify the perspective in which biblical and rabbinic views must be understood. For thorough interpretations, see G. F. Moore, *Judaism,* vol. i (Cambridge, 1927), pp. 357 ff.; also S. Schechter, *Some Aspects of Rabbinic Theology* (London, 1909), pp. 21 ff.

7. M. Abot 4.19. We follow the interpretation of J. Hertz, *Pirke Aboth* (New York, 1945), p. 77. The sentiment here expressed is, of course, unusual in rabbinic theology.

8. Tosefta Derek Eretz, Perek Haminim, 31 (*The Treatise Derek Eretz,* ed. by M. Higger [New York, 1935], text pp. 293 ff., translation pp. 110 ff.).

9. For biblical literature, cf. especially the Book of Jonah; for rab-binic literature, passages quoted by Newman-Spitzer, *The Talmudic Anthology* (New York, 1945), pp. 163 ff.

10. J. Berak. ix.l, 13a, line 17. In this and many other subsequent quotations, I have followed the translation of Montefiore and Loewe, *A Rabbinic Anthology* (London, 1938).

11. B. Berak. 33b.

12. Midr. Ps. on Ps. 123:1.

13. Lam. R. I, 33, on Lam. 1:6.

14. This is expressed with particular clarity in this passage: "R. Simeon b. Yohai said: . . . 'Only when Israel does God's will is His heavenly palace secure' . . . Nevertheless, R. Simeon b. Yohai also quoted, 'This is my Lord and I will praise Him' (Ex. 15:2), and he said: 'When I praise Him, He is glorified, and when I do not praise Him, He is, *as it were,* glorified in Himself' " (Sifre Deut., Berakah, 346, 144a).

15. It is, of course, well known that the rabbis interpreted the biblical *Elohim* as referring to the divine attribute of justice, and *YHWH* to that of mercy; cf., e.g., Pesikta (ed. Buber), 164a.

16. Gen. R. XII, 15. Cf., among numerous similar passages, the following: "Abraham said unto God, 'If thou desirest to maintain the world, strict justice is impossible; and if thou desirest strict justice, the world cannot be maintained. . . . Thou desirest the world and thou desirest justice. Take one or the other. Unless thou art a little indulgent, the world cannot endure' " (Gen. R. XXXIX, 6); cf. also Lev. R. X, 1.

17. Tanhuma (ed. Buber), Wayera, 49a.

18. Tanhuma (ed. Buber), Mishpatim, 41b.

19. B. Baba K. 50a; cf. also J. Shek. v. 2, 48d, line 35.

20. B. Hag. 16a.

21. Sifre Deut., Waethanan, 26, 70b. The whole of Israel is represented as making the same request (Midr. Ps. on Ps. 71:2).

22. Gen. R., Hayye Sarah, LX, 2.

23. Tanhuma B., Deut., Waethanan, 5a.

24. Midr. Ps. on Ps. 72:1.

25. This is indicated in Midr. Ps. on Ps. 72:1.

26. Cf., e.g., Deut. R., Nitztzabim, VIII, 6: "The law and all the implements by which it is carried out have been given, namely, modesty, beneficence, uprightness, and reward."

27. Cf., e.g., Pes. K. 158b: "If a mortal man uses broken vessels, it is a disgrace, but with God it is otherwise, for all His servants are broken vessels, as it is said, 'The Lord is nigh unto the brokenhearted and the contrite in spirit he will save' (Ps. 34:18)."

28. Cf. Raba's prayer: "O Lord! Before I was formed, I was without worth; and even now, having been formed, I am as if I had not been formed. Dust I am in my life; how much more at my death! Behold, I am before Thee a vessel of shame and disgrace. May it be Thy will, O Lord my God, that I do not sin; but the sins which I have already committed before Thee, wash them away with Thy great mercy, but not through tribulations and diseases" (B. Berak. 17a); cf. also B. Yoma 87b.

29. In Lev. R. Metzora, XVIII, 1, God is represented as demanding of man that he return his soul to God in the same state of purity in which it was given to him.

30. "If your sins are as high as heaven, even unto the seventh heaven, and even unto the throne of glory, and you repent, I will receive you" (Pes. R. 185a); cf. also Pes. K. 163b; Midr. Ps. on Ps. 120:7.

31. Lam. R., III, 60, on Lam. 3:43.

32. Cf. J. Berak. vi. 2, 7d, line 46: "May it be Thy will, O Lord our God and God of our fathers, that Thou put it into our hearts to perform a perfect repentance before Thee. . ."

33. Num. R., Behaaloteka, XV, 16.

34. Ab. R.N. (vers. I), XLI, 67a.

35. One of Dostoevsky's formulations of the nihilistic point of view, quoted by E. Frank, *Philosophical Understanding and Religious Faith* (New York, 1945), p. 38.

36. Frank, op. cit., p. 42.

37. B. Berak. 33b.

38. M. Berak. 9.5.

39. M. Berak. 2.2.

40. Deut. R., Nitztzabim, VIII, 6.

41. Num. R., Pinehas, XXI, 22.

42. M. Abot 2:21.

43. Cf. Immanuel Kant's celebrated dictum.

44. M. Abot 2.4.

45. M. Berak. 9.5.

5. Judaism and the Idea of Progress

1. This implication was clearly understood by the two profoundest proponents of the doctrine of necessary progress, Kant and Hegel. It is well-known that Hegel found himself compelled to accept this implication, consequently speaking of the "slaughter-bench" of history. What is not well-known is that Kant (to whom this conclusion was, in certain respects, intolerable) was in the end driven to abandon the doctrine of necessary progress. [Cf. my article, "Kant's Concept of History," *Kant-Studien*, 1956-57, pp. 381-398.]

8. The Dilemma of Liberal Judaism: The Problem of Authority

1. Any contribution of past "Jewish genius" is a contribution no doubt different from but not incommensurable with that of Greek genius. Why should the contemporary Jew have a qualitatively unique obligation to past Jewish contributions? The duty to assimilate Greek philosophy, if a duty at all, is incumbent, not on modern Greeks but on modern civilized men. This whole point is developed at greater length in my article, "Can There be Judaism Without Revelation?" [essay no. 4].

2. It may be noted in passing, however, that Rabbinic Judaism bal-

ances this insistence on the importance of learning with an insistence on the importance of religious motive.

3. See chiefly Kant's *Religion Within the Limits of Reason Alone* (transl. Greene and Hudson). Kant, who undoubtedly would have had a profound regard for Judaism had he possessed an adequate knowledge of it, thought of it as a mere external legalistic system—a notion which seems to have reached him, ironically enough, through Spinoza and Moses Mendelssohn.

4. This is the crux of the present, but not of every, inquiry into revelation. The question "Is revelation compatible with human freedom?" is logically secondary to the question "Can a modern man believe in revelation at all?" After all, while in the case of receptivity to a human other, one can *know* the existence of this other, in the case of receptivity to a divine Other, one can accept the existence of this Other, if at all, only *on faith.* But an inquiry into faith and revelation is not part of our present purpose, which is confined to inquiring into the compatibility between the liberal and the Jewish faith. See, however, the article previously referred to and also "Jewish Existence and the Living God" [essay no 7].

5. The distinction here made between law and commandment is indebted to a celebrated exchange of letters between Martin Buber and Franz Rosenzweig. See Rosenzweig, *On Jewish Learning* (ed. N. N. Glatzer, New York 1955), pp. 109 ff.

9. Apologia for a Confirmation Text

1. [This was written before the hippies made oddness fashionable, thus taking the sting out of it.]

2. [Roland Gittelsohn, *Little Lower than the Angels* (New York, 1951).]

11. Two Types of Reform: Reflections Occasioned by Hasidism

1. *Geschichte der Juden*, vol. xi (Leipzig, 1870), pp. 102 ff.

2. *Die Chassidischen Bücher* (Berlin, 1927), p. 130.

3. On this subject, cf. e. g. S. Minkin, *The Romance of Hasidism* (New York 1955), pp. 281 ff., and S. Dresner, *The Zaddik* (New York, 1960), pp. 15 ff.

4. For the Maimonides interpretation given in this paper, cf. *Guide for the Perplexed*, II, 35 and 39, and *Hilchot Yesode Ha-Torah*, VII, 6, VIII, IX. Cf. also my article "The Possibility of the Universe in Al-Farabi, Ibn Sina and Maimonides" (*Proceedings of the American Academy for Jewish Research*, XVI, 1947, pp. 39–70), which seeks to show that for the Rambam, creation is the *ratio essendi* of revealed authority, and revealed authority, the *ratio cognoscendi* of creation. The crucial difference between the "created" world of Maimonides and the "emanated" world of the Islamic Aristotelians is that the laws of the former may be interrupted by a free act of God.

5. For the effect of the modern view on historiography—a branch of knowledge of special concern for the religious thinker in the Jewish tradition—cf. R. G. Collingwood, *The Idea of History* (Oxford, 1946). Collingwood brilliantly expounds the difference between the pre-modern historian, who is prepared to accept documents as authoritative statements of what happened, and the modern historian, who regards all documents as mere sources aiding in the reconstruction of what happened. One of the earliest statements of the modern view is contained in David Hume's famous essay on miracles (*An Enquiry Concerning Human Understanding*, section X).

6. *Kuzari* I, 84 ff.

7. [I speak here only of rational explanation, and neither of phenomenological description nor of a listening faith.]

8. However, Mendelssohn (who, after all, remained an orthodox Jew) retained misgivings about a radical rationalist reform of Judaism —misgivings which, as we say below, are characteristic of most modern Jews retaining a positive Jewish identification. As is well known, while reducing Jewish *belief* to universal verities, Mendelssohn left room for revealed *law*. This left the theoretical basis of revealed law—of necessity itself belief—in a state of obscurity.

9. Thus while the Aristotelian God can know only Himself, and the God of the Islamic Aristotelians only the species of things in the world, Maimonides, ardent Aristotelian though he is, insists that God can know at least *human* individuals—thus defending a Jewish view of providence (*Guide for the Perplexed* III 20). We may refer, in this connection, to a point astutely made by Steven Schwarzschild. This is that, despite the Rambam's debt to the contemplative ideals of the *Nicomachean Ethics*, the last major statement in the *Guide* exalts the speculative knowledge of God, not for its own sake, but for the sake of a life of mercy and justice (*Judaism*, Winter 1961, p. 73).

10. Cf. further on this point, "Jewish Existence and the Living God" [essay no. 7].

11. The traditional belief in the Messiah does not entail the reduction of the individual to a mere means to the ends of history, especially if coupled with the belief in the world-to-come. In contrast, such a reduction always *was* entailed by the modernistic belief in necessary progress, at least when this belief is the sum total of eschatological expectation. This was clearly recognized, for example, by Kant (who for that reason refused to abandon belief in immortality for belief in necessary progress). Kant writes: "Befremdend bleibt es immer hierbei: dass die älteren Generationen nur scheinen um der späteren willen ihr mühseliges Geschäfte zu treiben, um nämlich diesen eine Stufe zu bereiten, von der diese das Bauwerk, welches die Natur zur Absicht hat, höher bringen könnten; und dass doch nur die spätesten das Glück haben sollen in dem Gebäude zu wohnen . . . ." (*Werke*, Prussian Academy edition, VIII 20).

12. The expression "God of the Greeks" is more aptly applied to current "Process" concepts than to the First-Cause concept of earlier Deism. For contemporary philosophers who, under the influence of contemporary science, adopt that concept—as well as those among us who follow their lead—hark back to Greek philosophy. In abandoning the inert matter of atomists and Newtonians for creative energy, contemporary science returns to the Greeks, who thought of nature as alive. And in identifying this energy with a divine Process immanent in the universe, modern thinkers take up ideas going back to the very first Greek philosophers. Further, they are often quite fully aware of this fact. Thus Bergson recognized his debt to Heraclitus, and Whitehead regarded all philosophy as a series of footnotes to Plato.

13. The interpretation of Hasidism here offered is indebted to many writers, such as Scholem, Minkin, Dresner. It owes its decisive debt, however, to Martin Buber. The writer is not unaware of the many criticisms which have been directed against Buber's interpretation of Hasidism. But he has found most of these unimpressive. The most common criticism is that Buber, instead of writing the kind of history which separates sources in painstaking analysis, has given the kind which is a creative synthesis. But the prejudices of positivistic scholarship to the contrary notwithstanding, there is always need for the latter as well as the former type of history, unless one is to be left, not with the spirit of the age or movement one seeks to understand, but merely with its dead bones. Moreover, while Buber's kind of history has great

dangers of subjectivity and distortion—which, incidentally, Buber himself has been the first to admit—Buber would seem to have coped with these with extraordinary success. His treatment of Hasidism shows him to be a thinker capable of practicing the empathetic openness which he preaches.

14. Cf. the following characteristic statement: "He who serves God in the 'great way' assembles all his inner power and rises upwards in his thoughts, and *breaks through all skies in one act*, and rises higher than the angels and seraphs and thrones, and that is perfect worship." (Quoted by G. Scholem, *Major Trends in Jewish Mysticism* [New York, 1961], p. 335; our italics).

15. The fact that neither the first (the Baal Shem) nor the last great Hasidic master (Nahman of Bratzlav) wrote books would seem symbolic of this faith. One must admit the existence in Hasidism of the kind of mysticism which dissolves the self into the infinity—a tendency no doubt inherited from the Kabbala. But one may question that this is a major trend in a movement placing so much stress on human action. For the concept of a mysticism of action, cf. Scholem, *op. cit.*, pp. 341 ff. and Buber, *The Origin and Meaning of Hasidism* (New York, 1960), pp. 198 ff.

16. Buber, *Die Chassidischen Bücher*, p. 157.

17. No doubt the aspect in Hasidism most alien to us (and also, perhaps, most responsible for the decline of Hasidism—cf. Minkin, *op. cit.*, pp. 335 ff.) is the exaltation of the Zaddik. Yet Rabbi Dresner's excellent study shows that even Zaddikism originally springs, if not from what we have called the basic aim of Hasidism, so at least from the Heaven-storming passion with which it seeks to reach it. For where passion seeks to "break through all skies in one act," and yet honesty discovers obstruction and failure, there the need springs up for a human mediator who might bridge that gap. And the Zaddik, finding himself placed into this mediating role, may respond with a rise to saintliness—or with a lapse into arrogance or even charlatanism.

18. While the Kant-interpretation here offered is simplified and even controversial (as regards personal uniqueness, not as regards human freedom), we obviously cannot pause to defend it. It may be mentioned, however, that although Kant denies the possibility of experience of God in the here and now, he refuses to follow contemporary Deism which reduces God to a universal verity indifferent to the here and now. Religion, for Kant, is hope; and this hope remains essentially related to the individual.

19. Kant distinguishes between scientific truths which take the form "it is certain," and moral and religious truths which take the form "I am certain."

20. Cf. my "Buber's Concept of Revelation," in: *The Philosophy of Martin Buber,* ed. Schilpp and Friedman (La Salle, Ill.: Open Court, 1967), pp. 273-298.

21. Cf. Buber, *Moses* (Oxford and London, 1946), p. 77: "The real miracle means that in the astounding experience of the event the current system of cause and effect becomes, as it were, transparent, and permits a glimpse of the sphere in which the sole power, not restricted by any other, is at work." Buber's doctrine of miracle—which makes it, not an exception to the natural, but a manifestation of God to the believer in the natural—is anticipated by the Baal Shem: "the first time a thing occurs in nature it is called a miracle; later it becomes natural, and no attention is paid to it. Let your worship and your service be a fresh miracle every day to you. Only such worship, performed from the heart with enthusiasm, is acceptable." (Newman and Spitz, *Hasidic Anthology* [New York, 1944], pp. 336 ff.)

22. Most great post-Kantian philosophers who are concerned with God at all are concerned, not with an abstract Deity but with a God capable of being *present.* Cf. e. g. Hegel's attempt to synthesize eternity with history, Nietzsche's insistence that God is dead, and Heidegger's that He is absent. (The important question to Nietzsche and Heidegger is not God's existence but His presence.)

23. Scholem, op. cit., p. 348.

14. The Revealed Morality of Judaism and Modern Thought

1. Cf., e.g., the famous passage in *Pirke Abot,* I 3.

2. *Bab. Talmud, Yoma,* 67 b.

3. *Fundamental Principles of the Metaphysics of Ethics,* translated by Abbott (London, 1926), pp. 59, 61. I have revised Abbott's translation. When possible, readily available English translations of Kant are quoted; otherwise, the Prussian Academy edition, 23 vols., 1900-56, is the source, and the translation is my own.

4. The "creative morality" interpretation of Kant, given by thinkers from Fichte to Hermann Cohen, has affected quite un-Kantian philosophies, such as those of Nietzsche and Dewey, as well as much popular moral and psychological thinking. Instead of documenting the view

that it is not Kantian, which I intend to do elsewhere, I refer only to
G. Krüger, *Philosophie und Moral in der Kantischen Kritik* (Tübingen,
1931).

5. A remarkable nineteenth century Jewish thinker neatly illustrates this dilemma. Samuel Hirsch subscribed to Kantian autonomous
morality. Yet he also believed quite literally in revelation. Aware of the
possibility of conflict, he sought to resolve it by interpreting revelation
(following Lessing) as divine education toward moral autonomy.
Hirsch's ingenuity in developing this doctrine does not save it from
ultimate failure. Revelation here is a divine guidance the sole purpose
of which is to emancipate man from the need for guidance, and hence
from revelation itself. Cf. my article "Samuel Hirsch and Hegel" in
Studies in Nineteenth-Century Jewish Intellectual History, ed. A. Alt-
mann (Cambridge, Mass., 1964), pp. 171-201.

6. Kant returns to this theme on countless occasions. We confine
ourselves to quoting one representative passage: "so far as practical
reason has the right to guide us, we shall not regard actions as obligatory because they are divine commandments. We shall regard them as
divine commandments because we are inwardly obligated to them"
Critique of Pure Reason, b. 847.

7. Prussian Academy edition, VIII, 405.

8. Cf., e.g., Gen. 12:1 ff.; Exod. 3:4 ff., and 19:5 ff.; Isa. 6:1 ff.;
Jer. 1:1 ff. When bidden to become a holy nation (Exod. 19:5-6), Israel
is, of course, already in possession of *some* commandments in terms
of which the content of holiness may be specified. Still, it is of the
greatest importance that the bulk of revealed commandments are yet
to come.

9. Isa. 6:8; Exod. 24:7. We follow the traditional interpretation of
the last passage.

10. Cf., e.g., Isa. 6:4; Jer. 1:6.

11. Whether or not *all* the 613 commandments of traditional Judaism
may be regarded as having permanence and intrinsic value is a large
question, and one transcending the scope of this essay.

12. Jer., 27.

13. Our brief remarks on this topic (*infra,* section VII) are not, of
course, meant to be an adequate treatment of this subject.

14. It is interesting to note that Kant and Kierkegaard use the same
Biblical tale—Abraham's sacrifice of Isaac—for opposite purposes: Kant
to argue that, since we must judge the claims of supposed divine voices
in the light of our moral standards, such voices must be *a priori* either
false or superfluous (Prussian Academy edition. VIII, 63 ff.; *Religion*

within the Limits of Reason Alone, translated by Greene and Hudson [New York, 1960], p. 175); Kierkegaard to argue that, if revelation is to be a present possibility, there must be, in an extreme situation, the possibility of a teleological suspension of the ethical (*Fear and Trembling* [New York, 1954]). Any Jewish interpreter of the Abraham story will surely be dissatisfied with both the Kantian and the Kierkegaardian accounts. But one must face the fact that if, as Kant argues, a revealed morality is necessarily heteronomous, there is no third possibility.

15. Cf., e.g., *Midrash Tanhuma*, Yitro, and many other passages, in hasidic as well as rabbinic literature.

16. Mic. 6:8. The point made in this section is perfectly expressed in a Midrash in which God is made to say, "Would that they had deserted Me, and kept My Torah; for if they had occupied themselves with the Torah, the leaven which is in it would have brought them back to Me" (*Pesikta Kahana*, XV). Liberal writers are fond of quoting the first half of this Midrash only, thereby perverting a profound statement of the morality of Judaism into a humanistic platitude.

17. *Bab. Talmud, Berakhot* 61b.

18. *Critique of Judgment*, tr. Meredith (Oxford, 1952), p. 110. The translation is mine.

19. According to one Midrash (*Tanhuma, Hukkat*), the righteous do not cease to fear God even though they have received His assurance. According to another (*Sifre Deut., Wa'ethanan*, No. 32), while everywhere else love drives out fear, this is not true of the love and fear of God.

20. In *Tanhuma, Behukkotai*, God is made to reject the offer of the angels to observe the Torah, on the ground that the Torah is appropriate only for human observance.

21. Cf., e.g., *Bab. Talmud, Berakhot* 31a, *Shabbat* 30b.

22. Isa. 6:6-7; Jer. 1:7-8.

23. As already indicated (*supra*, section IV), for reasons which are beyond the scope of this essay, Kant does not regard the divine will as an *absolute redundancy*. He does, however, regard it as redundant within a purely moral context.

24. *Midrash Genesis Rabba, Wayyera* LIII 7.

15. On the Eclipse of God

1. [Lest this controversial assertion be misunderstood, I should stress that it holds for the believer only. For the unbeliever or detached

critic, what is verified, or immediately verified, is good fortune or "religious experience"—and nothing else.]

2. [On the scope and limitations of this essay, see essay no. 1, sections IV and V.]

16. Judaism and the Meaning of Life

1. [*I and Thou* (New York: Scribner's), p. 110. Italics added.]

2. [Divine farness differs from a Heideggerian divine absence—a term used in this essay only to be rejected.]

3. [Cf. more fully, "The Revealed Morality of Judaism and Modern Thought," essay no. 14.]

4. [See essay no. 13.]

5. [On the scope and limitations of this essay, see essay no. 1, sections IV and V.]

17. A Jew Looks at Christianity and Secularist Liberalism

1. [*The Restless Church* is a volume of responses to Pierre Berton, *The Comfortable Pew* (Toronto: McClelland and Stewart, 1965).]

2. It is not overlooked, and should at this point be specifically stressed, that the synagogue too, when in the position to be tempted by numbers and power, is apt to yield to these temptations, as is illustrated by North American synagogues confined to the rich, and by the intolerance of the Jewish orthodox establishments of Great Britain and Israel of non-orthodox Jewish religious groups.

3. Roy Eckhardt, *The Journal of Bible and Religion,* vol. 33 No. 2 (April 1965), p. 124.

4. Frederick C. Grant, "Not All the Bishops Did Was Wise," *The Witness* XLIX, 35 (October 29, 1964), p. 9.

5. Eckhardt, op. cit., p. 126.

6. *Cf.* John A. T. Robinson, *Honest to God* (SCM Press 1963), chapters 2 and 3. Our few remarks are of course no adequate response to Bishop Robinson's earnest and thoughtful book.

7. Enlightenment ideas still have a strong and beneficial hold on the Anglo-Saxon mind. Thus the doctrine that all men are created equal is of the very life-blood of the United States, and the doctrine of the separation of State and Church is a virtual reality even where it is not,

as in the United States, a formal constitutional principle. Christians sometimes assail this latter doctrine, as a product of secularism. The contrast with the example of Germany might make them wonder whether, protect as it does *both* Church and State from mutual intrusion, it is not much rather the product of a sensitive religious conscience. They might also wonder whether, rather than look for opportunities of invasion of the State by the Church, they would not be better employed to safeguard the Church against intrusion from the State, an end best, if in the end not solely, accomplished by a sensitive religious conscience. But that such conscience must find expression in secular action is the main burden of this article.

18. On the Self-Exposure of Faith to the Modern-Secular World: Philosophical Reflections in the Light of Jewish Experience

1. In addition to the works discussed in this essay, see John A. T. Robinson, *Honest to God* (London, 1963); Pierre Berton, *The Comfortable Pew* (Toronto, 1965); William Kilbourn (ed.), *The Restless Church* (Toronto, 1966). I select these works from among many because of their wide popularity in their respective countries. *The Comfortable Pew* is a critique of the church that was commissioned by the Anglican Church of Canada, and *The Restless Church*, a response commissioned by the same body.

2. For an excellent example, cf. Milton Himmelfarb, "Secular Society? A Jewish Perspective," *Daedalus* (Winter 1967), pp. 220-36. The reader may form his own judgment as to the extent to which Himmelfarb's "long view" is inspired by contemporary Jewish experience.

3. "God has died in *our* time, in *our* history, in *our* existence." (Thomas J. J. Altizer, in *Radical Theology and the Death of God*, by Altizer and William Hamilton [Indianapolis, 1966], p. 95.)

4. Cf., for example, H. Jonas, "Heidegger and Theology," *The Review of Metaphysics*, Vol. 18, No. 1 (1964), 207ff. (reprinted in: *The Phenomenon of Life* [New York, 1966], pp. 235ff.); E. Borowitz, "Bonhoeffer's World Comes of Age," *Judaism*, Vol. 14, No. 1 (1965), pp. 81ff.; and my own "A Jew Looks at Christianity and Secularist Liberalism" [essay no. 17]. Cf. also, A. Wolf (ed.), *Rediscovering Judaism* (Chicago, 1965), by a group of writers united by their concern to seek out the classical sources of Judaism in their confrontation with the modern-secular world.

5. Cf. *infra*, Section IV of this essay.

6. I have attempted to view the confrontation of Christianity and secularist liberalism from the standpoint of contemporary Jewish experience and faith in the article referred to *supra,* n. 4.

7. Dietrich Bonhoeffer, *Letters and Papers from Prison* (London, 1953).

8. Ibid., pp. 163, 146ff., 163ff., 160, 157ff.

9. Ibid., p. 111.

10. [For a modification of the views stated in this section, see essay no. 1, n. 24.]

11. Cf. the articles listed *supra,* n. 4. Professor Jonas warns Protestant theologians against undue reliance on Heidegger's secularistic ontology, even though he finds it "awkward . . . to act as . . . defender of the cause of Christian theology," being both a Jew and "a mere child of this world."

12. Here and *infra,* I allude to a famous post-French Revolution slogan, according to which the Jew was to be permitted to remain a Jew "at home"—in the privacy of a purely religious conscience—on condition that he become "a man abroad," that he purge all remnants of Jewish national-cultural life from his public-secular existence. In pluralistic North America this artificial and illiberal dichotomy never took hold.

13. This statement is not, I think, the product of mere romantic optimism. I must, however, mention in passing that during the thirties Jews then in Germany, this writer included, were wont to make a saint of any Christian showing the slightest signs of resistance to Nazism; for example, of so questionable a figure as Cardinal Faulhaber, solely because he spoke up in behalf of Old Testament Patriarchs. (Cf. G. Lewy, *The Catholic Church and Nazi Germany* [New York, 1965], pp. 111, 276.) In those dark days it was a simple human impossibility to recognize enemies on *all* sides; and it would appear to be no accident that it took twenty years for works to appear that fully document the grim truth that while Nazi anti-Semitism is, of course, anti-Christian in essence, both this anti-Semitism and the attempted genocide in which it culminated would have been impossible except for centuries of Christian anti-Semitism; indeed, without considerable cooperation of Christians not all of whom were nominal. I trust I am not uttering a Jewish view only when I assert that the confrontation of this grim truth, now begun in some Christian quarters, is one of the major tasks of Christian thought in this generation.

14. Harvey Cox, *The Secular City* (New York, 1965).

15. Ibid., pp. 3, 26ff.

16. This is the title of a book by Milton Mayer (Chicago, 1955), which gives a portrait of ten Germans, all of them decent people and Nazis.

17. Cox, op. cit., p. 63.

18. An expression used by the nineteenth-century Jewish Hegelian Samuel Hirsch, in his critique of the utilitarian destruction of Roman religion in the later Roman Empire. With respect to religious pragmatism, there is an uncomfortable resemblance between the modern-secular world and the Roman Empire as viewed by Hegel himself; uncomfortable because Hegel sees Rome's all-encompassing utilitarianism as the source of its destruction.

19. Cox, op. cit., Part IV.

20. Ibid., p. 268.

21. Cf. Martin Buber, *Between Man and Man* (Boston, 1955), p. 15. For the interpretation of the Exodus passage, cf. Buber's *The Prophetic Faith* (New York, 1949), pp. 28ff., and his *Moses* (New York, 1958), pp. 52ff.

22. The claim that belief can no longer be genuinely alive is logically distinct from the claim that it is no longer intellectually legitimate. The latter claim is presently under review; the former will be discussed in Section V of this essay.

23. Paul Van Buren, *The Secular Meaning of the Gospel* (New York, 1963; paperback edition, 1966).

24. Ibid., for example, pp. 121ff., 132ff., 137ff., 141ff., 151ff., 163ff.; pp. 133ff., 137ff., 152ff., 168ff.

25. The fashion was started by J. Wisdom's "Gods," *Proceedings of the Aristotelian Society* (1945-46). Cf. also Van Buren, op. cit., p. 68.

26. Van Buren, op. cit., p. 68. From this reduction it follows that "today, we cannot even understand the Nietzschean cry that 'God is dead,' for if it were so, how could we know? No, the problem now is that the *word* 'God' is dead," ibid., p. 103.

27. That linguistic philosophy need not necessarily involve an empiricism destructive of Christian faith is illustrated, for example, in D. Evans, *The Logic of Self-Involvement* (London, 1963).

28. Van Buren, op. cit., pp. 198ff. The elimination is followed by this incredible statement: "The fact that the *language* of our interpretation of Jesus and Easter is different from that of Paul does not preclude the possibility that our *meaning* and Paul's may be the same" (italics ours).

29. Thomas J. J. Altizer, *The Gospel of Christian Atheism* (Philadel-

phia, 1966). Cf. also *Radical Theology and the Death of God,* by Thomas J. J. Altizer and William Hamilton; referred to as *RT, infra.*

30. Cf., for example, *RT,* p. 95: "We shall *simply assume* the truth of Nietzsche's proclamation of the death of God . . ." (italics ours).

31. *RT,* p. 95.

32. *RT,* pp. 20ff., 157.

33. This is argued in detail in my *The Religious Dimension in Hegel's Thought* (Bloomington: Indiana University Press, 1968).

34. *Gesammelte Abhandlungen* (Stuttgart, 1960), pp. 127, 129, 130.

35. Altizer, *The Gospel of Christian Atheism,* p. 147.

36. Cf. Robert Alter, "The Apocalyptic Temper," *Commentary* (June, 1966), pp. 61ff. Alter's article is an outstanding critique of the "savagely comical apocalypse in vogue in American fiction."

37. Altizer, *Gospel of Christian Atheism,* p. 22.

38. In fairness, it must be added that *The Gospel of Christian Atheism* in no way follows the kind of crude anti-Jewish line that attributes whatever is found inconvenient in Christian ethics and theology to Jewish influence. Cf. Altizer, op. cit., p. 45: "It is . . . Christianity that has reduced human existence to sin and guilt, confronting a broken humanity with a wholly other God who demands total submission to his numinous and judgmental power." If the "wholly other" God is Jewish, then this Jewish God has been essential to Christianity until the time of his "death."

39. The section just concluded is not intended as a comprehensive critique of the "God-is-dead" theology. I may, however, say in passing that I am puzzled to find William Hamilton in close association with Altizer. His ethically inspired optimism (and consequent repudiation of such writers as Ezra Pound); his intense concern with actual human suffering; his stance of "waiting for God": these and other themes would appear to associate him far more closely, on the one hand, with *The Secular City* and, on the other, with the doctrine of the "eclipse" of God (cf. *infra,* Section V); they would also appear to make the expression "death of God" in his case not readily intelligible. Cf., for example, *RT,* pp. 37ff.; 157ff.; also William Hamilton, *The New Essence of Christianity* (New York, 1966), especially pp. 44ff.

40. On the theme of this section, cf. also my "On the Eclipse of God" [essay no. 15].

41. Cf. Bonhoeffer, op. cit., pp. 126, 148.

42. Those currently inclined to dismiss Barth's neo-orthodoxy as

being in the end merely old-fashioned orthodoxy might find instructive his *From Rousseau to Ritschl* (London, 1959), a work showing a far deeper penetration of Hegel than is shown by those who invoke Hegel in their argument for the death of God.

43. Martin Buber, *I and Thou* (New York, 1958).

44. The brief summary of Buber's teaching just given is based, as well as on *I and Thou*, on other writings, notably those collected in *Between Man and Man*. The adequacy of Buber's teaching, here merely asserted, is argued for in my "Buber's Concept of Revelation," *The Philosophy of Martin Buber*, eds. Schilpp and Friedman (La Salle, Illinois, 1967), pp. 273ff.

45. Buber, *I and Thou*, pp. 75, 77, 99, 118ff.

46. Martin Buber, *Eclipse of God* (New York, 1952), pp. 89, 91.

47. Altizer refers to the possibility of a divine eclipse (*RT*, pp. 10, 107, 126); but despite much pondering, I cannot conclude that he has seriously considered it. Cf. *RT*, p. 126: "Buber asserts that the Jew can be safe in a time of God's eclipse because he exists in an eternal covenant that cannot be annulled by an act of man. The contemporary Jew can experience the contradiction of our existence as a theophany. However, not existing in an eternal covenant with God—if only because he exists in an Incarnate Word—the Christian cannot know the death of God as a theophany." Is the Jew "safe," and does Buber consider him so? Is a divine eclipse a theophany? Is not the Christian too in a covenant, the question of the "death" of God being precisely what is at issue? Finally, can Christian and Jew be as infinitely apart as is here asserted?

48. At a recent symposium "Toward Jewish Unity," S. Schwarzschild said: "The . . . point which I want to make . . . is a reference to an experience which many of us here shared last summer. . . . It was a gathering in the Canadian Province of Quebec . . . where a number of us, from all over the spectrum of Jewish life, gathered for a week's intensive study and conversation. . . . We discovered something at the end of the week . . . , namely, that the one man who spoke and protested and stormed the heavens and implicated Israel most tellingly for our generation and for our hearts, and for our hopes, and for our tragedy, was not a theologian, nor a professor, nor even a rabbi. The *de facto* High Priest of our generation turned out to be Elie Wiesel." (*Judaism*, Vol. 15, No. 2 [Spring, 1966], p. 157.)

49. Elie Wiesel, *Night* (New York, 1961), pp. 77ff.

50. Elie Wiesel, *The Accident* (New York, 1962), pp. 90ff.

51. Elie Wiesel, *The Town Beyond the Wall* (New York, 1964), p. 179.

52. Elie Wiesel, *The Gates of the Forest* (New York, 1966), p. 194.

53. Ibid., pp. 225ff.

19. A Response to Five Questions

1. [Cf. "The Revealed Morality of Judaism and Modern Thought," essay no. 14.]

2. [Cf. especially "On the Eclipse of God," essay no. 15.]

3. [Cf. "On the Self-Exposure of Faith to the Modern-Secular World," essay no. 18.]